The 386/486 PC
A Power User's Guide

2nd Edition

by
Harry Fairhead

PRESS

I/O Press

First Published 1990
Second Edition 1992
©I/O Press
Illustrations © David Conrad
ISBN 1 871962 22-6

British Library Cataloguing-in-Publication Data.
A catalogue record for this book is available from the British Library.

Typeset by I/O Press
Printed and bound in Great Britain by Billing & Sons Ltd, Worcester.

Preface

The world of the 386/486 has changed considerably since the first edition of this book, so much so that I have had to completely rewrite many of the original chapters. However, it is interesting to note that the 386/486 user is still confronted by many of the same problems. It is still important to know the difference between extended and expanded memory. Choosing or specifying a system suitable for a particular task is still a matter of clock speed, memory architecture and type of disk drive. We still do not have an operating system for the 386/486 that is completely satisfactory, and the choice between Windows and OS/2 makes life even more difficult.

I have to say that the struggle is worth it. The 386/486 is making an immense difference to the way that personal computers are used. Multi-tasking, GUI interfaces and multi-media are all commonplace and the PC is being used for tasks that traditionally needed a workstation. And all of this at a pace that has made the change look evolutionary.

Harry Fairhead
London
May 1992

Acknowledgements

I/O Press would like to thank the following companies for their help in the preparation of this book: DMST, IBM, IDS, Intel, Microsoft, Quarterdeck and SCO.

The cover illustration is used by kind permission of Viglen Ltd.
Viglen House, Alperton Lane, Alperton, Middlesex, HA0 1DX
Tel: (081) 758 7000 Fax: (081) 991 5115

Contents

The I/O Press Update Service

Subjects such as 386/486 hardware and software change so rapidly that there is little chance of publishing a definitive book that remains up-to-date for even a few months. To overcome this problem I/O Press is offering a free update service. All you have to do is to send a large (C5 size) self addressed envelope stamped with postage for 100gms to:

> I/O Press (386/486 Update Service)
> Oak Tree House
> Leyburn
> North Yorkshire
> DL8 5SE

There is no need to include any note, letter or proof of purchase. Your envelope will be kept on file until the first update becomes available.

Updates are anticipated for the release of Windows NT and the 586.

Chapter 1
The 386/486 Family

This chapter gives you an overview of the whole situation regarding the 386 (including the 486, 486SX and 386SX). The reasons for using a 386 are explained and the difficulties in getting the best out of such systems are described. Most of the ideas introduced in this chapter are explored in more detail later in the book.

The introduction of machines based on the 386 processor has resulted in a change in the way we use personal computers. Before the 386, PCs were not much more than competent word processors. If you wanted to do anything more ambitious then you either had to put up with a performance that produced long waiting times or make the move to a desktop super computer usually referred to as a 'workstation'.

The 386 family takes the PC into the workstation category and provides for a machine on which it is possible to tackle almost any type of application. It is powerful enough for a new breed of programs and even the simpler applications have taken a leap in terms of usability. Gone are the days of hard-to-use programs. Now, using systems such as Windows you can run more than one program at a time and do most things without ever having to touch a keyboard. The change is so great that it is sometimes hard to believe that the 386 PC is the same type of machine as the early PCs!

A good, though curious, example of this change is to be found in the games market. Although computer games are a frivolous application they are remarkably demanding of performance. Until recently you needed to buy a specially designed machine to reach the speed and graphics quality needed for acceptable games. Now the 386 PC is equal to any purpose built games machine. Indeed its ability to produce high quality sound and video enables it to be used as the basis of a multi-media machine on which you can read interactive books or give presentations that mix animated graphics and stereo sound.

However, every revolution has its price and in the case of the 386 family the need to be compatible with software and hardware designed for simpler machines has introduced many complexities. There is still much to do in setting up a 386 so that it works well with both the new and old generation of applications software. The range of processors in the 386 family also causes problems. Which one should you select for any particular job? It can be difficult to keep track of all the different varieties available, especially as they are only distinguished by serial numbers that seem little different.

A guided tour

Before moving on to consider some of the finer points of the current state of affairs it is worth introducing the major figures in the story. Computers differ in many different ways but one of the most important is the design of the *processor* that they use. The processor is responsible for actually running the programs and so its type and quality are vital to the performance of the machine. All of the PCs that we use today are based on a single family of processors - the Intel 80x family. This is a set of processors with different abilities and powers but all are based on the the founding member, the 8088. This was the processor used in the original IBM PC and its acceptance has ensured the continued dominance of the whole Intel 80x family.

To understand the genealogy of the Intel family you only need to remember that the bigger the number the more powerful the processor, and adding SX to the end means a cut down version. The earliest members of the family, the 8088 and 8086, are now virtually obsolete. The 80286, usually referred to just as the 286, is also heading towards being categorised as obsolete. The active members of the family are all based on the 80386 design. The 80386DX is the starting point. The DX was added to the number to make sure it wasn't confused with the 80386SX which is a cut down version. The 80486DX is a faster and more powerful version of the 80386DX and again the 80486SX is cut down version of this. Thus, at the time of writing, the 386 family in order of power is:- 386SX, 386DX, 486SX and the 486DX. Of course you can expect this list to be added to in various ways in the future but the important point is that the basic design remains the same.

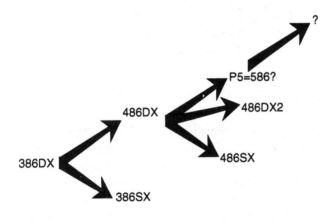

Figure 1.1
The 386 family

For various reasons the number of members of the 386 family is likely to increase by the addition of many minor variants. For example, there is already the 486DX2 to add to the traditional list but it is arguable if this really deserves to be treated as a distinct new member of the family as it is really only double speed version of the 486DX. There are a number of other small modifications to the 386/486 but the first real extension to the family is likely to be the 586DX, currently under development by Intel with the code name P5 and due for release some time in 1993. Even in this case it is important to understand that the basic 386 design will not be superseded, only enhanced. In general you can assume that new chips mean more speed or lower price, or both!

Evolution not revolution

The introduction of the 386 family has brought about, and is still bringing about, revolutionary changes in the way that we use PCs, but much of its success is the way that it softened this revolution. At many stages in the history of computing a revolution in computing power has come about as users have abandoned their existing hardware and software and adopted new. The first generation of almost practical personal computers were based on the Z80 and an operating system called CP/M. At the time it looked as though the status quo would last a thousand years but this entire generation of machines was swept away almost overnight when IBM announced the IBM PC in 1981. This was based on a completely different processor, the Intel 8088, and a completely new operating system, MS-DOS. While not perfect this really did offer a performance that allowed personal computing to be taken seriously. Even at the time of its introduction the design of the PC was considered old fashioned and at best conservative - still it resulted in millions of machines being scrapped.

This successful revolutionary change gave rise to the idea that users could be made to change their hardware and software if the benefits were large enough. In practice, and despite the best attempts of IBM and others, this hasn't proved the case. Instead of making a clean break with the past users have repeatedly preferred an upgrade path that didn't force them to throw out their existing hardware and software. Now it looks as though the size of the commitment to the PC is so great that all future changes will be a gradual step-by-step evolution. Although it has been extended, the original PC design is still very evident in the highest performance 386/486 based machines obtainable. There is the argument that we would have reached the current level of computing power much sooner if the PC architecture had been abandoned and a completely new start made.

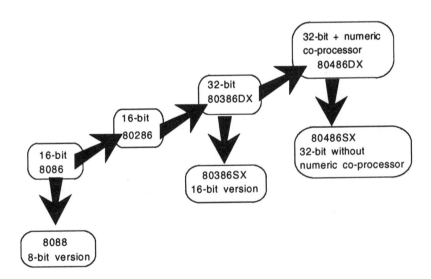

Figure 1.2
The complete Intel family

The legacy of upward compatibility

The evolution of the PC has certainly made the transition from the under-powered machines of the 80s to the desktop mainframes of the 90s but it has its disadvantages as well. The truth of the matter is that the 386/486 provides facilities that take it into the realm of the workstation but for most of the time it is being treated as a faster version of the original 8088! In other words, most of its power is simply ignored. This is the legacy of upward compatibility. Each new generation of processors has added features and facilities but not at the expense of compatibility with earlier processors.

The first improvement on the 8088 can be considered to be the 8086 even though they were created in the same period of time. The 8086 is a 16-bit version of the 8-bit 8088 and, from a software writer's point of view, it is identical but faster. As a result programs that run on the 8088 will, without modification, run on the 8086 only faster. What is more there

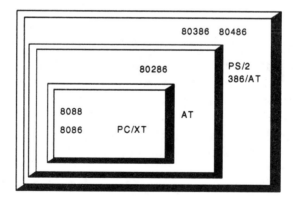

Figure 1.3
Upward compatibility - each new processor includes all the
features of the earlier processors

are no modifications that can be made that will make a program designed for the 8088 run any faster on an 8086. In this sense there is no hidden power in the 8086. Another way of looking at this is that a program written for the 8086 processor could be moved back down to the less powerful 8088 without making any changes. In this sense the 8086 is also downward, or backward, compatible.

In the case of 80286, the next processor that Intel produced, the story is very different. Although the 80286 is a 16-bit processor like the 8086, it contains many advanced modes of operation not shared by the 8086. You can take an 8086 program and run it without modification on the 80286 but the program will not make any use of the 80286's new features. As you might guess any program that is written for the 80286 that does make use of its special features cannot be moved down to an 8086 processor without extensive changes. In other words, the 80286 is upward but not downward compatible with the 8088 and 8086. The trouble with this situation is that very few software producers took the trouble or risk of producing software specially for the 80286 processor and so much of the power of this device has remained well and truly hidden.

The same situation holds with the 80386/486. It is upward compatible with the original 8088 and 8086 processors and that is how much current software treats it - as a fast 8088/86. The only difference between this and the 80286 is that now the hidden power is very great indeed. If you buy a small motor boat and insist on getting about by paddling it from one place to another then people will think that you are eccentric, but if you buy a high speed jet foil and treat it in the same way people will decide that you are mad. The same is true of the current state of computing. While it might have been fine to paddle the 80286, the 80386/486 deserves to be used fully. In later chapters the topic of how the extra power can be released is discussed in detail.

The 80286 - the false start

When Intel produced the 80286 it was to have been the first processor to put the power of a mainframe on your desktop. IBM even emphasised the point by calling the machine they designed to follow the PC the AT - standing for Advanced Technology. Although the design of the AT took the existing PC architecture and adapted it more towards a true 16-bit form, from the user's point of view it made little difference. Most, if not all, of the software available until recently treated the AT as if it was a faster version of the PC and there was no software designed to take advantage of its additional powers.

Even so the AT proved popular and with falling prices became the standard machine for serious work. The irony is that just at the time that the 386/486 became available at reasonable prices, the first software designed for the specially for 286 began to make an impact - for example OS/2, Lotus 1-2-3 Release 3 and Windows 3. Of course this software will run perfectly well on a 386/486 but it doesn't use them to the best effect.

In many ways it is best to see the 286 as a false start on the road to a desktop mainframe. It had many flaws that forced software designers to have to compromise and 'think small'. For example, the 286 still retains some of the 64KByte (Kilobyte) limitations of the original 8088. In a 286 system you can have almost as much memory as you want but only in 64KByte chunks or segments. In a 386 system each segment can be as large as 4 GBytes (Gigabytes) and this allows programmers to work without restriction. It also makes it much easier to move existing mainframe programs to 386-based machines. A detailed comparison of the 286's and 386's abilities quickly leads to the notion that the 386 is the processor that the 286 should have been and the sooner the 286 dies out the better.

Unfortunately the 286 still has a large, although no longer growing, user base. Even today manufacturers are still tempting the occasional user to buy a 286 by very low prices. There is also still a tendency for corporate purchasers to think that a 386-based machine is a luxury and only necessary for the most demanding application or user. In support of this notion it is frequently said that a 286 will run some applications as fast as a 386 and is cheaper. The error in this argument is that the performance comparisons are based on treating both machines as if they were just fast 8088/86 machines. In other words, if you don't use any of the special features of the 286 and you don't use any of the special features of the 386 but make them both pretend they are the older 8088/86 chip, there isn't much to choose between them!

It is already quite clear that the 386 is the dominant processor and will remain so for some years in one form or another. At the moment the penalty for owning a 286 is mainly to be excluded from taking advantage of the 386-specific modes of some software. In other words while there isn't much software that will refuse to run on a 286, there is an increasing amount of software that doesn't perform to its best on a 286. In the very near future you can expect both operating systems and applications software to abandon the need to be 286 compatible and move to a 'true 32-bit 386' form. When this happens the 386 will no longer be treated as just a fast 286 with one or two special extras by the software that runs on it - but as the full 32-bit powerful processor that it really is. This will reveal the gulf between the 286 and 386 once and for all.

To make this more concrete simply consider Windows. Windows 3 and even Windows 3.1 were both written for the 286 but with extra capabilities to make use of some of the features of the 386. The next version of Windows on the other hand, Windows NT, is being designed specifically for the 386 family and will not make any attempt to work with the 286. You can see that the very existence of the 286 and the need to be compatible with it has held back progress.

What to do with a 286?

Although there is no doubt that the 386 family has superseded the 286, many users will still have access to a 286 that is too young to be scrapped. The question that needs to be asked is exactly what are the operational differences between the 386 and the 286. There are a number of hardware based differences that limit the 286's performance:

» Larger memory limit of 64GByte as opposed to the 286's 16MByte limit. At the time of writing this isn't a real difference because most 386 machines have an upper limit of near 16 MBytes on the amount of memory that can be installed. Also notice that the 386SX, like the 286, is limited to 16 MBytes.

» Larger single segment addressing. The 386/486 can use memory in a single 4GByte segment but the 286 can only use it in 64KByte segments. At the moment this doesn't make much difference in practice because there is very little software that makes use of this ability. This situation is likely to change with the introduction of Windows NT and the interim 32-bit version of Windows.

» Powerful memory management which makes optimising the arrangement of memory for any particular application easy and fast. This makes a difference to the power of multi-tasking software such as Windows, OS/2 and Unix. For example, Windows 3 will make use of disk storage to increase the number of programs that can run at the same time only when it is working on a 386 based system. It can also only run DOS applications in re-sizeable windows on a 386. These differences are usually summed up by saying that Windows 3 can only run in 'standard' mode on a 286 but will work in 'enhanced' mode on a 386.

» Expanded memory is easier to create on the 386/486 than on the 286. This is a very real difference because it allows the memory configuration of 386 systems to be changed dynamically. A 286 system usually needs additional hardware to provide expanded memory.

» Virtual 8086 mode makes multi-tasking easier and more reliable. Again this accounts for differences between Windows 3 in standard and enhanced mode.

» The 386/486 is available with higher clock rates than the 286. In other words most 386 systems are faster than most 286 systems.

» The 387 numeric co-processor is faster than the 287. This difference makes programs that do a lot of arithmetic work faster on a 386 machine with a 387 fitted (or on a 486) than on the equivalent 286 plus 287 combination.

What all of these differences amount to is that if you are only interested in running MS-DOS based software then there is little to gain in struggling to change to a 386 (unless you want to use a 387 numeric co-processor). If on the other hand you do need to run 386 software and have a 286 then a practical solution to the problem is to add a 386SX upgrade board. The 386SX is a 16-bit processor exactly like the 286 but it will obey the full 386 instruction set and also has all of the sophisticated memory management options.

Although both the 286 and the 386SX are 16-bit processors you can't simply plug the new chip in place of the old. It requires some extra electronics and new BIOS ROM chips to make it work. As a result 386SX upgrades are either built on a standard expansion card or on a small printed circuit board that is cheaper but more difficult to fit.

If you compare the price of a 386SX upgrade card and a complete replacement motherboard then you will be surprised to discover that they are not that dissimilar. If you feel up to the challenge of fitting a new motherboard, and it isn't that difficult, then this is the course of action I would recommend. It salvages the disk drives, video and other adapter cards in the system and the result at the end of the day is a perfectly standard 386 system.

Intel's 386?

It is normal practice in the electronics industry to share the design of a chip with another manufacturer so that it can be 'second sourced'. The argument goes that second sourcing induces confidence that the product has a life beyond the original designer. Intel second sourced the 286 but with the 386, 486 and beyond Intel has decided to keep its design to itself by not signing second sourcing deals and by threatening to stop any manufacturer from infringing its patents and copyrights.

For some time this gave Intel a total monopoly on the 386/486 market and resulted in higher prices. Other manufacturers had to work hard to construct their own 386 designs from scratch but eventually they did. The availability of 386 chips from sources other than Intel had two effects. The first is that the price of the 386 fell rapidly and the second is that Intel shifted its emphasis onto creating special purpose and enhanced versions of the 386 and 486 for which other manufacturers had no equivalents.

Some of the marketing ploys used by Intel are bound to confuse and puzzle the onlooker unless they are seen in the context of trying to keep customers loyal to Intel. For example, the 486SX is a lower specification 486DX but Intel only introduced it as a way of drawing customers away from the newly introduced lower cost 386DX chips produced by other manufacturers. In fact the early 486SX chips were simply full 486 chips with the numeric co-processor section disabled! The 486SX quickly settled down to look more like a respectable member of the family but the fact still remains that Intel wouldn't have produced it if there had been no competition. Another interesting twist in the 486SX story is that in order to add a numeric co-processor, the chip that you install next to it, the 487SX, is actually a full 486DX processor! In this situation the original 486SX sits in its socket doing nothing much at all.

In an effort to turn the 'empty socket' next to the 486SX into a marketing advantage, Intel invented the idea of offering users an upgrade chip which they could fit in place of the 487SX to boost performance still further. The increased performance is achieved by a technique called 'clock doubling'. This is explained in more detail in the next chapter but essentially it succeeds in doubling the rate at which the processor works without the need to make any changes to other parts of the machine. This is such a good idea that Intel extended it to the other members of the 386 family so, for example, you can now buy the 486DX2 which is identical to the 486DX but runs twice as fast.

Intel's competitors are also producing new and improved versions of the 386 family. There are already faster 386DX and 386SX chips from sources other than Intel. At the time of writing the first non-Intel 486 chips have arrived on the market. There are also likely to be some interesting innovations. For example, the chip manufacturing company Cyrix has just announced the 486SLC which is a 486-like processor that can be used to replace a 386SX with a claimed 20% to 40% speed improvement. Of course many of these innovations are being challenged by Intel as patent infringements and there are many law suits pending.

From chips to systems

The 386/486 is a powerful device but tapping its power when making the transition into complete systems poses a number of problems. When the 286 was introduced IBM modified the existing PC architecture to produce the AT. The modifications were fairly small and mostly upward compatible with the original PC design. In other words, apart from a few well understood exceptions, what would work with a PC would work with an AT - hardware and software alike. The AT quickly became a de facto standard to which other personal computer manufacturers conformed.

With the introduction of the 386 a similar modification to the AT architecture seemed to be called for - after all if there was a change in going from 8 to 16 bits then surely as large a change is needed in going from 16 to 32 bits. IBM took this apparent need for change as a way of trying to gain control of the PC market. Instead of basing their new design on the existing AT they choose to produce something quite new and different - the PS/2.

While the PS/2 range is closely related to the AT design, in that nearly all software that will run on an AT will run on a PS/2, it is incompatible at the hardware level. The PS/2 range uses MCA (Micro Channel Architecture) to connect additional hardware instead of the ISA (Industry Standard Architecture) used in the AT. MCA has a lot of performance advantages but IBM chose to make it a proprietary technology and so most other manufacturers were deterred from using it.

The alternative approach to the PS/2 was to simply use a 386 in place of a 286 in a traditional AT design, modified as little as possible. Initially the problem was that different manufacturers made the necessary modifications in slightly different ways. In the main this didn't matter too much and only affected the way that additional memory was added. As memory technology progressed even this difficulty tended to vanish and a 386 design that is, from the user's point of view, identical to an AT evolved.

This AT/386 design has all the advantages of being hardware compatible with the original AT but has the disadvantage of not being able to deal with high speed add-on cards. In other words ISA is not as fast or as flexible as MCA. Whether this is a real problem or not depends very much on the application you are interested in. There is an argument that ISA isn't used to its full capacity in most systems anyway! Even so this criticism resulted in a group of manufacturers defining a new improved version of ISA - EISA (Extended Industry Standard Architecture). EISA offers many of the advantages of MCA but it is upward compatible with ISA and so you can use existing AT style hardware with it.

Much of the fuss concerning which type of machine to buy is irrelevant. The key fact to remember is that the effect of ISA, MCA or EISA depends on what add-on you require and in many cases it isn't critical, see Chapter 3. For example, if you are plugging in a card to provide an additional printer port then, from a performance point of view, it doesn't matter which bus you are using because they are all fast enough to cope with the data rate of a printer. On the other hand, if you want to connect a high speed disk drive then you might need MCA or EISA to achieve the performance you desire.

The situation isn't quite as clear cut as 'if you need a high speed disk you need MCA or EISA'. In practice the speed of operation of a disk using ISA can be improved by selecting IDE, SCSI or ESDI drives (see Chapter 6) and this might be all that is necessary for the application. Another confusing factor is that one of the main tasks for which MCA was designed, that of connecting additional memory that will work at the full speed of the processor, has largely become redundant. Part of the reason has been the introduction of special add-on boards with high speed connections to the processor just for memory extension but the main reason is that the amount of memory that can be fitted to the main system board has increased to the point where memory expansion seems an unnecessary concept!

The pros and cons of the different architectures can be summarised as:

» ISA 386-AT - Low cost, lots of existing add-on cards but limited in its maximum performance.

» EISA 386-AT - Higher cost, not many add-on cards as yet but upward compatible with ISA, higher potential performance, not backed by IBM.

» MCA PS/2 - Higher cost, higher potential performance, backed by IBM.

As things have turned out the dominant architecture has proved to be the ISA-386. The reason is that for most applications this provides more than enough power and flexibility. In some specialised situations the EISA 386-AT is an advantage and these are discussed later in this book. The MCA PS/2 has proved to be of interest only to dedicated IBM customers. It is too early to say that the MCA PS/2 design is obsolete but it certainly doesn't seem to have a bright future. Unless there is a radical and unforeseen change in the PC market the MCA bus and the PS/2 have to be seen as another failed attempt at forcing a revolution on the PC-using community. This isn't to say that the EISA 386-AT can be hailed as the victory of evolution over revolution. As already stated the plain fact is that the majority of 386-AT designs use and need nothing more sophisticated than the ISA bus. All of these topics are taken up in more detail in the next chapter.

The software choice

Until recently the only software choice open to a PC user was which version of MS-DOS (PC-DOS) to run! MS-DOS was designed to work with the 8088/86 and is subject to the well known 640KByte limit on memory. In addition all of the programs that run under MS-DOS were written for the 8088/86. As has already been mentioned, the 286 and the 386 can pretend to be high speed versions of the 8088/8086 and as such can quite happily run MS-DOS and all of the programs that run under it. If all you want to do is run MS-DOS and MS-DOS programs then the only factor that affects performance is processor clock speed and in this case you could do just as well with a 286 system with a fast enough clock. However, there are still reasons to prefer a 386-based system and these are concerned with its use of memory.

» Memory management

Even if you intend to stay with MS-DOS you can still benefit from a 386 machine by adding a memory manager such as QEMM or 386MAX or by using EMM386 which is included with MS-DOS 5. The 386 has the ability to rearrange the layout of memory in a machine. A memory manager can make use of this ability to move parts of MS-DOS such as network drivers etc. out of the usual 640KByte area and so increase the proportion of it that is available to applications programs. This is usually referred to as making use of Upper Memory Blocks (or UMBs) which are discussed in more detail later.

» Expanded memory

Expanded memory is a type of memory used by older MS-DOS programs needing to use more than 640 KBytes. In non-386 based machines expanded memory has to be implemented using additional hardware. In the case of a 386, however, its ability to reorganise memory can be used to implement expanded memory using nothing but software. You can buy utilities that do nothing but create expanded memory - so called Limulators - but in most cases this ability is incorporated into a full 386 memory manager of the type described in the previous section.

» DOS extenders

Some software, Lotus 1-2-3 Release 3 being the best known, makes better use of the 386 by incorporating DOS extenders. In this case you can only run the application on a 286 or 386 under MS-DOS but the application has access to all of the memory installed on the machine. In other words DOS extenders are nothing more than a way around the 640KByte limit.

To get the best out of the 386 there is no doubt that you have to move to something beyond MS-DOS. There are various alternatives some of which don't involve a complete abandonment of MS-DOS.

» DOS multi-taskers

A DOS multi-tasker makes use of the 386's ability to look like more than one complete 8088/86 system to run multiple copies of MS-DOS and applications. The best known DOS multi-taskers are Windows 3 and DESQview. Both will allow you to run multiple DOS applications and switch between them but Windows 3 goes somewhat further. It also supports its own type of application that isn't limited by the 640KByte barrier. In this sense Windows 3 is halfway to being a completely new operating system that replaces MS-DOS.

» New operating systems

The most attractive solution from the technical point of view at least is to get rid of MS-DOS and all its limitations and start again with a more appropriate operating system. This is exactly what Microsoft and IBM intended to happen when they designed OS/2 but for various reasons the first versions of OS/2 were eclipsed by Windows 3. Only IBM is currently making any effort to develop OS/2 as a challenge to Windows 3. OS/2 Version 2 was written specifically for the 386 and it will run MS-DOS, Windows and OS/2 applications on a nearly equal footing. Microsoft have more or less abandoned OS/2 to develop Windows NT which is a completely new operating system that will run MS-DOS and Windows applications on a 386 and perhaps even on other types of processor. So at the time of writing the competition is between Windows 3.1 and OS/2 Version 2 but in the longer term the battle line-up will change to be Windows NT versus OS/2.

» Unix - an existing operating system

As well as the new operating systems for the 386 there is also Unix. Unix has been available for over 20 years on a wide range of different machines and it has been tipped to replace

MS-DOS for as many years. This wasn't a particularly realistic prediction until the appearance of the 386. The 386 is much more like the type of machine for which Unix was developed and for the first time Unix can be implemented on a personal computer without any difficulty. Unix has many committed supporters and this accounts for the number of times it has been put forward as a replacement for MS-DOS. There are many arguments in favour of Unix but its most important advantage is usually overlooked. Unix is a machine independent operating system. That is, it is possible to run Unix on everything from a 386 PC to a super computer. At the moment if you need a computer more powerful than a PC you have no choice but to leave behind the world of MS-DOS, Windows and even OS/2 - there is just no continuity. With Unix, on the other hand, a manufacturer can offer a range of machines that all use the same operating system, hence the enthusiasm for Unix. Unix is discussed more fully in Chapter 14, but my personal opinion is that it now has little chance of becoming a serious threat to the popularity of either Windows NT or OS/2. However, this is not to say that it is without its uses!

Key points

» The 80386 family of processors have such significant advantages over the older 286 processor that the 286 is now best considered obsolete along with the earlier 8088 and 8086 based machines.

» In choice of hardware and software, the PC community has repeatedly chosen evolution in preference to revolution. This has slowed down the rate of progress towards utilising the full power of the 386 family but it has protected the investment in the past.

» The 386 family looks certain to remain the dominant processor type for some years.

» There are three general 386/486 machine designs - the MCA PS/2, the ISA 386-AT and the EISA 386-AT. The ISA 386-AT is by far the most popular with the EISA 386-AT being used where its extra power is needed.

» MS-DOS treats the 386/486 as if it was an 8088/86 chip complete with all of its limitations. To get the best from it you have to make use of memory managers, DOS extenders and DOS multi-taskers.

» Windows 3, as well as being a DOS multi-tasker, is halfway to being a 386-specific replacement for MS-DOS.

» For the longer term future a true 32-bit, 386-specific operating system seems certain to be the best choice. The possible candidates are Windows NT, OS/2 and Unix.

Chapter 2
System Performance

There is no single factor that makes a computer system powerful. Even systems based on the same processor running at the same speed show considerable differences in their ability to tackle particular tasks. This chapter explores these differences and explains how to assess a machine's qualities.

One of the main reasons for using a 386 based machine is to run sophisticated programs as fast as possible under all conditions. In practice this is not just a matter of opting for the 386 or 486. There are many design decisions that have to be made that affect the speed at which programs run and it is important to understand which aspects of the complete system impinge on your application. You may even find that a slower processor is up to the task that you have in mind if coupled with the correct peripherals. Many of the ideas introduced in this chapter are developed in more detail later in this book. You will also find a number of technical boxes that deal with general issues and you can choose to read or ignore these as suits your curiosity or requirements.

MIPS

A processor obeys the instructions which make up a program. How fast the program is carried out depends on how many instructions the processor can obey per second. Following this idea to its logical conclusion you might think that it would be possible to give each processor a speed rating in terms of the 'number of instructions per second' it can obey, analogous to a 'miles per hour' rating for a car. Unfortunately this isn't possible because not all instructions that the processor is called on to obey take the same amount of time. In other words, how many instructions per second a processor can execute depends on the particular instruction in which you are interested! For example, to make the comparison between two different processors seem favourable in a particular direction all you have to do is count how many simple instructions per second one can execute compared to how many complex instructions the other manages. You might think that this sleight of hand would be easy to detect, but in practice it is not so easy to determine what is a simple and what is a complex instruction when dealing with two completely different processors.

The idea of a measure of the number of instructions per second can be rescued by introducing a standard mix of instructions that can be used to find out how many instructions on average the processor will obey in a second. This corresponds to the often quoted measure of processor speed - MIPS or Millions of Instructions Per Second. So a machine that is capable of say 2 MIPS will obey 2 million instructions per second on average.

Average MIPS is a useful measure of how fast a processor runs but it can still be misleading. For example, suppose a processor was very good at a particular operation - addition say - and your application used this operation very heavily. The fact that it was exceptionally good at addition would only increase the MIPS rating a little, but it would have a powerful impact on your application! The point is that MIPS is an

Risc v. Cisc

There are two very general types of processor in use - *risc*, Reduced Instruction Set Computers and *cisc*, Complex Instruction Set Computers. Processors such as the 386 family are cisc processors. They have a large and powerful set of instructions which programs can use. For example the 386 can perform a multiplication or division in a single instruction where many other processors take tens of instructions to do the same task.

It is difficult to see how there could be any alternative to the progression of increasingly powerful cisc processors. The philosophy of risc design, however, is that a complex instruction set is difficult to implement efficiently and most of the time programs only use 10% or fewer of the available range of instructions. Instead of trying to implement a full cisc instruction set efficiently, the risc approach is to concentrate on just the 10% of the instructions that are used often. The resulting processors have a small but very fast instruction set. Risc processors have proved that they can match and surpass the performance of cisc chips such as the 386 while being much simpler and cheaper to build.

The future of the risc versus cisc argument is difficult to predict. It is likely that PCs based on risc designs will become more common as 386 software such as Windows NT is designed to also run on risc processors. However, a more subtle effect of the risc philosophy is on the future generation of cisc chips. The 486, for example, gains much of its speed by optimising the speed of the most commonly used instructions. This is of course exactly the principle used in designing a risc processor! It is going too far to say that the 486 is a cross between a cisc and a risc processor but it weakens the argument that to reach increased processing power we have to move to risc at the expense of cisc.

average measure of performance but your applications may be very specific in their use of a processor's instruction set. The result is that it can be difficult to predict how much effect an improvement in the MIPS rating will have on the speed of your particular application.

The first desktop computers offered performances below 0.5MIPS. Today's 386/486 based systems offer performances in the region of 10MIPS. At these levels of performance desktop computers can be used for tasks that traditionally needed a mainframe or a workstation such as real time solid modelling, animation and complex equation solving.

Clock speed and Landmark speed

A simpler measure of performance, and one more often quoted than MIPS, is *clock speed*. Every computer has a master clock which serves to co-ordinate everything that happens. An instruction will always take an exact number of clock pulses to complete and so how fast a program runs is directly dependent on the clock rate. Clock rate is measured in MHz or Mega-Hertz. (Hertz was a pioneer of radio transmission and the international measure of frequency is named after him.) Roughly speaking 1MHz is one million clock pulses per second and you can use the measure of clock rate to deduce the running time of a program on different machines. For example, if you are running a program on a machine with a clock rate of 1MHz and it takes one minute then changing to a 2MHz machine of the same type will mean that it only takes half a minute to complete.

Well, to be strictly accurate this reasoning only holds if the program's running speed is only affected by the rate at which the processor obeys instructions and in practice this isn't the case. For example, if the program in question spends a lot of time waiting for you to type on the keyboard or for a slow disk drive to deliver up its data then doubling the clock speed

The problems of speed

Compared to the typical 1MHz and 2MHz clock rates used in the first desktop computers, the 33MHz and 40MHz clock rates in use today pose some interesting problems for designers and users. The difficulty stems from the fact that current clock rates are well into the radio frequency range. For example, some FM radio stations transmit on frequencies lower than 80MHz and stations in the long wave band use frequencies as low as 0.1MHz! The reason why this becomes more of a problem as clock rates increase is that the efficiency of an aerial increases with frequency. This means that the copper tracks connecting the chips that make up a computer radiate significant amounts of radio frequency noise as the clock rate increases. If you have tried listening to a radio near to a computer you will have heard the problem.

However, the problem isn't to do with radio interference, this can be reduced by using a specially treated metal case, the problem is that the radio emissions cause distortion of the pulses that the copper tracks carry and lead to interference or 'crosstalk' between tracks. You can think of it as the copper tracks becoming increasingly leaky as the clock rate goes up. It is possible to do something about this by careful layout of the printed circuit board but many early machines used printed circuit boards that were designed for slower speeds and were often unreliable. Today there is no real problem with clock rates up to 40MHz but there is some doubt about the possibility of pushing the rate any higher without unreasonable increases in cost. (This is one reason for the use of clock doubling circuits to increase a 25MHz external clock to 50MHz.)

Another common practice that can cause problems is using chips above their recommended clock rate. The frequency at which a chip is guaranteed to work is usually a very conservative estimate of actual maximum operating frequency. Before true 40MHz processors were available it was a common practice for manufacturers to select the higher quality components from a batch of 33MHz parts and push them to 50MHz. This sometimes resulted in a machine that would refused to work if the room temperature was too high!

doesn't result in the program taking half the time. Even so clock speed is a valuable measure of potential performance. The point is that it determines the rate at which instructions are obeyed. Doubling a machine's clock speed halves the time a program takes to run in the best possible case.

If you are comparing identical processors then clock speed is a good measure but it isn't as meaningful between processors. Even so clock speed is still quoted as a way of showing how machines based on the Intel family have increased in power. The original PC had a clock speed of 4.77MHz and the first AT 6MHz (quickly increased to 8MHz). The fastest 286 machines used clock speeds of 10MHz, 12MHz, 16MHz and even on occasion 20MHz. 386 systems have been available in clock speeds of 16MHz, 20MHz, 25MHz, 33MHz and even higher. The 486 has been manufactured in 25MHz, 33MHz and 40MHz versions.

At this point you might be wondering why every processor, especially those in the 386 family, isn't available at every clock speed. The answer is that manufacturers have an obvious desire to rationalise the range that they offer and this goes for chip and machine manufacturers. This means that processors

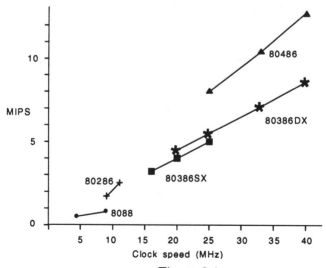

Figure 2.1
Clock speed and MIPS for the Intel family

are produced in a range of clock speeds that tries to eliminate overlap in processing power. For example, the 20MHz 386DX died out when the 25MHz 386SX became available. In this case the 386SX version was as powerful and cheaper than the DX version. Thus while a complete listing of all the clock speeds that have ever been produced makes interesting reading it isn't likely to correspond to the range available or desirable at any given time.

To get some idea of how clock speeds and MIPS compare and how the different processor types offer different ranges of power then see Figure 2.1.

Clock speed is the simplest measure of the speed of a processor and it works very well as long as you confine your attention to a single type of processor. However it is prone to misrepresent the speed of a processor if the number of instructions that are obeyed per clock pulse is modified. For example, you could modify a 386 chip to execute its instructions in half the number of clock pulses. This means that you could have two 386 chips with the same clock speed but one would have twice the MIPS of the other! If you think that this is entirely theoretical it is worth mentioning that the

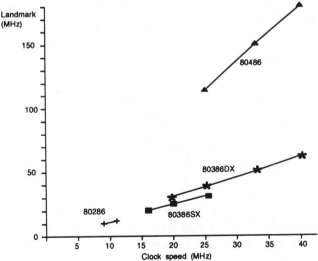

Figure 2.2
Clock speed and Landmark speed

486 is in many senses nothing more than a 386 that executes an important subset of instructions in fewer clock cycles and the 486DX2 doubles the external clock speed so in effect obeying all instructions in half the time!

To compensate for the possibility of there being different numbers of instructions per clock pulse it is useful to use the Landmark speed. This is simply the speed that an original 286AT would have to be run at to give the same performance. The Landmark speed is good in the sense that it does provide a reasonably realistic measure of performance but it can also be used to mislead if a manufacturer quotes a clock speed that is in fact a Landmark speed. A typical set of Landmark speeds quoted for a range of machines from one manufacturer can be seen in Figure 2.2. Notice that this graph is also influenced by other design aspects than the type of processor. For example in the case of the 486 machines a cache (see Chapter 4) was used to produce an even greater speed increase over the 386SX and 386DX machines.

Data transfer rates

Clock speed and MIPS both reflect the potential processing power of a machine but the processor is not the only component in a real machine. A typical system is comprised of a processor, memory, a video display and disk drives.

In running a program data has to be moved between these system components - from memory to processor, from memory to disk, from processor to video etc.. Connections are made between the different components by sets of wires called buses. In practice a *bus* is more than just a set of wires, it also includes sets of rules or *protocols* that govern how data should be transferred, what its destination is etc.. Another name for a data bus is a data highway which is more descriptive of its role in transferring data from one system component to another.

The speed of these transfers between the components of a system affects how long a program takes to run. Different programs will make demands on different types of data transfer. For example, a database program will spend much of its time transferring data from disk to memory and vice versa whereas a DTP program will spend more of its time transferring data to and from the video display. The importance of high data transfer rates between the different system components depends very much on the type of work that a program is engaged in. In an ideal world a system would optimise the transfer rates between all system components but in the real world this results in a very expensive machine! A more realistic approach is to optimise those transfer rates that are critical to the application.

Data transfer rates are usually measured in either MBytes per second or MBits per second and it is important to be aware of which measure is in use. 1MByte per second is eight times faster than 1MBit per second.

There are two factors that affect data transfer rates - *clock speed* and *band width*. Clock speed is simply the rate at which a unit of data can be transferred and band width is the size of the unit of transfer. In other words, at each clock pulse an item of data is transferred but the total amount of data transferred can be increased by sending more per clock pulse. In physical terms band width corresponds to the number of wires in a bus available for data transfer. In simple terms it needs one wire connection to transfer a single bit of data between two units.

Bits and Bytes

Most computer users are familiar with the idea of bits and bytes. A *bit* is the smallest unit of storage that a computer can make use of. In most cases a bit can be thought of as storing a 0 or a 1 but it can record any yes/no, on/off (that is any two-state) information. Information that is more complicated can be stored by using groups of bits. For example, two bits can store four items of data coded as 00, 01, 10 and 11. It is not difficult to work out that n bits can store 2^n items of data.

Although each memory location in a computer could be designed to store just one bit this would be hopelessly inefficient. In practice most computers store 8 bits per memory location. The reason is that 8 bits can store 256 different symbols and this is enough to represent a reasonable sized alphabet, including special characters and graphics symbols. So common is this unit of 8 bits that it has been given a special name - the *byte*. You can think of one byte as just enough storage to hold a single character. In other words 1 byte=1 character.

There are other units of storage that are useful enough to have special names. Half a byte, that is four bits, is often referred to as a *nibble*. Two bytes or 16 bits is called a *word*. Four bytes or 32 bits is called a *double word* or a *long word*. Eight bytes or 64 bits is called *quad word*. The 386/486 processor works with data in all of these forms and one or two less common forms. Character handling generally involves working with bytes of data. Accurate (floating point) arithmetic generally involves double words, quad words or a special ten byte format. The 386DX and 486 can store and retrieve as much as a double word in one operation. This is one of the reasons they are said to be 32-bit processors. The 386SX and the 286 are 16-bit processors and can only store and retrieve a single word in one operation. In principle 32-bit processors should be twice as fast as 16-bit processors but this advantage is only realised if a double word is actually needed at each memory access. On average they are faster but not by as much as the factor of two that theory would suggest.

Early personal computers based on the 8088 were 8-bit machines that transferred eight bits, one byte or one character per clock pulse. In other words, they were based around an 8-bit bus. Later 286 based systems transferred data 16 bits, two bytes or two characters at a time, i.e. they had 16-bit buses. Now 386 based systems transfer data at 32 bits, four bytes or four characters at a time and they use a 32-bit bus. You can see that even at the same clock speed the 286 transfers data twice as fast as the 8088 and the 386 transfers data twice as fast again.

The rule is that for high data transfer rates the bus connecting two system components should be as wide as possible and should be clocked at as high a rate as possible.

There is a subtle point to be considered before moving on to other matters. The width of a bus and the speed of its clock represent only the maximum achievable data transfer rate. There may be many practical situations where data is transferred at rates much lower than this maximum. For example, if you have a 32-bit bus which is capable of transferring four characters at a time, then you are under-utilising it if you only want to transfer a single character. In other words, you may find a 32-bit bus actually being used to transfer a 16-bit word or a single byte.

The clock speed of a bus can also be deceptive. For example, if two system components have to go through an elaborate exchange of data to establish contact with one another then

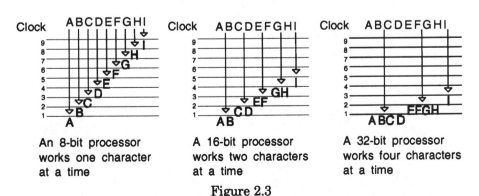

Figure 2.3
The speed of processing depends on the amount of data that can be handled in one operation

Why does memory always double?

Many users are puzzled by the fact that memory capacity tends to double rather than increase in regular units. This doubling is a natural consequence of the way the processor selects or addresses particular memory locations. Data is transferred between the components of a computer system via a data bus but it is often necessary to determine the exact location that data will be stored in or read from using an associated address bus. An address bus is a collection of wires which communicates an address or memory location to be used in the data transfer.

The simplest address bus has a single wire capable of selecting one of two memory locations depending on whether it carries a 0 or a 1.

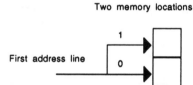

Two memory locations

If a second address line is added, to make a two-bit address bus then a single location out of four memory locations can be selected. The second address line selects which group of two memory locations is being addressed and then the first address line selects which of the two it is.

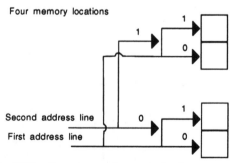

Four memory locations

It is not difficult to see that each time you add an address line the amount of memory that can be addressed doubles. The 286 and 386SX processors have 24 address lines and so can address up to 16 MBytes, whereas the 386DX and the 486 have 32 address lines and can address up to 4 GBytes.

this can represent a significant overhead in transferring modest quantities of data. An everyday analogy to this is that the time it takes to make a one-minute international phone call is usually considerably longer than one minute due to the time it takes to connect. Simple minded reasoning would say that you can make 60 one-minute phone calls in an hour but without exceptional preparation the actual number of calls is certain to be much less. The rules that a bus uses for data transfer are called its protocol and it is quite possible for a single bus to have a bus protocol that includes more than one way of transferring data.

How many buses?

For the highest speed of transfer it is necessary to use a dedicated bus between each system component but in practice this would prove too complex. Instead a single bus is often shared between a number of components. Traditionally this bus served to connect the processor to memory, the video, the disk drive and whatever else was connected.

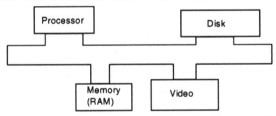

Of course, using a single bus in this way implies that data can only be transferred between two system components at any one time but this was no disadvantage to early personal computers. It also had the advantage that, as long as a standard was defined for the bus, all of the system components could be connected in the same way. For example, in the early days of personal computers the S100 bus became a de facto standard and you could buy plug-in printed circuit cards that held memory, disk controllers, printer ports, video controllers, indeed everything you could want including the processor itself!

More modern designs have tended to abandon this single external bus design in favour of using an internal bus to

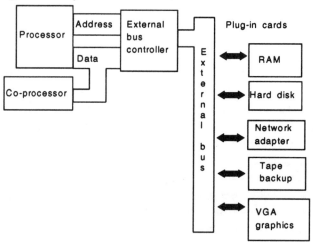

Figure 2.4
A traditional design using a single external bus

connect memory and even some other standard system
components, leaving the external bus for system components
that really are 'optional extras'. This approach has the
advantage of economy for the manufacturer and of higher
efficiency for the customer. As the internal bus isn't available
for use by the outside world it doesn't have to conform to any
standard and so it can be based on a modern design and take
advantage of any advanced features of the devices it is
connecting.

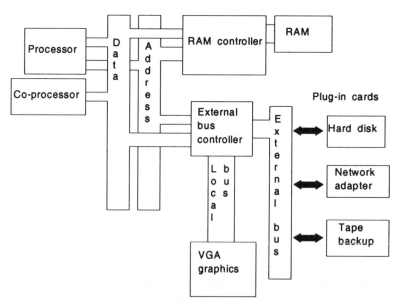

Figure 2.5
A modern design using one external and two internal buses

Surprisingly, this approach hasn't really been taken to its obvious limit of using using a local bus for disk and video. The only reasonably common example is the now defunct Amstrad PC2386 which used an internal bus to connect the processor to memory, disk controller, video controller, serial port and parallel port. Anything additional to this list was added via a standard ISA bus. As will be explained in the next chapter, this use of an internal bus for memory has made many of the arguments about the type of standard external bus - i.e. ISA, MCA or EISA - irrelevant in many situations. The majority of machines have taken the attitude that the advantages of being able to exchange sub-systems such as disks controllers and video have made the use of the expansion bus preferable to an internal bus. This attitude is very likely to change in the future because of the increasing demands for high speed transfer. In short, the internal bus design may still have its day!

Inside the chip - SX and DX2

It is not just in the whole machine that the clock rate and the bus width determine the speed of data transfer, the same is true when you look inside the processor chip. The processor is a sort of complete computer system in miniature (or should it be in microture!), It makes use of a data bus to transfer data internally and the clock is used internally to synchronise all operations. In most cases the external data and clock are simply brought inside the chip without any changes, but it doesn't have to be this way. For example, the full 386DX uses an internal 32-bit data bus that is identical to the external 32-bit bus. However, the 386SX makes use of a 16-bit external data bus even though it uses a full 32-bit bus internally. The chip has some additional electronics to manage the conversion of data from 32 to 16 bits and vice versa - see Figure 2.6.

This use of a smaller external bus makes the 386SX cheaper for creating a system in a number of different ways. Of course there is a cost in performance in that it now takes twice as long to transfer a full 32 bits. The impact of this isn't quite as great as you might imagine because the majority of software

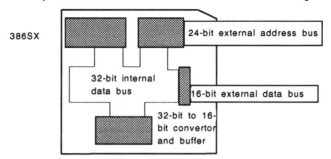

Figure 2.6
The 386SX uses a 32-bit internal bus and a 16-bit external data bus

is still written using a 16-bit machine and so most data transfers turn out to be 16-bit anyway! This isn't quite so true when using software specially written to make use of the 386's 32-bit capabilities. It may be that as the proportion of 32-bit software increases the perceived performance gap between the 386SX and 386DX will grow. Notice that unlike the 386SX, the 486SX doesn't make use of a smaller data bus. It is a 'cut down' version of the 486DX but its reduced performance is due to the loss of the built-in numeric co-processor.

As well as changing the data bus size it is also quite possible to make use of a different internal clock. The 486DX2 is a standard 486DX processor but with the addition of a clock doubling circuit that makes the internal clock twice as fast as the external clock. This means that once data gets inside the processor instructions are completed in half the time but externally the data transfers etc. operate at the usual speed. This means that the power increase isn't the doubling that you might otherwise predict, it's more like a 50% gain in speed. Intel are planning clock doubled versions of most of the 386 family as user-installable upgrades to existing machines.

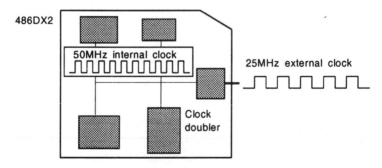

Figure 2.7
The 486DX2 uses a clock doubler to speed up internal operations

How many processors?

Another change in the design of a modern personal computer is the use of separate processors for different tasks. The idea of a numeric co-processor was mentioned in Chapter 1. This is an additional processor that handles all arithmetic instructions. If the numeric co-processor isn't fitted then the main processor does the arithmetic but it takes longer. There is no reason why the same principle shouldn't be extended to graphics co-processors, disk co-processors, etc.. Numeric co-processors are special only in that they have been available for a long time and are generally connected to the processor via a separate internal bus. Indeed, numeric co-processors work so closely with the processor that they need a specialised bus. Other types of co-processor don't always share this closeness with the main processor and can be fitted to a standard external bus.

In a simple system the processor is always in charge of data transfer over the bus but if other devices have sufficient power there is no reason why they shouldn't take control of the bus. The device that has control of the bus is called a bus master and modern external buses such as ISA, MCA and EISA allow multiple bus masters, although with different degrees of ease and sophistication. In a shared bus which allows only the processor to act as bus master all data has to pass through the processor. For example, if you want to transfer data from disk to memory then each item of data is read from disk into the processor and then from the processor to the memory.

The advantage of having multiple bus masters is essentially to allow other system components to transfer data directly between themselves without having to involve the processor. A secondary reason is to allow another processor to take over the bus and so control the entire computer. This is one way of upgrading machines without having to start again from scratch.

An alternative but related method of by-passing the processor in data transfer to memory is to use DMA (Dynamic Memory Access). In this case a system component, a disk controller

Measuring memory
K, B, G and T

You can refer to any memory location by giving its address. For example, the first memory location has an address of 0, the second has an address of 1 and so on. As the amount of memory that can be accessed doubles with every address line that is used, numbers such as 2, 4, 8, 16, 32, 64 ... 1024 tend to occur. As 1024 is the closest power of two to 1000 it is used as a convenient larger unit of memory. That is 1KByte (1 KiloByte)= 1024 Bytes. In the same way 1024 KBytes is 1 MByte (1 MegaByte). Notice that this means that 1 MByte isn't simply a million Bytes but 1048576 Bytes instead, that is more than 47 KBytes more than you might have expected! (Be aware, however, that on occasions when it suits them, hard disk manufacturers sometimes take 1 MByte to mean 1000 KBytes)

Until recently the MegaByte was the only unit necessary to measure the amount of storage that desktop computers could use but now two larger units, the GigaByte and the TeraByte are in increasingly common use. So now you also need to know that 1GByte (1 GigaByte)=1024 MBytes and 1 TByte (1 TeraByte)=1024 GBytes.

In terms of Bytes the standard units of memory are:

          1 KByte = 1024 Bytes
          1 MByte = 1048576 Bytes
          1 GByte = 1073741824 Bytes
          1 TByte = 1099511627776 Bytes

Most people can cope with 1 GByte of storage but 1 TByte is a different matter. The standard 386/486DX can work with up to 4 GBytes of memory which should be enough for a while. However, it is possible to build 386/486 systems with some added hardware that can work with up to 64 TBytes of memory. To put this in perspective this is enough memory to allocate every person in the UK around 1 MByte of personal storage! Needless to say there has been no need to construct a system with TeraBytes of storage - yet.

say, can ask a special sort of co-processor, a DMA controller, to transfer data from it directly to memory. A DMA controller can generally be set up to transfer data from more than one device to memory but each one requires a dedicated DMA channel. DMA is a good system in theory but unfortunately the original PC design was particularly weak on DMA because it allowed so few channels. The AT design improved on this situation by providing more DMA channels but by this time designers had tended to ignore DMA.

In a simple system with only one device, i.e. the processor able to control data transfer on the main bus, there is no great advantage in minimising bus use. If the processor isn't using the bus then it simply stays idle. In more advanced systems, with more than one device able to control transfers over the bus, the question of bus utilisation becomes important. For example, if the main processor makes use of the bus for close to 100% of the time in transferring data to and from RAM then there will be no way that any device can use the same bus to transfer data. This situation is often referred to as 'lockout' or 'bus hogging' and any device, not just the main processor, can be guilty of it.

Wait states

One complication of bus transfer rates is the *wait state*. If a bus attempts to transfer data faster than a device can cope with the data then it is obvious that it will have to wait until the device is ready. This is a wait state. If the bus is being used by the processor to transfer data to and from slow memory, or whatever, then the duration of the wait state is usually quoted in terms of number of clock pulses. So for example, if you have a 20MHz 386 working with one wait state for memory access then this means that the processor will wait for one clock pulse each time it accesses the memory. Obviously, a 20MHz 386SX with zero wait states will be faster than a similar system with one wait state which will be faster than a system with two wait states etc.. This is easy enough to understand. The complicated part is saying how much faster or slower a machine with a wait state is. For example, which is faster - a 25MHz machine with one wait state or a 20MHz machine with zero wait states? This question takes us further into the intimate relationship between the processor and memory than is covered in this chapter and so the answer will have to wait until Chapter 4.

Measuring the FPU - MFLOPS

The numeric co-processor or FPU (Floating Point Unit) is definitely the most important co-processor at the moment and many programs benefit from using one. In the same way that the speed of the main processor, the CPU, can be measured in MIPS, the speed of the FPU can be measured in MFLOPS - Million FLoating Point Operations per Second. This is an average measure of FPU power and is as liable to misinterpretation as MIPS. In particular it is possible to create numeric co-processors that are better than average at common types of arithmetic, such as scalar products, but this doesn't show up in a raw MFLOPS rating.

At the moment there are five possible numeric co-processors that can be used with 386 systems, the 287, the 387, the Weitek Abacus and the 387 compatible FasMath 83D87 and IIT-3C87. These have MFLOPS ratings that range from .3 MFLOPS for the 387 to .9 MFLOPS for the Weitek Abacus.

Benchmarks

As you should be able to see by this point, the question of how fast a computer is is a very difficult one to answer. The speed and power of the processor is only one aspect of system performance. Speed of data transfer between system components and the existence of co-processors for particular tasks all affect how quickly a machine will run a program.

At each stage it is easy to say what will maximise performance, for example a numeric co-processor will speed up a program that does a lot of calculations and the fastest available disk controller is desirable for a database program. However, in practice real programs use the facilities of a machine in different proportions and real machines are compromises. Given two machines, one with a fast processor, the other with a fast disk, it is usually difficult to say which will run any given program quicker. In other words not only is it difficult to rank machines in order of power, but it can be difficult to rank them for a specific application on the basis of their specification alone. A partial solution to this problem is to run a *benchmark* program on each machine. A benchmark is simply a standard program that is used to compare machines. There is no such thing as the perfect benchmark and there is certainly no single benchmark that can accurately summarise a machine's performance. Another problem is that once a benchmark becomes accepted manufacturers can look at it and attempt to find ways of running it faster that are so specific that the improvements don't carry over to other programs - so effectively invalidating the benchmark.

Even though it is impossible to find a single benchmark to summarise the performance of a processor, it is clear that its performance at any task must depend on a mixture of four factors - its CPU, its FPU, its disk, and its video power. It is possible to create benchmarks that measure the power of each of these system aspects separately. Any real application will make use of these facilities in different proportions. For example, spreadsheets use the CPU and FPU a lot, the disk and video a little, desktop publishing uses the CPU and the video a lot and so on.

It is not difficult to see that it is reasonably sensible to think of each type of application as having a 'demand profile' that gives the percentage of each type of a machine's facilities that it uses on average. For example, you might say that the overall speed of a spreadsheet application depends 40% on CPU speed, 30% on FPU, 10% on disk and 20% on video. Of course these percentages may not be exact and may change over time. For example, if a DTP program uses disk to store temporary information then its disk weighting may be higher than average for the task. Similarly the new generation of spreadsheet programs tend to make more use of disk and video than the previous generation and so their profile for the task is different. Typical applications profiles are given in the following table:

Application	CPU	FPU	Disk	Video
Word processing	high	low	medium	medium
Spreadsheet	high	high	low	medium
Database	medium	low	high	low
CAD/CAM	high	high	medium	high
DTP	high	medium	medium	high
Scientific	high	high	medium	medium
Program development	high	low	high	low

Standard benchmarks

There are a great many standard benchmarks in use and it is very easy to become confused by performances quoted in so many different terms. In most cases, however, it is important to realise that these benchmark results are relative. That is, they can only be used to compare different machines of the same type and say which one is better than another.

The following is a list of well known benchmarks:

Byte benchmarks - a standard set of test programs used by Byte magazine to test machines. A new set of benchmarks was introduced in 1988. The performance on each test is normalised so that an IBM 286AT (8MHz) rates 1.0. The benchmarks are a mixture of special low level test programs and standard applications programs.

Dhrystone - a standard benchmark program that tests aspects of machine operation not covered by the Whetstone. The one thing that the Dhrystone does not measure is floating point arithmetic.

Landmark speed - the clock speed that a traditional 286/AT machine would have to operate at to give the same performance as the machine under test (discussed earlier in this chapter). Many users confuse Landmark speed with clock speed and some manufacturers make use of this in the way that they quote Landmark speeds in place of true clock speed.

Linpack - a collection of Fortran routines designed to solve linear equations. Tests floating point speed.

MIPS Rating - Dhrystones normalised so that the VAX 11/780 computer rates as 1. Sometimes called VAX MIPS.

Norton SI - a System Index introduced as part of the Norton Utility package. Originally designed for the 8088/86 and sometimes said to give misleading results for the 286 and 386/486 processors. The PC/XT has an SI of 1.0.

PC Magazine benchmarks - a range of programs that test individual system components. Results are reported as time to complete each test.

PCW benchmarks - a collection of six test programs. The individual results are combined to form an index normalised so that the PC/XT has an index of 1.

Power Meter - an automated testing package providing a range of standard and customised benchmarks. Many results are reported in PMU - Power Meter Units - scaled so that the bigger the result the better the performance.

Savage - a complicated calculation that involves trigonometric and other transcendental functions which should evaluate to 1.

Sieve - a standard method of finding prime numbers. The full title is the Sieve of Eratosthenes and it is used mainly to test language compilers.

Whetstone - a Fortran floating point calculation. Used to test speed of numeric calculation. Usually reported as Whetstones per second.

Key points

» MIPS and clock speed are two reasonable measures of processor power as long as they are used within a single processor family.

» The data transfer rate between the different components of a computer system also determines its overall speed of operation.

» The data transfer rate depends on the width of the data bus and the clock rate.

» A single shared bus is the traditional way of connecting system components. This has been superseded by the use of local buses for high speed components such as RAM and in some cases the video controller.

» It is possible to use a different data bus width and clock rate inside a processor. For example, the 386SX uses a 32-bit internal but only 16-bit external data bus. The 486DX2 double the external clock for internal use.

» Modern high performance designs make use of co-processors to share the load with the main processor. This presents design problems in how to share the common bus efficiently and fairly between each of the system components.

» Even with a high speed bus there is still the possibility that wait states may slow the actual data transfer rate.

» Benchmarks are test programs that are used to compare the performance of computer systems.

Chapter 3
The External Bus

In this chapter we examine the need for an external bus and look at the four standards - PC bus, ISA, EISA and MCA. The type of bus that a machine has can limit the type of application it can handle efficiently. However, there are also lots of situations where the type of bus has no effect whatsoever and it is important to know when it is a critical choice.

The original IBM PC in its most basic form was a very weak machine and it relied heavily on the idea of expansion options to make it into something useful. For example, one of the early models could only have 256KByte of memory fitted to its main board. If you wanted to expand this to the limit of 640KByte then you had to buy an extra printed circuit board to accommodate the RAM chips. This board plugged into a special connector or slot towards the back of the machine. The collection of expansion slots is generally referred to as an *expansion bus*. Eight such slots were generally available for expansion options that included, in addition to memory, video boards, disk controllers, printer ports, modem ports etc.. If it hadn't been for this remarkable expansion capability it is arguable that the IBM PC would have become extinct very rapidly.

Most owners ran their machines with the nearly all of the expansion slots full and finding a spare slot for something new often proved difficult. This experience tended to drive home the idea that the provision of expansion slots in quantity is the mark of a good machine. Perhaps it should be remembered that a full set of expansion slots is a good indication that the original machine was severely lacking in basic features in the first place!

Today the number of expansion slots that a machine needs varies greatly according to its intended purpose. It used to be the rule that all machines needed the standard eight slots. The reason for this was that you needed a slot for the video, one for the hard disk controller, one for a floppy disk controller, one for the parallel/serial interface card, one for memory expansion and three more just in case. This counting has changed due to the availability of multi-function expansion boards. For example, nearly all hard disk controllers now incorporate a floppy disk controller. Indeed, you can buy a single expansion card that includes a hard disk controller, a floppy disk controller, a serial port, a parallel port and a games port. In addition, most machines no longer use the external bus for memory expansion. This not only reduces the number of potential add-on cards needed by one, but greatly changes the role of the external bus, as will become clear later. Putting all of these changes together results in the typical machine using only one slot for a combined disk controller, one for a video card and perhaps one other for serial, parallel and games ports.

The PC bus

The original PC was an eight-bit machine based on the 8088 processor and this was reflected in the design of its expansion bus. The PC bus was an eight-bit design originally working at the slowish speed of 4.77MHz. Although other manufacturers have pushed this speed up, in line with processor speeds,

8MHz is generally considered to be the safe upper limit and has now become the norm. It introduced the now familiar 62-pin printed circuit card edge connector and the long narrow plug-in cards that go with it. At first all PC plug-in cards were full length but over time half length and even third length cards have become more common.

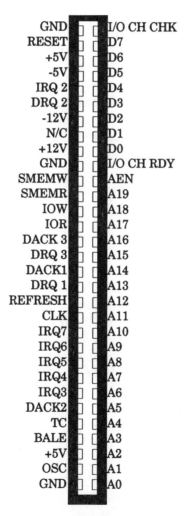

Figure 3.1
Standard PC bus expansion connector

By today's standards the PC bus is not only slow, it is primitive. It has no facility for an expansion card to take over the bus, i.e. to become a bus master, it has only six interrupt lines and only 20 address lines. Of these shortcomings, having only six interrupt lines proved most difficult to live with, especially as most of these were already allocated. Twenty address lines are enough to control only 1 MByte of memory but as this represented the maximum amount of memory usable by the 8088 and 8086 systems at the time this was not a problem. In fact, seen in the light of the systems that it was designed to work with, the PC bus was very reasonable. You could use it to add any type of peripheral - graphics, disk, modem etc. - without it becoming a bottleneck on your machine's performance. You could even use it to add additional memory that would work at the same speed and be treated in the same way as any memory fitted to your computer's main board, but this is more a reflection of the slowness of the machines of the time rather than the speed of the bus.

ISA

When IBM introduced the 286 AT the only immediate shortcoming of the existing PC bus was that it was 8-bit and the new machine could deal with data 16 bits at a time. Had the PC bus been left unmodified the only real consequence would have been that devices plugged into the expansion bus would have had a slower data transfer rate than anything connected directly to the processor. In practice this second class status was unacceptable, particularly where memory expansion cards were concerned, and IBM augmented the PC bus, to produce what we now call the ISA (Industry Standard Architecture), in a very clever way. They simply added a second printed circuit board edge connector just in front of the original connector and used it to add the extra eight data lines and four new address lines. The eight data lines made the ISA bus a full 16-bit bus, as used by the 80286. This means that in principle devices connected via the ISA bus are at no disadvantage when it comes to data transfer rates. The extra four address lines also take the amount of memory that can be added via the bus up to 16 MBytes (i.e. 24 address lines) and this is the largest amount that the 80286 can handle. In other words, with this one simple change the ISA bus is made equal to the performance of the ATs of that period.

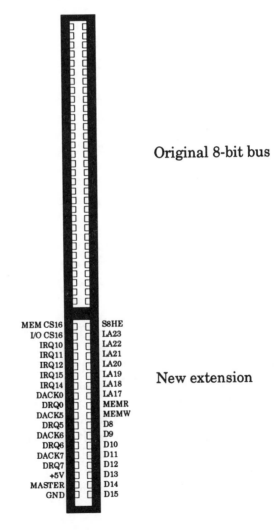

Figure 3.2
ISA 16-bit extension to the PC bus

As well as matching the 80286's design, the ISA bus also added features to ensure backward compatibility with the PC bus. The objective was to allow existing 8-bit PC style add-on cards to be plugged into the large printed circuit edge connector, leaving the smaller 36-pin connector empty. Most manufacturers also fitted a mixture of full ISA and PC expansion slots in their machines. It was reasoned that not all cards needed or could benefit from a 16-bit slot and so they saved the cost of the additional connectors.

In practice backward compatibility with the PC bus was achieved but the need for it caused a number of inefficiencies in the way that the ISA bus works. Obviously, to get the best out of the ISA bus you need to use a 16-bit card, but how does the processor know the difference between an 8-bit card and a 16-bit card? To allow the processor to decide which type of card it is dealing with, other control lines were added to signal whether a transfer was to be 8 or 16 bits. In fact an add-on card has to signal before the processor starts the transfer that it is a 16-bit card. If it doesn't then the processor transfers data eight bits at a time and the speed advantage is lost.

The difficulty with this scheme wasn't immediately apparent but it stems from the need for a card to detect that it is about to be used. The ISA bus duplicates four of the address lines on the original PC bus on the additional connector but in a fast 'un-latched' form that allows a card to detect that it is about to be used and send the 'I am a 16-bit card' signal if it is. The trouble is that with only four fast copies of the address lines, a card can only pin down the address that is about to be used to the nearest 64KByte of memory and this is a little vague. To be sure that it about to be used, an add-on card has to claim a 64KByte block of memory all for itself - and many found this unacceptable. In addition to make use of 16-bit data transfers the software needed to be re-written. As a consequence many apparently 16-bit adapter cards spend much of their time working eight bits at a time.

Another problem is that the ISA bus was never defined in any publication or document produced by IBM. As a result, and despite its name, it has proved difficult to standardise and improve. Most manufacturers have taken the attitude that increasing the speed of the basic 8MHz ISA bus is a dangerous occupation. In machines with processors that run faster than 8MHz the bus is run from a different clock, so slowing external bus transfers. This split speed working is the norm for all ISA 386-ATs.

The ISA bus also added some additional and much needed interrupt and DMA control lines. It also added a *bus master* line that could be used to allow an add-on board to take over control of the entire machine. However, this bus master facility was slow and really only allowed an add-on to take over the whole machine on a long term basis - i.e. you could use it for a second processor but not to allow a graphics controller to take over for a few milliseconds every now and again.

The need for change

The introduction of the 80386 caused a similar reappraisal of the ISA bus to that caused by the introduction of the 80286 with respect to the PC bus. There was a certain inevitability about this process that may not have been entirely rational. The argument was that if an 8-bit processor needed an 8-bit external bus and a 16-bit processor needed a 16-bit bus then the 32-bit 386 certainly needed a 32-bit bus of some sort. The ISA bus isn't as sophisticated as the buses found in mini and mainframe computers. It is also true that the ISA bus is slow and lacks features by these same standards. However, the real question was, and is, whether 386/486 based machines really need a more powerful bus than the ISA bus? At the time the answer seemed to be yes because of one single factor - the ISA bus was too slow to allow memory expansion to be fitted using it. It also only has 24 address lines limiting the memory expansion to 16 MBytes whereas the 386DX has 32 address lines.

The 286-AT had introduced the custom of adding memory by way of expansion cards, but the typical 286-AT worked at 8MHz and in this case the ISA bus was fast enough. Even early 386 machines worked at 20MHz and needed to make 32-bit data transfers between the processor and memory. Clearly the ISA bus was too slow and too narrow and had insufficient address lines for this class of machine, let alone for the 40MHz 386/486 machines that were soon to follow. Notice, however, that the ISA bus is much more suited for use with the 386SX which can only make use of a 16-bit external bus.

The RAM bus

What changed this general consensus about the inadequacy of the ISA bus for the 386/486 family was the integration of increasing amounts of memory on the motherboard. This was connected to the processor via an internal high speed 32-bit bus. At first manufacturers found it necessary to incorporate special 32-bit memory expansion bus slots. These usually took the form of a pair of full length PC connectors - the first was a standard PC bus and the second contained the extensions needed to cope with 32-bit memory transfers. There were even some special high speed 16-bit memory slots added to fast 386SX designs. The disadvantage of this arrangement is that each manufacturer's expansion card was different and so there was a complete loss of standardisation.

What saved us from a standards chaos was the introduction of *memory modules* in the form of SIP or SIMM packages. These are small printed circuit boards with a small number of memory chips fitted (see the Chapter 5). SIPs and SIMMs reduced the cost of memory, but their most important contribution was the standardisation that they brought to memory packaging. The connections to SIP and SIMM modules were standardised by an electronics industry committee, as is common with many electronic components. In this case, however, the standards effectively became the standards for an internal memory bus with the SIP or SIMM modules playing the role of tiny memory expansion cards! Using SIPs or SIMMs, 16MBytes or more can be fitted in easy stages to a suitable motherboard. You can also buy the SIPs and SIMMs from a wide range of vendors. If this isn't a standardised memory bus then I don't know what would be!

The point of all this is that although the ability to add memory via an external bus is sometimes important, it is no longer the burning issue that it once was. It is certainly not the single reason for the replacement of the ISA bus by something better.

Future buses

Once memory is removed from the external expansion bus, the need for a new improved bus becomes less pressing but it doesn't go away entirely. It is possible to find special situations and applications where the need to transfer data either more quickly or more intelligently than the ISA bus can manage becomes a problem. (You will find detailed arguments about which applications need which type of bus later in this book.)

It is thus worth knowing what specific defects should be put right in its successors. The most obvious restrictions have already been mentioned. In particular, any new bus should be a full 32-bit bus with 32 address lines, giving it the power to work with as much memory as the 386/486 is able to handle. Of course there is the argument that 32-bit data and 32-bit addressing is nothing more than a temporary high point and any new bus working to these specifications will soon have to be improved. It is likely to be some time before processors that use more than 32 bits become the norm because, even in the mini and mainframe world, machines are based on 32 to 48-bit designs. This is because after 32 bits there is very little to be gained in terms of speed and power by increasing the number of bits, and other methods of increasing power have to be used.

The only other desirable features are some way of efficiently transferring control to another devices, i.e. bus mastering, and better interrupt and DMA facilities.

There are only two candidates to succeed the ISA bus - the EISA bus and the MCA bus.

The EISA bus

Although later on the scene than its direct rival, the MCA bus, the EISA (Extended Industry Standard Architecture) bus is directly based on the ISA bus. Indeed it was a conscious effort on the part of a number of manufacturers to provide an improved bus that was backward compatible with ISA as a reaction to the totally new and incompatible MCA bus. The first problem that the EISA designers had to solve was to find some way of extending the physical connectors used in the ISA bus to accommodate the additional signals. In practice this proved very difficult, with crazy suggestions such as 'out-rigger' boards being used to plug into EISA sockets mounted at the side of the traditional slots. Fortunately, a good solution was eventually found in the form of double depth or bi-level modified ISA edge connectors. (This was designed by the electronics company Burndy who also supply IBM with MCA connectors!)

At first sight an EISA connector looks exactly like an ISA connector. You can also plug any ISA board into an EISA slot and expect it to work as it would in an ISA slot. The secret of the EISA slot is only revealed when you plug an EISA card into it. This has a small notch cut into it that allows it to be inserted further than an ISA card. The extra connectors that EISA uses are present at the bottom level of the slot and don't make contact with an ISA board. The EISA signals are threaded between the standard ISA signals on the add-on card. This threading has been carefully arranged to improve the immunity of the bus to interference between adjacent signal lines. Even so, it is important to realise that the EISA bus retains the basic clock speed of 8MHz. This has to be so to enable it to work with existing ISA add-on cards. In other words, a 386/AT or 486/AT machine will still engage in split speed working, keeping its EISA bus at 8MHz no matter how fast the processor clock runs.

The EISA bus is a full 32-bit bus complete with 32 address lines giving it the same capabilities as the 386/486 processor. For backward compatibility it also has control lines that an add-on board can use to signal to the processor that it is capable of performing an EISA 32-bit transfer or an EISA/ISA 16-bit transfer. To make this more workable all of the address lines are available in a fast non-latched form making it possible for any card to determine if it is about to be used and so signal the type of transfer it can cope with. If none of the

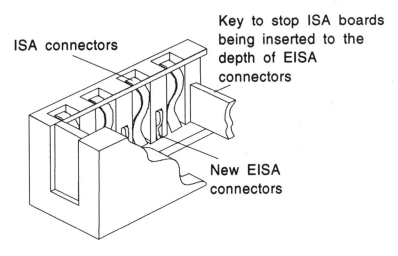

Figure 3.3
The bi-level EISA connector showing the internal detail

lines are used then the bus reverts to an 8-bit transfer. That is, EISA is not only ISA backward compatible, it is also compatible with the original PC bus.

Other improvements include the introduction of shareable interrupt lines and an efficient bus mastering system. The shareable interrupt lines have been achieved by changing existing interrupt lines to be level rather than edge sensitive, as in the case of the ISA bus. A level sensitive interrupt allows the processor to scan the add-on boards to discover which of them needs attention.

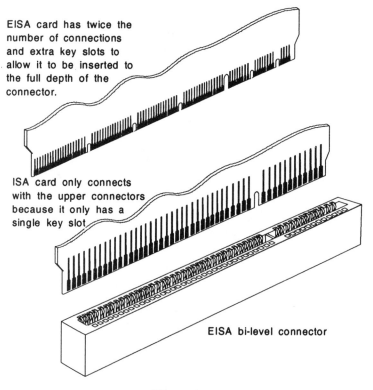

EISA card has twice the number of connections and extra key slots to allow it to be inserted to the full depth of the connector.

ISA card only connects with the upper connectors because it only has a single key slot

EISA bi-level connector

Figure 3.4
How the EISA connector can accept ISA and full EISA cards

The only disadvantage of this scheme is that you cannot mix ISA cards and EISA cards on one interrupt line. In other words, only EISA cards can share. The bus mastering facilities are particularly powerful. A bus master can gain control of the bus very quickly and can then transfer data directly between other devices. The EISA hardware will take care of any problems of a 32-bit bus master trying to talk to a 16-bit device. In addition, the EISA hardware will arbitrate between multiple bus masters to make sure that the most important get a fair share of the bus's time.

In theory the EISA bus can transfer data at 32MByte/s (i.e. 32 bits or 4 Bytes x 8MHz) in short bursts but 25MByte/s is a more typical sustained transfer rate.

To make life easier for the user, each EISA card has a unique product identifier code that the processor can read to determine which card is where. In principle this makes configuring EISA software and hardware easier than configuring ISA software and hardware. In practice, though, things aren't generally quite so smooth. You need a utility program to configure the bus to the adapter cards and this can be almost as tricky as hardware configuration. The EISA configuration file is supplied along with any EISA cards that you buy. More of a problem is the fact that you need an EISA configuration file for any ISA standard cards that you install and this is most definitely not supplied with the card. You still have to set the switches on the card correctly, but without the configuration file the EISA bus refuses to notice the presence of the card. You can usually obtain a suitable configuration file from the manufacturer of the machine but only for very common cards. Failing this, you have no choice but to write your own configuration file. As the EISA bus increases in popularity the quality of installation software is also improving.

The MCA bus

Perhaps the most important fact about the MCA bus is that it is completely incompatible with the ISA bus. This is both its advantage and its disadvantage. Not having to be compatible with any earlier design, it was possible to start again and produce something simple and fast. The price for this is simply that the existing range of ISA boards cannot be used in an MCA-based system.

MCA was introduced by IBM as a replacement for the ISA bus in its 286 and 386 based PS/2 machines. It is more complex than the EISA bus because it is implemented as a 16-bit and as a separate 32-bit bus. In other words, there are two grades of MCA bus. The 16-bit version is used in 286 and 386SX PS/2 models because there is no point in using a 32-bit expansion bus with a 16-bit processor! However, even in 386 based PS/2 designs a mixture of 16-bit and 32-bit expansion connectors are used. The 16-bit MCA connectors are used for lower performance devices and the 32-bit MCA connectors are used primarily for memory and other high performance devices.

There is an additional, but minor, complication in that there is also the possibility of a video extension being added to any single MCA bus slot. The video extension allows any extra video card to override the internal VGA and make use of the machine's video output hardware. The video extension makes it possible to extend the display modes offered by the internal video hardware without having to replace it. Only one of the MCA expansion slots in a machine has the video extension because the internal hardware can only be overridden by one external adapter. The same effect can be achieved on the ISA and EISA bus by adding a 'video feed through' connector to any video cards in the system. None of the MCA buses can achieve the same result by adding an extra connector to the video card itself.

Thus inside an MCA machine you can find as many as three distinct types of expansion slot - see Figure 3.5. The 32-bit MCA has many of the same specifications as the EISA bus. It is a full 32-bit data bus with 32 address lines. The 16-bit version is similar to the ISA bus. That is it has a 16-bit data bus and a 24-bit address bus. The main technical difference between MCA and EISA is that MCA is an asynchronous bus whereas EISA is a synchronous bus. A *synchronous bus* works at a fixed clock rate no matter how fast a device can transfer data. An *asynchronous bus*, on the other hand, takes its timings from the devices involved in the data transfer and does not depend on a fixed clock. When the receiving device has the data it signals back to the sending device for more data. Clearly an asynchronous device has to be more complex than a synchronous one but it is potentially more efficient.

The original MCA specification resulted in a maximum transfer rate of 20MByte/s which is of course slower than the EISA maximum of 32MByte/s. IBM, however introduced a new method of data transfer using the existing MCA bus that increases the data rate to 160MBytes/s.

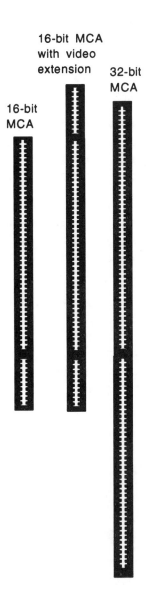

16-bit MCA with video extension

16-bit MCA

32-bit MCA

Figure 3.5
Three different MCA connectors

They also introduced additional modes to allow other devices to take over the MCA bus more effectively and efficiently. These developments emphasise the way IBM made use of MCA in an attempt to keep one step ahead of the competition without much regard to the actual needs of the user. Indeed, there are many parts of the MCA bus that are 'undefined' or 'reserved for future use' and this stopped many manufacturers from producing MCA designs for fear that IBM would simply change the rules and make existing MCA machines look out of date.

Other improvements included a change in the way that interrupts were handled. The ISA bus uses edge triggered interrupts but the MCA bus uses level triggered interrupts. This allows systems that use a large number of interrupts to be more efficient and more reliable.

MCA cards also have a unique identifying number which can be used by software - POS, Programmable Option Select - to simplify installation. As in the case of the EISA bus this software configuration of adapter cards can be almost as troublesome as the hardware configuration needed for ISA adapter cards.

Choosing the bus

After this review of them, it seems fitting to deliver judgement on the three buses. The issue facing any prospective 386/486 buyer is which type of bus to look for in their machine. Of course, there is the small matter of cost to consider as well as performance. Obviously, the aim is to find the lowest cost machine that will do the job well and continue to do that job for a reasonable number of years - typically five.

The lowest cost bus to buy and run is currently the ISA bus. It has been around a long time and looks set to be around for a long while yet. There are more ISA add-on cards than either MCA or EISA cards. EISA is marginally easier to design and so in principle it should be cheaper than MCA, but market forces have as much influence on actual costs as manufacturing costs. Intel make chip sets allowing manufacturers to implement both MCA and EISA expansion bus machines. At the time of writing it looks distinctly likely that the cost of the EISA chip set will fall to the point where an EISA-based machine will cost as little as an ISA-based machine of equivalent specification. When this happens there will at least be no penalty in buying an EISA machine.

MCA adapter cards are much smaller than either PC bus or ISA/EISA bus cards and this can cause designers a problem in crushing all the electronics needed into the space provided. The MCA design was produced with the idea that manufacturers would use high density surface mounting components to reduce the space needed, but this is an expensive construction method for small runs or prototypes.

As far as performance goes MCA and EISA are more or less equal, although there are many who would argue the superiority of one over the other. The point is that they are in the same class when it comes to transfer rates and sophistication and any slight difference will have little impact on observable performance. In other words, once you decide that you need something more than ISA the choice between

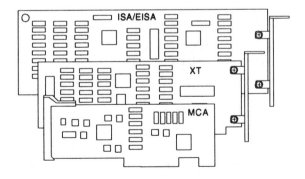

Figure 3.6
Three different sizes of add-on card

EISA and MCA will be based on something other than performance.

The EISA bus has one single powerful advantage over MCA - it is backward compatible with ISA and this is enough for a clear cut recommendation in its favour. The MCA bus is only worth considering if you are committed to buying IBM machines. It even seems credible that IBM could produce an EISA based machine in the future - after all they still supply ISA based machines!

In other words, the choice is really between the ISA bus and either one of the MCA or EISA buses. To discover what determines the choice it is necessary to examine the transfer rates encountered in a typical system.

Bus saturation

An external bus may be slow by the standards of what else is available but to have a negative effect on a system's performance it is necessary for it to saturate - i.e. for the data rate demanded to exceed the data rate the bus can handle. To investigate the situations in which an external bus might saturate, it is necessary to compare typical transfer rates achieved by today's hardware with the maximum transfer rates offered by each bus.

In Figure 3.7, CPU and RAM transfer rates are estimated for a 33MHz 386. Obviously a faster clock rate would increase these in proportion. A 486 can reach *burst transfer rates* (i.e. peak rates that can only be sustained for a short time) of over 100MByte/s for short periods. The disk transfer rates quoted are typical of fast IDE, SCSI and ESDI drives and controllers. Disk rates could increase in the future to as much as 20MByte/s by using the SCSI 2 bus or perhaps something even better. The video data transfer rates quoted are based on the time to completely rewrite a screenful of data for a super high resolution VGA mode (1024 x 768pixels in 256 colours) in the

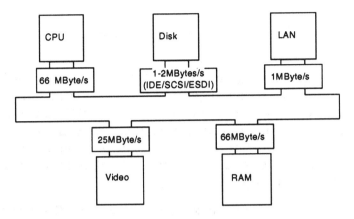

Figure 3.7
Typical bus transfer rates

time it takes to show one TV frame. In other words, it is the data transfer rate needed for real time animation at the stated resolution. Obviously this data rate can be much reduced by redrawing only the part of the screen that changes or by accepting lower screen refresh rates. For example, if you assume that half a second is a reasonable time to wait for a screen redraw, then the data rate drops to only 2MByte/s, and if you are happy to make do with only 16 colours then it drops to 1MByte/s and so on. The transfer rate quoted for the LAN adapter is based on a standard 10MBit/s Ethernet system. This is also the average transfer rate. In a server it could well be desirable for the peak transfer rate to be ten times higher than the 1MByte/s quoted.

The maximum data transfer rates on the three standard buses are:

» ISA can manage a maximum of approximately 6.5MByte/s when working at the standard 8MHz.

» EISA can achieve burst transfers at approximately 33MByte/s but 25MByte/s is a more reasonable sustained transfer rate.

» 32-bit MCA can work at 20MBytes/s and in the new burst transfer mode at 160MByte/s.

Comparing these rates to those needed by the different components of the system, it is immediately clear that only the MCA bus using its highest speed transfer mode comes anywhere near being able to support the data transfer between processor and memory. Of course, this advantage is entirely illusory because it is more cost effective to move memory off the external bus and connect it to the processor using a local bus as already discussed.

Once the processor and memory have their own bus over which to communicate, the picture looks very different. Clearly disk drives and LAN adapters don't risk overtaxing the ISA bus, let alone the EISA or the MCA bus. The only critical component is the video adapter and this could be handled by the EISA or the MCA bus. However, in practice this high video transfer rate isn't needed for all applications and once again the ISA bus seems perfectly acceptable. If you change the specification to a higher resolution video board, say 1024x1024 with 24-bit colour, then the story is very different and in this case the ISA bus saturates, making the EISA or MCA bus preferable. Even so it is arguable that the video transfer rate is so high that a better solution is to move the video hardware onto a local bus.

Thus in a single-user/single-tasking system the ISA bus is good enough for all applications with the possible exception of high performance graphics of the sort found in CAD or illustration workstations.

This conclusion changes, however, if you consider a multi-user or multi-tasking system. In this case what matters is the degree of processor saturation as well as external bus saturation. In a single-user/single-tasking system there is little point in freeing the processor from the job of transferring data because there is nothing else for it to do other than stand idle. In a multi-user or multi-tasking situation this isn't the case because the processor can get on with another task while a bus master transfers data. The ISA's lack of sophisticated bus mastering means that the CPU saturates long before the ISA bus does. If you add multiple bus masters into the equation then a disk drive and a few network controller cards can saturate the ISA bus by trying to transfer data at the same time. This makes it necessary to move to the EISA or MCA bus to achieve the necessary throughput of data. The most common situation in which multi-tasking is encountered is in a network server. This has to deal with requests for data from a number of workstations and the faster it can do this the better. Thus the EISA or MCA bus makes a considerable difference to the performance of a network server, if not to the workstations connected to it. Notice that Windows 3 and other DOS multi-taskers only benefit from EISA or MCA if they are being used with more than one active program. In most cases they are used to swap between programs in such a way that only one is active at any given time.

To summarise:

» The ISA bus is good enough for all single-user/single-tasking applications with the possible exception of high resolution graphics.

» The EISA and MCA bus have performance advantages for network servers and other multi-user/multi-tasking machines.

In the future the cost difference between EISA and ISA machines may make it possible to simply buy one type of machine, i.e. EISA, for all situations. Even in this case it is likely that the cards plugged into the average machine will be ISA leaving EISA cards for use in network servers.

Key points

» There are three standard expansion bus designs: the original ISA bus used in the AT, the upward compatible EISA bus, and the incompatible MCA bus.

» The EISA bus is a full 32-bit design that extends the 16-bit ISA design. ISA adapter cards can be used in EISA slots. This means that a machine with nothing but EISA slots can accept 8-bit or 16-bit ISA cards as well as full EISA cards.

» The MCA bus is available in a 16-bit and a 32-bit version, each of which uses a different connector. There is also a video extension to the 16-bit connector. This means that to accommodate all types of MCA cards a machine has to have at least three types of expansion connector.

» On the basis of data transfer rate alone there seems to be little reason, as yet, to abandon the ISA bus as long as it isn't used for system memory. That is, as long as system memory is added via the main board, the speed of the expansion bus is not critical.

» ISA machines are still suitable for the majority of single-user/single-tasking systems with the exception of high performance graphics.

» Only multi-user/multi-tasking systems benefit from the use of either the EISA or MCA bus.

Chapter 4
Memory Speed

After the processor, memory - its amount, type and speed - is the most critical component of any system. In this chapter the hardware and performance details of 386/486 system memory are described. Memory expansion is dealt with in the next chapter.

The amount of memory that a system has limits the practical size of a program that you can run. It is true that a program that is larger than the available memory can always be run by splitting it into smaller chunks and running these as required, but this introduces a significant performance degradation. A second limitation is that the speed that a processor offers can only be made use of if the memory can deal with data transfers at the same rate. There is little point in coupling a fast processor with slow memory.

With memory prices falling the amount of memory is no longer the major problem for 386/486 users but there are still some small difficulties to look out for. A much bigger problem is memory speed. Put simply, the 386/486 processor is capable of running at much higher speeds than current reasonably priced memory. You can buy memory that runs as fast but it is prohibitively expensive to use in the sort of quantities that a typical 386/486 system needs. For this reason a large part of this chapter is devoted to explaining the different ways that manufacturers have used to speed up memory systems. This discussion is of little interest if you already have a 386/486 system - you are unable to change the method that a machine uses to handle memory - but it will help you appreciate your machine's weaknesses and strengths and might help you configure it appropriately. If you are about to buy a 386/486 system then the type of memory it has is a crucial indicator of how fast you can expect it to work.

The effect of wait states

The original PC worked at only 4.77MHz, a speed that even the more leisurely memory chips of the time found easy to keep up with. That is, whenever the processor wanted to write or read data from the memory it could. With the introduction of the 8MHz and faster 286 machine, this situation changed. At first the slow memory problem was solved by the introduction of wait states. (The idea of a wait state was introduced in Chapter 2, it is simply a clock cycle in which the processor is forced to be idle to give time for a slower device to catch up. The processor knows that it has to use wait states because the device it is trying to use signals that it needs a wait state.)

The 386/486 processor typically takes two clock cycles to read or write memory. This means that adding a single wait state makes it take three clock cycles so slowing it down by 33%. A better way to think about this is to ask how much slower a clock speed with no wait states would be in order to equal the performance with wait states. For example, if you are using a machine that runs at 20MHz with one wait state this will be equal to a 13MHz machine with no wait states. The effect of one and two wait states on the clock speed of various standard clock rates can be seen in the table that follows.

Speed	1 Wait state	2 Wait states
12MHz	8	6
16MHz	10	8
20MHz	13	10
25MHz	16	12
33MHz	22	15

Notice that these are worst possible case figures. In practice a 386/486 memory access may take longer than two clock cycles and there are instructions that don't access memory at all. However, these figures do provide an indication of how powerful an impact wait states can have on a system.

The situation is very similar to the use of a different internal and external clock as described in connection with the 486DX2 in the previous chapter. In the case of the 486DX2 the internal clock rate is doubled; in the case of wait states the external clock rate is reduced. You can see from the table that adding two wait states is exactly the same as halving the external clock rate.

To give you some idea of how fast memory chips have to be to keep up with a 386/486 it is worth saying that in a 16MHz system the RAM chips can be accessed as fast as every 125ns. (1 ns or one nano-second is .000000001 of a second.) The calculation is simply that at at 16MHz the time between clock pulses is 62.5ns (i.e. 1/16MHz) and the processor can access memory every two clock pulses, giving a fastest time of 125ns. You can perform a similar calculation for any clock speed.

The speed of memory chips is also measured in nano-seconds. The usual quoted figure is the chip's access time, that is the time it takes to read or write data to a location. From this you might think that 100ns chips, which are readily available, are all that are needed to make a 16MHz system run without wait states. However, there is a complication in that the quoted access time for a RAM chip is simply the time it takes to read or write one item of data. If you want to use it more than once then it needs a little time between each access to get itself ready - the precharge time. What actually matters is the RAM chip's total cycle time, i.e. the time for it to be used and ready to be used again, and this time is usually a good percentage more than the access time. So a chip with an access time of 100ns could have a cycle time of close to 200ns and therefore if used in a 16MHz 386 system it would need at least one wait state. The cycle time needed for memory chips for some typical processor clock speeds can be seen in the table below:

Clock Speed	0 wait states	1 wait state	2 wait states	3 wait states
16MHz	125	187.5	312.5	375
20MHz	100	150	200	250
25MHz	80	120	160	200
33MHz	60	90	120	150
40MHz	50	75	100	125

Taking into account that access times have to be roughly half the indicated cycle times, the possibility of obtaining fast enough memory chips to produce zero wait states is remote. What this table reveals is that this is only feasible for 16MHz machines and while it is indeed possible to build 16MHz 386/486 machines without wait states by using fast memory (70ns or better), there are much cheaper ways of solving the problem almost as effectively.

Dynamic and Static RAMs

Many users are confused by the terms *dynamic* and *static* RAM. In practice the difference isn't as important as the jargon might lead you to believe. In short:

» Static RAM is fast, expensive and not available in very large quantities

» Dynamic RAM is slower, cheaper and available in very large quantities

The technical details of the difference between these two types of RAM is also interesting. Static RAM uses two transistors to store a single bit of data. The transistors are connected together in a way that makes sure that only one of the two transistors can be on and the other off. Which transistor of the pair is on determines whether a 0 or a 1 is stored at that location. Dynamic RAM uses only a single transistor to store a bit of data. The transistor acts as a switch to control the storage of a small charge on a capacitor. The size of the charge determines whether a 0 or a 1 is stored at the memory location. The only problem with the dynamic RAM arrangement is that the charge slowly leaks away because it is impossible to make a perfect capacitor that stores charge without loss. If a dynamic RAM chip was used in the same way as a static RAM chip then after data was stored in it the charge would start leaking away and eventually the data would be lost. The solution is to arrange for the dynamic RAM chip to be read before the data is lost and then rewritten to restore it to full charge. This is called *refreshing* the dynamic RAM and it imposes a certain level of overhead in using dynamic as opposed to static RAM. You should now be able to see where the names static and dynamic come from. Static RAM retains its data as long as the power is applied without the system having to do anything about it whereas dynamic RAM has to be 'kept on the move' so to speak. You will also come across the jargon terms SRAM, DRAM and refresh, the meanings of which should now be obvious.

It is also worth being aware of how difficult it is to get accurate wait state information from manufacturers. Most would rather claim zero wait states than have the marketing disadvantage of admitting that their machine was slower than it should be. The truth is that no matter what the manufacturer may claim there are no machines on the market at the present time running faster than 16MHz that work with true zero wait states! In the absence of accurate information from manufacturers the only thing that a prospective buyer can do is to discover the memory speed and access method used and try to deduce the likely number of wait states on any given machine.

The statistical approach

Instead of trying to optimise the access time of the entire memory in a machine a different approach makes use of the observed behaviour of programs to optimise the access time of the section of memory actually in use. This idea relies on the fact that most programs use a small area of the memory for a given amount of time, and then move on to use another small area. If you could see into your computer's memory and each location glowed according to how much it was being used, what you would see is small bright patches changing their location slowly as the program entered different phases of activity. In other words, programs tend not to use the memory evenly and if a memory location has just been used then it is much more likely that it, or a memory location near it, will be the next to be used rather than just a random location anywhere in the memory.

There are four broad methods of making use of this locality of reference to speed up memory access:

» memory interleave

» page mode

» page interleave

» cache

None of these methods guarantee to eliminate wait states. Instead they reduce the average frequency with which wait states are required. Thus in systems that employ these methods it makes sense to talk of statistical wait states. For example, a statistical wait state of .5 means that on average half the memory accesses require a full wait state. From the point of view of speed this is exactly the same as saying that each memory access requires a wait state of half the duration of a normal wait state.

Memory interleave

Memory *interleave* is one of the simplest methods of avoiding wait states. If the processor accesses memory locations in a strict progression one after another then zero wait states can be achieved by providing memory in two banks - one providing odd memory locations and one providing even memory locations.

Obviously using two physical banks in this way doubles the time each bank has to deliver up its data and so enables slower chips to be used without generating wait states. Of course the

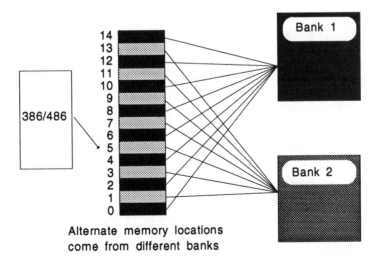

Alternate memory locations
come from different banks

Figure 4.1
Two-bank memory interleave

flaw in this argument is that it only works if the processor always accesses memory in the order an odd followed by an even address. If this isn't the case then the same bank will be used in succession and a wait state will be needed. It is difficult to be precise about the average number of wait states needed using interleaving but if the memory naturally needs 1 wait state then interleaving will reduce it to around .5.

One important point to notice about interleaving is that it depends on having two physical banks of memory. If your machine has only a small amount of memory fitted - 1 MByte say - as a single bank then it can't use interleaving. In this case adding an additional 1 MByte of memory to form a second bank can result in a faster machine.

It is possible to extend the interleave idea to more than two banks of memory being used in succession but this increases the complexity of the system without giving a proportional increase in performance. However, many machines do support up to four banks interleaved in various ways. Notice that many machines describe the memory devices installed as forming bank 0, bank 1, bank 2, etc. but these don't necessarily use interleaving. It is often convenient to label the smallest blocks of memory that can be fitted to a machine in this way no matter how they are used. It can sometimes be difficult to work out the best way to install memory in a machine so as not to place limits on the maximum amount of memory that can be installed while still managing to make use of interleave. This topic is discussed more fully in the next chapter.

Page mode

It is a quirk of the design of DRAM memory chips that once you have accessed a particular location it takes about half the normal time to access any memory location within the same memory region or *page*. How large a page is depends on the particular DRAM chips being used but it is typically 2 KBytes or larger. In other words in a page mode design the first access to any 2KByte page incurs a wait state but any subsequent access to this 2KByte page, the active page, does not. So if memory accesses are sequential a wait state will only occur when a page boundary is crossed.

The problem with this method is that, despite the tendency for memory accesses to be clustered in small regions, programs generally use two active areas of memory - one for the program's code and one for the data. These areas are very likely to be in different pages and so wait states will be generated more often than a simple-minded analysis might suggest. In practice, page mode tends to reduce 1 wait state to about .8 of a wait state on average, which is not a very good performance even though the implementation isn't difficult.

Page interleave

The basic principle of interleaving memory access to a pair of banks has already been described as a way of reducing wait states to about .5. An even greater reduction can be produced by combining interleave with page mode to give *page interleave*. If two banks of memory are available and each is accessed using page mode then a memory access to the same page in the same bank as the previous access generates no wait states. This works exactly the same as in simple page mode. The additional benefit of interleave is that if the next access is in a different page and in a different bank then no wait state will be generated. In simple page mode every access to a different page generates a wait state. In interleaved page mode the only access that causes a wait state is to another page in the same bank as the active page.

Page interleave mode can reduce 1 wait state to .4 of a wait state and because it is relatively easy to implement - the Chips and Technologies standard 386/486 chip set supports it for example - it is a very good solution to the slow memory problem. Once again, as in the case of simple interleave, page mode interleave can only be used if you have enough memory installed to make it possible to form more than one bank.

Cache

A *cache* is like a sophisticated extension of page mode access. An additional block of very fast (SRAM) memory is used as a working store for the processor to read and write data directly without wait states. If the processor wants to access a particular data item and it is in the cache then the cache provides it. This is called a *cache hit*. If it isn't in the cache then the main memory has to be accessed and wait states are introduced. This is a *cache miss*. When data is accessed from memory the data is not only made available to the processor, it is also stored in the cache so that next time the processor asks for it the cache can provide it without generating any wait states.

If the cache were unlimited in size then after a short time all of the memory locations that a program needed would be in the cache and the program would run without any wait states at all. In practice, of course, cache is limited in size. RAM chips fast enough to implement cache are expensive and so typical cache sizes are 16 KBytes, 32 KBytes, 64 KBytes or 128 KBytes, which are small compared to the typical 4 MBytes found on a 386/486 system. Even so, as long as a cache is large enough to hold the memory locations that a program uses most - the program's working set - it can often reduce wait states to as little as .1 of a wait state.

Caches differ in the way that they store and find data in the cache RAM and in the way that they re-use cache locations that already have data stored in them. Roughly speaking there are three types of cache - direct mapped, set associative and fully associative - listed in order of increasing complexity and efficiency. In practice what matters more than the method used is the size of the cache RAM and so most manufacturers have opted either for a direct mapped or set associative cache. The fully associative cache is prohibitively expensive to implement and seems to have little to offer in terms of performance.

Another difference between caches is the amount of data stored in each cache location. This is called the cache's *line size*. A simple-minded design would have each location within

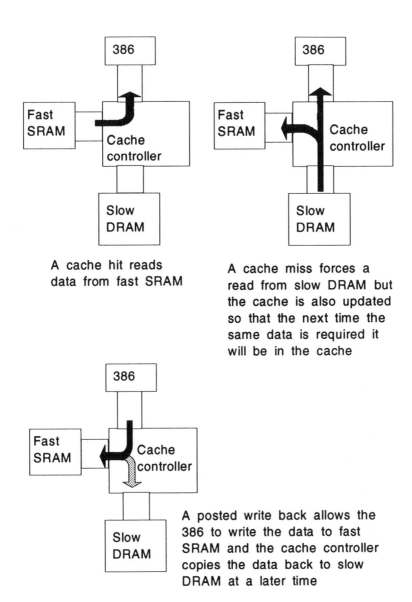

A cache hit reads data from fast SRAM

A cache miss forces a read from slow DRAM but the cache is also updated so that the next time the same data is required it will be in the cache

A posted write back allows the 386 to write the data to fast SRAM and the cache controller copies the data back to slow DRAM at a later time

Figure 4.2
Cache operation

Cache technology

You can get very bogged down in arguments about different types of caching methods when at the end of the day what really matters is getting a good increase in performance for a reasonable cost. The basic problem in designing a cache controller is in allocating cache memory locations to main memory locations. The most complex option is to allow any main memory location to be stored anywhere in the cache memory. This is called an *associative cache* and it requires each cache location to store not only the data that it holds but the address that the data occupies in main memory.

The simplest option is to assign each cache location a fixed group of main memory locations. For example, the first cache location could be assigned to store the main memory locations 0, 9, 19, 29 ..., the second cache location could be used to store 1, 10, 20, 30 ..., and so on. This is called a *direct mapped cache* because each main memory location has only one possible place that it can be stored in the cache. If the processor wants memory location 9, for example, the cache controller knows at once that it only has to look in the first cache location to see if it is present. Of course the problem with a direct mapped cache is that collisions occur. For example, what if the processor needs memory location 19 but memory location 9 is already stored in the cache? Memory locations 19 and 9 are both assigned to the same cache location. In this case memory location 19 would be brought from main memory and would overwrite location 9 in the first cache location. In other words, memory location 9 would be lost from the cache even though there might still be plenty of unused locations in the cache. You should be able to see that this wouldn't happen in a fully associative cache.

A sort of halfway house between these two methods is to be found in the *set associative cache* where more than one fixed cache location is assigned to each main memory location. For example, in a two-way set associative cache each main memory location has two possible places that it can be stored in the cache. Clearly a two-way set associative cache would deal with the problem of storing memory location 19 in the cache without overwriting location 9 (see the figure on the opposite page).

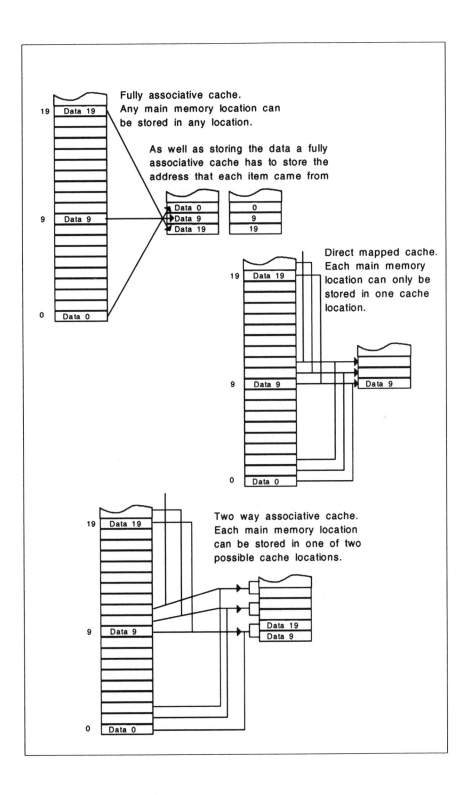

Fully associative cache.
Any main memory location can
be stored in any location.

As well as storing the data a fully
associative cache has to store the
address that each item came from

Direct mapped cache.
Each main memory
location can only be
stored in one cache
location.

Two way associative cache.
Each main memory location
can be stored in one of two
possible cache locations.

the cache the same size as the basic unit of storage used by the machine, i.e. 32 bits or 4 Bytes for the 386DX. However there are advantages in making the line size larger. The reason for this is that if a memory location is required by the 386 then a large line size will result in memory locations around the one required being transferred to the cache. As the principle of program locality says that memory locations close to one that has just been used are likely to be needed in the very near future, this tends to increase the cache hit rate. In addition it is often possible to organise the main memory to work with a full cache line in one read or write operation, so speeding things up still more.

Caches handle requests for data from the memory in more or less the same way but they can differ greatly in the way they handle writes to the memory. Some simply allow the processor to access the memory directly and so always introduce a wait state on every write - this is called a write -through cache. A better idea is to use a posted write cache. This accepts the data from the processor without a wait state and then allows the processor to get on with its next job while it gets on with the slower job of actually writing the data to memory. This is a good scheme which goes wrong only if the processor encounters a cache miss or wants to write data to the memory before the cache controller has had time to finish writing the data to memory. In this case the processor has to wait until the write cycle is complete. This problem can be avoided by use of a *writeback cache*. In this case data is written to the cache with no wait states and the main memory is updated only when it becomes necessary, for example when the cache location is needed to hold some other data item. At the moment posted writes are the norm but the higher performance of the writeback cache is starting to be incorporated in newer designs.

There are complications in the use of a cache concerned with how to keep its contents up-to-date if there are other devices that can write data directly to memory. For example, what if the processor is using a memory location that is currently stored in the cache and a disk controller reads data from disk directly into that memory location. When the processor next accesses that location it will be supplied with data from the cache, which is not the same as the data now in memory. This problem is generally referred to as cache coherency and all cache hardware is designed to deal with the problem. The simplest method is to mark the entire cache invalid if any other device writes to memory. This may be simple but it isn't efficient. A slightly better method is to mark only the altered memory locations that are in the cache as invalid. An even better method is for the cache to monitor what is being transferred to memory and keep itself up-to-date so that no cache locations have to be marked as invalid. Current systems use each of the three techniques. Clearly if you are using an advanced disk controller, video controller or other device then how the system's cache handles the coherence might have a significant impact on performance.

An alternative method of maintaining cache coherency, which is surprisingly simple, is to regard the cache as belonging to the memory rather than the processor. In this situation every

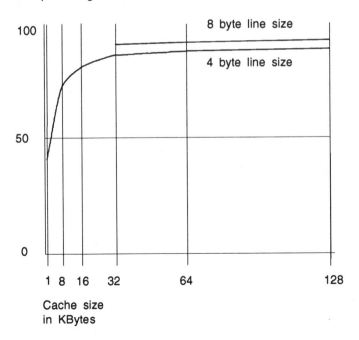

Figure 4.3
Graph of percentage hit rate against cache size

access to memory would go through the cache rather than non-processor accesses by-passing it. Although this is a simple idea manufacturers seem strangely reluctant to take it up.

A cache can reduce 1 wait state down to .03 wait state or less. The most important factor determining the reduction in wait states is the size of the cache as can be seen in the graph.

You can also see in Figure 4.3 that cache sizes follow a law of diminishing returns. Once a cache is larger than the program's working set there is little to be gained in making it larger. Also notice that increasing the cache line size has a bigger effect on hit rate than cache size once the cache is bigger than the working set.

Slow or very slow memory

Even if a machine uses a well designed cache, page or page interleave technique, occasionally the main memory will have to be accessed with wait states. In this case it is very important to ensure that as few wait states as possible occur. For example, if you use 100ns DRAMs in a 33MHz machine then three or even four wait states will be necessary when an interleave failure or cache miss occurs. All the figures for wait states quoted for the various memory management techniques have assumed that only one wait state is necessary in the worst possible case. In practice you will find machines that need more than one wait state and then the appropriate figures for the average wait state are as given below:

Wait states	interleave	page mode	page interleave	cache
1	.5	.8	.4	.03
2	1	1.6	.8	.06
3	1.5	2.4	1.2	.09
4	2	3.2	1.6	.12

You can see that reducing wait states to a minimum before using sophisticated memory access methods does make a difference. Two machines that are using the same memory access method, cache say, but turn in different benchmark performances are likely to be using different speed memory chips.

One way of using slower memory chips in a cache based system is to combine caching with interleave or preferably page interleave. There is nothing stopping memory being organised on a page interleave basis even if there is a cache memory used by the processor for most accesses. The effect of page interleave is to reduce the average number of wait states needed to service a cache miss. For example, if a system's memory normally needs 1 wait state then using page interleave will reduce this to .2 of a wait state and if a cache has a hit rate of 98% then the effective average wait state will be something like .004 of a wait state. In practice the performance will not reach this impressive level because cache misses that need to access the memory will tend to be those accesses that break the principle of program locality, i.e. outside the program's working set. Even so the gain in performance is worth the extra effort of combining page interleave with a cache.

Once you understand all of the different methods of speeding up memory access it becomes clear that cache based systems are to be preferred followed by systems that use page interleave.

To give you some idea how important memory design is in a real system, disabling the 64KByte cache on a 20MHz machine, leaving only a page mode memory system, reduced the MIPS from 4.3 down to 3.3, reduced the Whetstones per second from 64.3 KW/s to 50 KW/s and almost doubled the time that programs took to run.

Standard cache hardware

Although some manufacturers build their own cache hardware most opt to use one of the small number of ready built cache controller chips. The most popular of these cache controllers is Intel's own 32385 which is also the device integrated with the 386 to produce the 486. Other common cache controllers are the Austek cache controller and the Chips and Technologies 82C307. The basic characteristics of each of these caches is listed in the table below:

Cache	Type	Write cycle	Max cache size	Line size
82385	Two-way	Posted write	32KByte	4Byte
486	Four-way	Posted write	8KByte	16Byte
82C307	Two-way	Posted write	32KByte	32Byte

The 82385 can also work with 64KByte and 128KByte caches by using external circuitry.

Pipelining

The 386 is a very sophisticated processor and in an attempt to speed up memory access it can be run in a pipelined mode. In pipeline mode the processor attempts to access the next memory location before it actually needs it. The 386 has enough storage on-chip to hold four memory locations and pipelining attempts to keep this buffer full. You can see that this is a sort of crude on-chip cache. The problem with it is that pipelining assumes that the processor will always want the very next instruction in memory and this isn't always the case. In other words, sometimes the pipeline will retrieve an item of data from memory that the processor doesn't use. A bigger fault with pipelining is that it can actually slow down memory writes because these have to wait until the, possibly unnecessary, pipeline read completes.

You can see that pipelining is a mixed blessing. Add to this the fact that some early 386 chips had pipeline mode faults that made machines crash in admittedly rare situations, and that most manufacturers failed to implement pipelining properly, and you might feel that it is to be avoided. To cater for this the 386 has a pin that can be used to signal that it shouldn't use pipelining and most main boards contain a jumper that can be set to disable pipelining. This said, most systems do run marginally faster with pipelining enabled and I have yet to encounter a system crash due to its use.

The 486's cache

The 486 differs from the 386 in that it has a version of the 32385 cache controller built in on the same chip. You can see this as a natural extension of the 386's pipelining and four-word buffer. The 486's cache controller works with 8 KBytes of SRAM built into the chip. This is quite a small amount of cache RAM but the 486 uses a 16Byte line width which is double the usual 8Byte width and it is four-way associative, rather than two-way. For these reasons Intel claim a 96% hit rate, which is very good for an 8KByte cache.

Even though the 486's cache is better than its 8KByte size may suggest, many manufacturers have added their own external cache with larger amounts of SRAM to work with in association with the internal cache to provide a two-level cache. Of course, once again page interleaving can be used to speed up the external DRAM memory and some manufacturers, e.g. Hewlett Packard, are claiming that this used with just the on-chip cache produces results that are as good as adding larger caches.

Because it has an on-chip cache the 486 doesn't need or support the pipeline mode of the 386. However, it does offer a additional memory access method - *burst mode*. In burst mode the 486 will transfer consecutive memory locations one per clock cycle. This is twice as fast as the 386 can manage and it provides an ideal way of transferring data from external memory to the cache. Each time there is a cache miss the burst mode can be used to transfer 16 Bytes (i.e. four 32-bit words) to the cache in just five clock cycles. By arranging memory into two or more banks of interleaved memory this transfer can be arranged to always occur with zero wait states - as the four words are always taken from consecutive locations.

386SX

The 386SX, being a 16-bit version of the 386, is very similar from the point of view of memory access to the 286. The lower speed 16MHz and 20MHz versions of the 386SX tend to use simpler, and so cheaper, methods of memory access. Many SX machines use a page interleave design for near zero wait states with 100ns DRAMs. With the fall in the price of DRAM you will even find 70ns chips being used to produce true 0 wait states! For 386SXs running at 25MHz a cache becomes a sensible choice. Indeed the electronics needed for a cache has dropped in price to the point where both 20MHz and 25MHz 386SXs using cache cost little more than 16MHz non-cached designs.

Clock doubling and cache

In the case of a clock doubled processor such as the 486DX2, the quality of the memory matters even more than for a normal processor. The processor is running at twice the speed of the external memory and any delays following a cache miss thus have a greater effect on performance. Each memory wait state is now the equivalent of two missed instructions, not just one! In a sense this makes every wait state seem twice as long from the processor's point of view.

To get the best from a 486DX2, it should be used with a large secondary cache of 128 KBytes and the wait states on a cache miss should also be minimised by using the fastest DRAM modules available.

Shadow RAM

All this discussion of ways of speeding up access to RAM has ignored the fact that large chunks, typically 128 KBytes, of a machine's memory will be made up of ROM or EPROM which is generally very slow indeed. ROM is used to hold all of the standard system routines - the BIOS and Video BIOS - and so even though they might appear to be a small area of memory when compared to the megabytes a system might have they are used very often. Thus speeding up ROM access has a large impact on the overall performance of a system. One of the simplest ways of achieving this is to transfer the contents of any ROMs into DRAMs that are positioned at the same location. This is called shadow RAM or, less often these days, slushware. (The reason for this odd name is that software permanently coded into ROMs is usually referred to as firmware and so transferring it to more temporary accommodation in the form of DRAMs makes it slushware.)

The early implementations of shadow RAM used specially built hardware that couldn't easily be changed. This resulted in DRAM being used as shadow RAM whether you liked it or not. Later implementations, for example those using the Chips and Technologies AT/386 CHIPset, allow shadowing to be turned on or off and even selectively enabled to shadow BIOS but not the video BIOS, for example. As shadowing ROM in this way has such a powerful effect on system performance you might be wondering why you would want to switch it off. The answer is that many systems use a full 256 KBytes of DRAM to shadow as little as 32 KBytes of ROM. If you are short of memory then it might be better to disable shadowing and accept the slowdown to gain additional memory. However, not all shadow RAM that is disabled is recoverable. You could find yourself in the situation of having disabled the shadowing but still unable to use the RAM that you have apparently freed for any other purpose. The important point is that for maximum flexibility shadow RAM should not only be capable of being disabled it should also be recoverable. Finally, it is worth saying that shadow RAM is an important and highly desirable system feature in that it certainly returns its cost in terms of system performance. The effect of shadow RAM is discussed more fully in Chapter 10.

Multi-tasking and multi-user effects

In the discussion of the use of cache memory, and indeed page and page interleave, the idea that a program makes use of a small set of memory locations - its working set - was used to explain why such techniques work. Of course, if there is more than one program working with the same memory then there will be more than one working set. This means that the total size of the working set will be larger and it will be split over more discrete areas. This reduces the efficiency of a cache of any given size and reduces the efficiency of page mode memory.

MS-DOS is a single-user/single-tasking operating system and so in the case of a simple MS-DOS 386/486 system only one program can be running. If, however, you use MS-DOS with Windows 3, DESQview or use OS/2 or Unix the situation is different because these are all multi-tasking systems, and in the case of Unix multi-tasking/multi-user. If you use such systems to run a large number of programs at the same time then you should be aware of the possible loss of efficiency.

It is possible to construct 'horror stories' that demonstrate that, given a few programs of the wrong sort, the caching mechanism can be almost totally disabled. In most real cases you can expect a 5% to 10% reduction in cache hit rate. This isn't as bad as you might expect because much of the time the system is executing shared code that forms part of the operating system. However, the message is clear - for a multi-tasking/multi-user machine the largest possible cache size should be used.

Selective caching

Many systems that use caching allow the user to determine which areas of memory are cached and which aren't. Some regions are also automatically excluded from caching. For example, in general it isn't sensible to cache I/O ports or video RAM. Also expanded memory that is provided by hardware should not be cached. (See Chapter 10 for an explanation of expanded memory.) The reason is that the block of memory in the page frame can be changed without the cache being updated. However, expanded memory that is produced using a LIMulator (explained in Chapter 10) should be cached because this is managed by the normal 386/486 memory management methods and caching will safely speed up its operation. If you know a great deal about the operation of a particular program then you might be able to make use of the cache RAM more effectively by restricting the range of memory on which it operates. In this case access to non-cached memory would incur wait states. In most cases it is simpler and just as efficient to leave the cache in its default state.

Cache - the universal solution

Although other methods of decreasing wait states work quite well, the falling cost of implementing a cached solution has made it the method of first choice. As already mentioned, machines such as 20MHz and 25MHz 386SXs are increasingly implemented as a cached design. The modern 386DX usually has a 64KByte or larger cache and even the 486DX/SX is rarely seen without a secondary cache of 64KBytes to 128KBytes. Part of the reason for this is that manufacturers can avoid having to go into the fine detail of the design of their machine - to say that it has a cache of a particular size satisfies most prospective purchasers. To a certain extent this is a reasonable approach in that once you know that a machine has a cache of a reasonable size you can be certain that cache misses, and so wait states, only occur around 1% of the time. This makes other features of memory organisation the fine detail that most users can afford to ignore.

Key points

» The 386 and 486 support data transfer rates that are too fast for the current generation of RAM chips.

» The simplest, but slowest, machines deal with slow memory by introducing wait states.

» Faster systems use page mode RAM or interleave memory access between a number of banks to reduce the occurrence of wait states. The two techniques can be used in combination.

» The fastest systems use cache memory. A 20MHz machine with cache is roughly equal to a 25MHz machine using interleave.

» The main criterion in determining how good a cache is its size. A second important parameter is line width.

» Page interleave memory can be used with cache systems to reduce wait states when a cache miss occurs.

» The 486 has an 8KByte on-chip cache and supports an additional memory access method, burst mode, that can be used to reduce wait states following a cache miss to next to nothing.

» Shadow RAM is an important contributor to system speed but it may use 256KBytes or more to shadow 32KBytes of ROM.

Chapter 5
Memory Upgrade

Upgrading and configuring memory is a perennial problem no matter how new a machine is. This chapter describes the theory and practice of memory upgrade.

After speed the next most important aspect of a memory system is how easy and economical it is to increase its capacity. Adding memory can actually make a machine run faster by reducing the need to make use of slow disk storage for data and programs that otherwise wouldn't fit into memory!

Many users initially buy machines with 1 to 4 MBytes of RAM only to discover that falling RAM prices and the increasing demand of software for memory space force them to consider adding more memory. It is difficult to believe that only a short time ago we were working with 64 KBytes of memory and now 64 MBytes doesn't sound unreasonable or astronomically expensive. MS-DOS 386/486 based systems typically need a minimum of 1 to 2 MBytes, Windows 3 needs 2 to 8 MBytes and OS/2 8 to 12 MBytes but it is rare to find any system that cannot make use of extra memory.

Adding extra RAM is in most cases easy, just a matter of opening the case and plugging in some chips. The only complication is deciding what type of chips to buy and exactly where to plug them in. However, some users encounter a slightly different and almost shocking problem - to increase the total amount of memory fitted to their machine they have to remove some, if not all, of the existing memory! At first this seems to be a paradoxical situation but, as will be explained, it is a perfectly reasonable and sensible consequence of the 386SX using a 16-bit external bus and the rest of the family using a 32-bit external bus. An understanding of how this affects the addition of memory can save you from starting with a memory size that forces the original chips to be removed as part of an upgrade.

Types of RAM chip

RAM chips are made in a range of different sizes and the amount of memory that can be packed into a single chip is increasing all the time - usually doubling every few years. At the time of writing individual chips are available in 256Kbit, 1Mbit and 4Mbit capacities at a reasonable price. The 64KBit chip that used to be so common has vanished from all new systems and is considered obsolete by suppliers. This isn't unreasonable as 64Kbit is a very small amount of memory when compared to the Megabytes that are currently in use.

To a very great extent the amount of memory that can be placed on a single chip has become less relevant with the introduction of multi-chip modules. Instead of buying a single chip to plug into a circuit board, it is standard practice to mount several chips together on a small circuit board of their own and treat this assembly as a single component. This use of multi-chip modules has reduced the cost of memory per Megabyte by reducing manufacturing costs, but of course you have to buy more at one go! If you are worried about the increased unreliability of multi-chip modules, after all if one chip fails you have to replace the entire module, it is worth saying that the reliability of memory devices is so high that it scarcely makes any difference!

Currently memory comes packaged in three different forms: one single chip variety - DIL (Dual In-line Package, also known as DIP) - and two types of multi-chip modules - SIMM (Single In-line Memory Module) and SIP (Single In-line Package). The most familiar of these three is the DIL, which is the archetypal chip of any description.

DIL chips

DIL chips supply relatively small amounts of memory even though they might sound big when measured by the total number of bits they provided. For example, a 256K DIL chip is 256K bits - not bytes - of storage and so you need nine of them to make a full 256KBytes of storage. Why nine? Surely a byte is only eight bits? Since the first IBM PC, it has been the rule that every byte of memory has an associated error detection or parity bit. This isn't used to store data, it is simply stored as a check that what was stored hasn't changed due to power fluctuations, cosmic rays or just to detect a bad chip. So although eight bits make one byte, most PCs use nine bits to store a byte with error checking, see the technical box, *Parity*. In practice it is possible for a machine to dispense with parity checking and so only need eight bits to store a byte, but this is still relatively uncommon.

So 256Kbit DIL chips store 256K bits and you need nine of them for 256KBytes of storage and 1Mbit DIL chips store 1024K bits and you also need nine of them to form 1 MByte of storage. The only complication is that you will occasionally come across chips that store 256Kx4 bits. These are simply reorganised 1Mbit chips so that two chips can be used to provide 256Kx8 bits of storage. This type of chip is sometimes used as an economical way of providing the first 1 MByte of storage on 386SX machines. Notice that in this case another type of chip has to be used to supply the ninth parity bit. This explains why some 386SX machines need two 256Kx4bit chips and one 256Kx1Bit chip for every 256KBytes of memory fitted.

Installing DIL chips is usually simply a matter of plugging them into standard DIL sockets. This is made easier if the legs of each chip are straightened using pliers or by pressing against a rigid surface. If you are at all worried about the mechanical process of inserting chips then it would be worth buying a chip insertion tool. This automatically straightens the legs of each chip and pushes it into the socket evenly. You must make sure that you insert each chip the correct way round. One end of a DIL chip is usually marked by a small semi-circular indentation or a small dot. This should be lined up with a similar mark on the chip socket or main board. Some chip sockets are marked by a semi-circular indentation and some by having one corner flattened. If you insert a DIL chip the wrong way round and turn the machine on there is a good chance that the chip will be permanently damaged. For advice about handling chips read the technical box, *Static and handling precautions* before even ordering the new chips that you need!

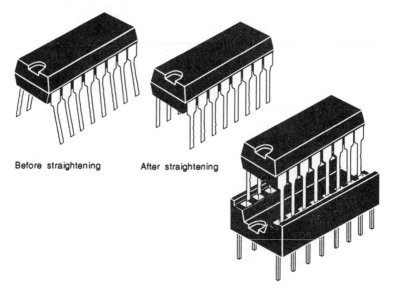

Before straightening   After straightening

Figure 5.1
Standard DIL chip and socket

As well as standard DIL sockets you may also come across combination sockets. These come in two types - dual 18/16-pin and 20/18-pin. The 18/16-pin sockets can accept either 16-pin 256Kx1bit or 18-pin 1Mx1bit chips. The 20/18-pin sockets can accept either 20-pin 256Kx4bit or 18-pin 1Mx1bit chips. You should be very careful to make sure that you use the correct section of the socket for each type of chip and this can be difficult on a crowded mainboard.

The most common cause of failure in upgrading DIL memory is bent pins. After inserting each chip you should always check that all of its pins are correctly home in the socket. It can be very difficult to see a bent pin because the bend usually happens at the point that the leg would otherwise disappear into the socket. This makes it look as if the chip is correctly inserted when it isn't. It can also sometime make an intermittent contact with the metal of the socket resulting in it working sometimes but not always. The only sure way of checking for bent pins is to remove the chip and examine it. A chip extraction tool can help with this job just as a chip insertion tool can stop it happening.

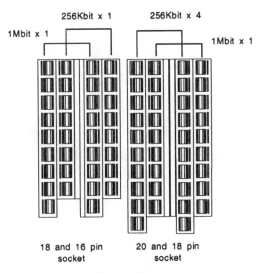

Figure 5.2
A combination DIL socket

SIMM and SIP modules

SIMMs and SIPs are easier to use than DIL chips because they are actually small printed circuit boards with enough memory chips mounted to make byte-wide memory. For example, a 1MBitx9 SIMM or SIP will contain enough chips to provide a full 1 MByte of parity checked memory.

The advantage of SIMM or SIP memory is that it occupies less space and is easier to install than the large number of DIL chips that it replaces. The only disadvantages are that SIMM and SIP memory is marginally more expensive than the equivalent number of chips and one faulty chip on a SIMM or SIP means replacing the entire module rather then just the chip. In practice, memory is reliable enough for this not to be a serious concern and overall they are a cheaper way of reaching larger memory capacities. Machines that use DIL chips usually have to resort to expensive memory expansion boards to reach the same memory capacities.

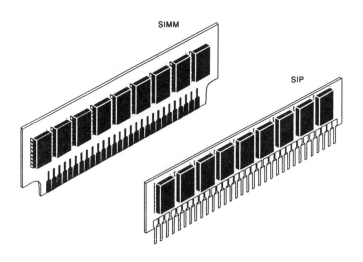

Figure 5.3
SIMM and SIP memory

SIMMs are inserted into small printed circuit sockets and it is usual for a number of such sockets to be grouped together to form a memory expansion area. There are two types of SIMM sockets - push-in and rotate. Using the older push-in sockets it can take considerable force to fit insert a SIMM. The more modern SIMM socket allows a SIMM to be fitted almost without any force being applied. You place the SIMM in the socket at about 30 degrees and then push it back into place. A clip at either end of the socket then holds it in place. The clip has to be released before the SIMM can be removed. SIMMs have to be inserted the correct way round but that's the only possibility of error.

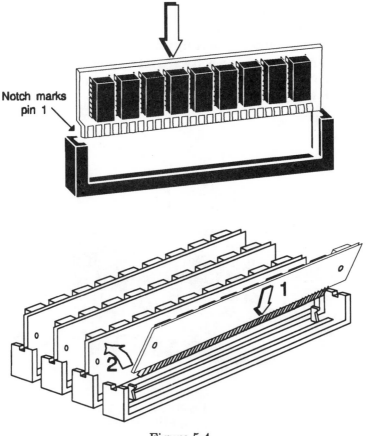

Figure 5.4
Old and new SIMM sockets

SIPs are slightly more difficult to insert as you have to make sure that all of the pins are correctly aligned over the holes in the socket and it is possible to bend the pins if you push too hard. After aligning the pins, a steady even pressure should cause the SIP to slide slowly into place. It is important to insert the SIP the correct way round. Most SIPs and SIP sockets are marked with a dot at one end which should be lined up but you should check your machine's manual. There are also two different types of SIP packages with 30 or 32 pins.

Of course, you can only use the type of memory package that your machine can accept, but some machines are versatile enough to take a mixture of DIL and SIP/SIMM memory. If you do have a choice then you should always choose the mixture that gives you the maximum potential RAM without having to remove any memory that is already fitted. Many machines have to be informed of exactly what type of device you are using, either by setting jumpers or dip switches on the mainboard or by using a software setup program. The modern approach is towards machine auto-configuring by sensing the amount of memory fitted.

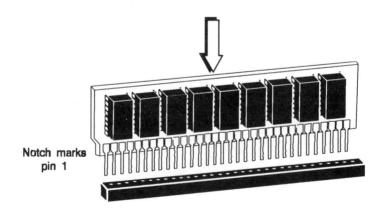

Figure 5.5
Inserting a SIP module

Parity

The first personal computers were mainly used for recreation and the consequences of any undetected error was slight. However, if a machine is used for business or any serious purpose it has to incorporate some method of error detection. The simplest and most commonly used method is *parity checking*. This involves adding an extra bit to every byte of data stored so as to make the number of 1 bits even. This is called *even parity* checking as opposed to making the total number of 1 bits odd i.e. *odd parity*. For example, if the data is 011101100 then the parity bit is 1 because there are five 1s in the data and making the parity bit 1 makes the total six which is even. If the data is 10100000 then the parity bit is 0 because the total number of 1s is already even. Each time data is read from memory its parity is checked. If a single bit has changed, either a 0 turning into a 1 or a 1 into a 0, since the data was stored then the total number of 1 bits will not be even and a parity error will be detected.

The problem with parity checking is that while it is certain to detect a change in a single bit, if two bits change then this leaves the total number of 1 bits even and a parity error will not occur. However, in modern computer systems the probability of a single bit error is so small that the probability of two such errors in the same memory location is vanishingly small. Indeed, such errors are so rare that it is arguable that parity checking itself is redundant.

As it takes eight bits to store a single byte, adding an extra bit for parity checking makes the total number of bits needed equal to nine. This is the reason that 386/486 systems need nine 1MByte chips or 9x1MByte SIPs or SIMMs for every MByte of memory. This means that if you have 8 MBytes of memory you also have an additional 1 MByte dedicated to parity checking! In some machines you can disable parity checking and make use of the unused chips to increase the amount of memory available. As transient memory errors are very rare, and the memory is tested for permanent faults every time you switch the machine on, you might consider this a reasonable trade -off.

Reading the chips

One of the most intimidating aspects of trying to buy extra RAM is the way that chips, SIPs and SIMMs are described in catalogues and manuals. Part of the problem is due to each manufacturer assigning their own product codes to each type of chip they produce. This assignment is fairly arbitrary and so you shouldn't expect too much sense in the sort of numbers marked on a chip but they can provide a general guideline to the chip's type.

The first part of a chip's part number usually indicates the amount and organisation of the memory that the chip provides. The same amount of memory can be organised in many different ways. For example a chip that stores 1Mbit can be arranged to provide 128Kx8bits (i.e. 128KBytes), 256Kx4bits, or 1Mx1bit of storage. As most computers can only work with memory locations that can store a complete byte, the organisation of the chip indicates the smallest number that can be used to increase memory capacity. For example, you could use one 128Kx8bit chip to increase memory by 128KBytes, but you would need at least two 256Kx4bit chips (i.e. 256KByte) and eight 1Mx1bit chips (i.e. 1 MByte). (This ignores the complications of needing a parity bit and memory banks, see later.)

The final digits of a chip's part number generally give its speed in nano-seconds but often leaving out or adding in extra zeros. For example, the product code for an 80ns chip might end in -80, -08 or just -8 as the manufacturer chooses!

Often you will find chips listed simply by their organisation and speed. For example, 256Kx4 120ns DRAM, 1Mx9 80ns SIMM, 256Kx1 100ns SIP etc.. On other occasions you will find their full part numbers quoted. For example, a 41256-80 is a 256Kx1bit 80ns DRAM, 41464-12 is a 64Kx4bit 120ns DRAM and a P21010-08 is a 1Mx1bit 80ns DRAM. From these examples you can see that there is some connection between part numbers and chip types - but not enough to be certain without looking them up! If you are at all in doubt about the type of memory that your machine needs then check its manual or contact one of the specialist memory suppliers listed at the end of this book.

RAM speed

The final part of the specification of a memory upgrade is the speed of the devices needed. As already described in the previous chapter, access speed is measured in nano-seconds or ns. The slowest devices have access times of 150ns to 120ns. Medium speed devices are 100ns and fast access chips are 80ns, 65ns and 60ns. In most cases it isn't possible to look at the design of a machine and easily deduce the speed of RAM chips needed. Indeed some systems will allow you to use one of a number of speeds by imposing additional wait states for slower chips. If a machine uses page mode memory access then it may even be more stringent in the type of chips it uses than simply specifying an overall access speed.

The simplest solution to finding out what type of chips your machine needs is to look in the manual! Failing this you could open the case and look for the area where the existing memory is installed and read the device code on one of the chips - see *Reading the chips*. You can usually recognise where the memory devices are either because they will be the only SIP/SIMM devices or because they will be arranged in a regular rectangular array of identical DIL chips.

It doesn't really matter if you use chips that are faster than your machine needs. They won't make it work any faster and they will cost more but at least they will work. This is one solution if you simply cannot find out what speed of memory device to use. On the other hand, using chips that are slower than your machine needs will cause memory errors to be reported during the Power On Self Test (POST) routine. It is even possible that if the chips are only a little slower than your machine needs then they will pass the POST routine but fail intermittently later on when your machine has warmed up a little. (RAM chips are more tolerant of being worked faster when they are cooler.)

Most machines have to be informed, either via jumpers, dip switches or software setup, of what speed chips you are using so that they can use the appropriate number of wait states. Once again introducing more wait states than necessary will

Static and handling precautions

DRAM chips, and a great deal of electronics in general, are very sensitive to static. Indeed a machine can be damaged by a static discharge in normal use, let alone when the cover is off. Static is a high voltage charge caused by friction on highly insulating materials such as nylon. People just walking about on a nylon carpet can carry charges of many thousands of volts just waiting to run to earth through any convenient conductor. This static discharge doesn't harm humans, even though in extreme cases they may actually feel the shock, because it is a very low current discharge, but it can pack enough power to destroy a sensitive electronic component.

Static in offices can be reduced by avoiding known static-producing materials and by keeping the humidity normal. (Indoor plants have a valuable role to play in regulating the humidity in non-air conditioned rooms!) If you have a static problem then you can fit static mats at entrances and in front of computer desks. A static mat is simply a conductive mat that is connected to earth via the water or heating system.

Static precautions have to be much more stringent when you are handling any electronics, components or boards, out of their protective metal case. Most chips and complete boards are delivered in static protection tubes, bags or on foam backing. As long as they are within this packaging they are safe from static. Before you start any hardware modifications you should prepare yourself and your working area. If you are taking a board out of a machine then you should lay aluminium foil on the surface of your desk and discharge it and yourself by touching an earthing point - a radiator or water pipe will usually do. If you are working on a board inside a machine, the mainboard say, then it is usually enough to touch the metal case of the machine now and again. If the case isn't metal then touching an earthing point every few minutes is a good idea. You can buy special static handling equipment in the form of desktop static mats and conductive wrist bands complete with a wire to connect you to an earthing point but working while touching an earthing point, in the form of a radiator or pipe, is usually good enough.

simply slow your machine down. However using too few wait states will make it fail with a memory error on POST or produce intermittent errors later on.

Memory banks

So far we have concentrated on identifying the type and speed of memory device that is needed, but you cannot add extra memory in any amount. For example, it seems reasonably obvious that you cannot add a single 1MBit chip. The reason is simply that supplying 1 bit of each storage location in a Megabyte of memory doesn't allow you to store a complete byte in any of the locations. To be of any use, each location has to have a full complement of 8 bits (9 including parity) and so you have to fit memory devices to give this number of bits at each location. For example, by fitting eight (or nine including parity) 1MBit chips. Another way of saying this is that memory has to be at least eight (or nine) bits wide.

This restriction of fitting memory in whole bytes seems reasonable enough, but the 386SX gets data from memory in 16-bit chunks and the rest of the 386 family works in 32-bit chunks. The argument about fitting memory in complete eight-bit blocks also applies to the 16- and 32-bit blocks used by the 386SX and rest of the 386 family. That is when the processor tries to retrieve a 16-bit or 32-bit item of data from memory all 16 or 32 bits have to be there!

In other words:

» for the 386SX you have to add memory in 16-bit wide chunks

and

» for the 386DX, 486DX and 486SX you have to add memory in 32-bit wide chunks.

The smallest chunk of memory that you can add to a machine is usually referred to as a bank and so the 386SX uses 16-bit banks and the rest use 32-bit banks.

The number of banks and the type of memory device that a machine accepts can have important implications for memory expansion. For example, suppose you have a 386SX machine with four SIMM sockets taking either 256Kx9Bit, 1Mx9Bit or 4Mx9Bit SIMMs. Simple minded reasoning suggests that you can reach any memory capacity by fitting mixtures of different types of SIMM in each socket (for example, two 256Kx9Bit SIMMs, one 1Mx9Bit SIMM and a 4Mx9Bit SIMM to give a total of 5.5 MBytes). In fact you cannot and this configuration would most definitely be illegal! The reason is that although there are four SIMM sockets these are organised as a pair of banks each consisting of two of the sockets. Each bank has to be filled or empty, i.e. you can not have a half-used bank and it has to be filled with the same type of memory device. This severely restricts the possible memory configurations and certainly makes the example configuration illegal!

Once you realise that memory devices have to be added in whole banks, many of the strange rules that apply to which memory sizes are reachable and which are not become clear. Some machines are even more restrictive than this and demand not only that you fit the same type of memory device to each bank but to all of the banks. In this case configurations such as 2x256Kx9Bit SIMMs in bank 0 and 2x1Mx9Bit SIMMs in bank 1, giving a total of 3.5 MBytes, would be illegal.

You can also see that having a limited number of banks can stop you reaching the maximum configuration of any given machine. For example in the case of a 386DX or a 486, each bank would have to consist of four SIMM sockets. If there are two banks then fitting all 4Mx9Bit SIMMs would produce a total of 32 MBytes. However, if the machine was initially delivered with 4 MBytes of RAM fitted then this could only be supplied as four 1Mx9Bit SIMMs, i.e. filling one bank. Notice that it is impossible to supply this small amount of memory in any other way as a single 4Mx9Bit SIMM wouldn't fill a whole bank. When you subsequently consider the upgrade options you can only fill the second bank with more 1Mx9Bit SIMMs, giving a total of 8 MBytes, or if you are allowed to mix the type of memory device, use four 4Mx9Bit SIMMs, giving a total of 20 MBytes. To reach the maximum memory you would have no choice but to remove the initial bank of 1Mx9Bit SIMMs.

The same arguments apply to the use of DIL chips, only in this case the numbers involved are larger. That is for a 386SX, a bank of DIL chips consists of 16 (18 including parity) 1-bit devices and for the 386DX and 486 a bank consists of 32 (36 including parity) 1-bit devices. With chips having to be fitted in multiples of 32 or 36 you can start to see the advantages of memory modules!

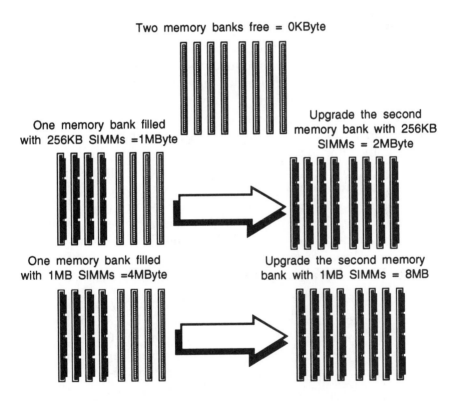

Two memory banks free = 0KByte

One memory bank filled with 256KB SIMMs =1MByte

Upgrade the second memory bank with 256KB SIMMs = 2MByte

One memory bank filled with 1MB SIMMs =4MByte

Upgrade the second memory bank with 1MB SIMMs = 8MB

Figure 5.6
The memory upgrade path for a 386DX or a 486

Mainboard or expansion board?

Early 386 machines depended on the use of expansion boards to hold the majority of their RAM. This was mainly due to the low capacity of memory chips available at the time and hence the large number needed to produce any reasonable sized memory. The only problem with expansion boards is the type of connector/bus used to plug them into the mainboard. For the 386/486 the familiar ISA bus used on the 286/AT is grossly inadequate for memory expansion, being limited to 16 bits. In the case of the 16-bit 386SX, however, memory expansion via the ISA bus is a possibility. To overcome the shortcomings of the ISA bus most manufacturers have opted for proprietary 32-bit bus connectors. In the case of the 386SX there have even been proprietary 16-bit bus connectors. These are fast enough to support memory expansion but they have the disadvantage of not being standardised. If your machine uses a 32-bit proprietary memory expansion bus then you have to buy plug-in cards that are made specially for your machine and usually by the same manufacturer. This single source situation is only a problem in that it restricts your shopping around, keeping prices high, and you run a small risk of not being able to obtain expansion cards if by any chance the manufacturer should go out of business. However, some machines, notably those made by IBM and Compaq, have sold in sufficiently large numbers for third party manufacturers to offer lower cost alternatives.

The only way of providing standard 32-bit memory expansion cards is to use either the 32-bit MCA or EISA bus. Both these standards have been extensively described in Chapter 3. Briefly, they are both suitable ways of extending memory, both perform roughly equally and both can be out-performed in terms of simplicity, cost and speed by memory installed directly on the mainboard.

Indeed, this last comment could be applied to most memory expansion adapters. The most economical and efficient form of memory is that installed on the mainboard of your machine, and the upper limit on the amount of memory installable without expansion adapters is an important consideration in choosing a machine. If your machine does need memory expansion adapters then you can generally buy them fully populated, i.e. complete with chips, or with 0 KBytes installed i.e. without chips. If you want a trouble-free life then buy expansion boards fully populated, but if you want to save money then buy boards and chips separately. The process of installing memory chips onto an expansion board is the same as installing them on the mainboard. In many cases the cost of a memory expansion card is close to that of a replacement mainboard, complete with the amount of memory you require, and upgrading in this way is often a sensible alternative.

Finally, don't fall into the trap of confusing expanded memory, EMS or LIM memory boards with the sort of memory boards used to extend the memory in 386/486 based systems. Expanded memory is described in detail in Chapter 10 but briefly 386/486 systems use extended memory as opposed to expanded memory hardware. Any expanded memory that may be required can be produced by using software that converts extended memory to expanded memory. If this important topic is worrying you then turn to Chapter 10.

Increasing cache memory

Systems that use cache often, but not always, allow you to upgrade the size of the cache memory as well as main memory. It is important to understand that doing so will increase the speed of your machine but not the total amount of memory available to programs - cache memory is entirely separate from main memory. It is a buffer between slow main memory and the fast processor.

It is also important that you use exactly the type of memory chips specified by the manufacturer - this is very critical to the reliable operation of your machine. Notice also that cache memory is very fast SRAM, not DRAM as used in main memory. In nearly all cases when you fit extra cache memory you have to change the configuration of the machine by changing jumpers or switches on the mainboard.

Expanding page interleave systems

The organisation of page and page interleave memory was described in Chapter 4 as a way of increasing the speed of systems when using slow memory devices. The only problem with interleaving is that it requires more than one bank of memory to work and so memory upgrades must be planned with this in mind. In other words, you can expand memory by a single bank but you have to expand in pairs if you want to take advantage of the speed increase provided by interleave or page interleave. This also explains the very common restriction on fitting the same type of device to pairs of banks. If a pair of banks is being used to provide alternate memory locations then each has to supply the same amount of memory!

For example, if a 386SX machine can support a maximum of eight 256Kx9Bit or 1Mx9Bit SIMMs (i.e. it has four banks) then there is a very real problem in deciding how a 2MByte machine should be configured. A 2MByte machine could be realised by using eight 256Kx9Bit SIMMs or a pair of 1MByte SIMMs. Using the eight 256KByte SIMMs would produce a faster machine because the multiple banks of memory could be used in interleave mode to reduce wait states. Unfortunately, this configuration makes it impossible to increase the memory without starting again. The alternative arrangement of using two 1MByte SIMMs has the advantage that expansion is just a matter of plugging in more 1MByte SIMMs. The disadvantage is that, being a single physical bank of memory, interleaving cannot be used and so the system will run slower. In nearly all cases it is better to accept the slower machine that results from using a single bank with larger capacity memory modules. The reason is that memory upgrade is usually inevitable and so it makes sense to prepare for the future at the expense of present performance.

A real example

To give you some idea how complicated decisions about memory upgrade can be and the importance of planning for the future it is worth considering a real example. A 386 machine was bought on the basis that could be expanded to 16 MBytes. The machine was delivered with 1 MByte installed with the expectation that it would be expanded to 4 MBytes and eventually to 8 MBytes as the need arose.

When the day arrived for the memory to be increased from 1 MByte to 4 MBytes it was discovered that the original 1 MByte had been installed using 256Kx1bit chips. The mainboard could take up to two interleaved banks of memory consisting of 18 chips in each bank. There was also an optional memory expansion card that could be used to fit an additional two banks. Each bank could use either 256Kbit or 1Mbit DIL chips with the restriction that pairs of banks, that is bank 0/bank 1 and bank 2/bank 3, used the same type of chip. A bank filled with 256Kbit chips would provide 1 MByte and filled with 1Mbit chips would provide 4MByte. Clearly the manufacturer had no choice but to use 256Kbit chips in bank 0 to provide the 1 MByte requested and the most obvious upgrade path to 4 MBytes was to add 256Kbit chips into banks 1, 2 and 3. This route also had the advantage that, with four banks populated with chips, memory interleaving could be enabled and the machine would be faster. However, this would have meant purchasing a memory expansion card and reading the small print in the manual suggested that memory provided by the card would not be as fast as memory fitted to the mainboard. In addition, once all banks had been fully populated there would have been no way that the memory could be further expanded without replacing 256Kbit chips with 1Mbit chips.

Considering the extra cost of the upgrade card and the extra cost of future upgrades, a better option was to remove the existing 256Kbit chips in bank 0 and replace them with 1Mbit chips. The only disadvantages of this were the waste of 18 256Kbit chips and the inability to use memory interleave to speed the machine up. However, when the machine was upgraded to 8 MBytes, by adding a further 18 1Mbit chips to bank 1, memory interleave could be used. Further expansion beyond this point would need the memory expansion card and there is no way to avoid this problem.

Key points

» Memory upgrade can be by installing chips on the mainboard or by installing complete memory add-on boards. Mainboard memory upgrades are cheaper and simpler.

» RAM devices come in three basic forms - DIL chips, SIMM and SIP modules. DIL chips are slightly cheaper, but are more difficult to install and cannot achieve the same total memory capacities without the use of expansion cards.

» It is important to use memory devices that are fast enough for your machine. You can use devices that are faster than needed, but this isn't an advantage and doesn't make your machine work any quicker.

» The need for parity checking increases the number of bits needed to store a byte from eight to nine.

» The smallest amount of memory that you can fit is a bank.

» In the case of the 386SX a bank is 16 bits wide, i.e. a pair of SIMMs make up a bank.

» In the case of the 386DX and the 486 a bank is 32 bits wide, i.e. four SIMMs make up a bank.

» Memory interleaving makes it an advantage to populate memory banks in pairs to optimise the speed of your machine. However, it is better to avoid filling pairs of banks with low capacity devices that then have to be removed to achieve further memory expansion.

Chapter 6
Disks

The type of hard disk that your system uses affects its performance in real applications as much, if not more, than the speed of memory access. Choosing a hard disk to complement the power of your machine and to suit the application you have in mind is not an easy matter.

At the current stage of development of personal computers, software is heavily dependent on the use of hard disks to supply the large amounts of permanent and working storage needed. The speed of a hard disk has a considerable impact on the performance of a system. It is true to say that most systems can be speeded up more by a change of hard disk than by any other fine tuning. Even a machine inferior in terms of processor speed and memory access time can be lifted into another class by the addition of an above average disk system.

To discover how much effect disk performance has on your applications you have to estimate the proportion of time they spend in reading and writing disks. This may not be a simple measurement nor the same in all situations. For example, you may think that a word processor will only read a text file when it is first opened and then hold it in memory until it is time to save it back to disk. This may be true for small documents that can fit in memory, but there may be a point at which the document is too large to be handled in one piece and then part of it will be left on disk in temporary files. Multi-tasking operating systems, such as Windows 3 or OS/2, also make use of disk storage to hold programs that are temporarily swapped out of memory. When memory is in short supply, or when you are running a large number of applications, the time taken to swap programs to and from disk can be appreciable.

You can gain a crude measure of how much an application is using the hard disk by simply watching for how much of the time the disk activity light is on. If it flashes only at the start and end of processing a file then the only time advantage to be gained is in saving and loading. On the other hand, if the light also flashes as you are working, then your application is either using the file in small sections or is creating temporary work files and a faster hard disk would lead to an overall improvement in performance.

In general the applications where disk performance is critical are:

» Database - especially multi-user or networked database.

» CAD/DTP - many, but not all, graphics oriented programs make extensive use of temporary work files to create images.

» Network fileserver - being shared, a networked disk drive needs to be fast no matter what the real applications are.

» Program development - if you are working with a compiler that makes extensive use of libraries to build a program.

A fast disk is of little interest if you are using a word processor unless you are working with very large documents, but it can speed up operations such as spell checking. Also, as spreadsheet programs rarely use temporary files the impact of a fast hard disk is limited. The obvious exception to all of these rules is when you are using running these applications under a multi-tasker such as Windows.

Disk and controller

The first important idea is that a hard disk installation is made up of two components - the disk drive itself and the controller. The disk drive is the physical part of the system that actually stores the data and the controller allows the machine to access that data. You can change the speed of operation and the total storage capacity by choosing a disk drive but you can only affect the speed of data transfer by choosing a controller. It is also important to realise that in most cases a disk drive is made for a particular type of controller and therefore the choice of drive and controller are not independent.

A mistake often made by users taking an upgrade path from a PC/XT to a 386/486/AT is to think that they can use an existing hard disk plus controller in the new machine. Superficially it looks as though it should work because the ISA and EISA expansion bus includes the original eight-bit connector and most other PC/XT cards will work in an AT. The difference is that the AT uses specific software to handle the controller and this software is contained in ROM (EPROM) on the disk controller board. Thus a PC/XT controller has a ROM specifically for the XT and an AT controller has a ROM specifically for the AT. It might be possible to upgrade an XT disk controller for use in an AT but the result would be poor compared to the real thing. To be more precise, a true AT controller uses the full 16-bit version of the ISA/EISA bus to achieve higher data transfer rates than the original 8-bit ISA controller. The conclusion is that you should buy an AT disk controller even if you plan to keep your original drive as part of an upgrade.

Interfaces

An interface is a connection between two pieces of electronic equipment. In the case of a disk drive, disk controller and computer there are three pieces of equipment involved and so two interfaces - one between the disk and the disk controller and one between the disk controller and the computer.

The interface between the disk controller and the computer is usually just one of the ISA, EISA or MCA bus designs that have already been discussed in detail in Chapter 3. Alternatively, the disk controller can be built directly on the mainboard and this allows the designer to use any interface that improves speed or cuts cost as required by the design objectives. Even so many mainboard disk controllers still use essentially the ISA, EISA or MCA bus, albeit in a cut down form, to connect to the memory and processor and so their performance is often close to their plug-in equivalents.

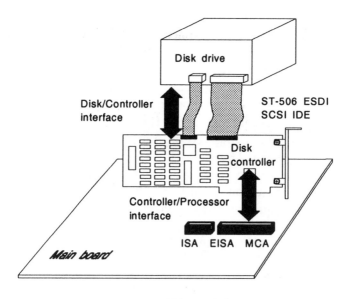

Figure 6.1
Disk interfaces

The interface between the disk drive and the disk controller represents the new element under discussion. There are essentially four types of disk interface - ST-506/ST-412, SCSI (Small Computer System Interface pronounced 'Scuzzy'), ESDI (Enhanced Small Device Interface pronounced 'Esdee') and IDE (Interface Design Enhancements). The ST-506 interface also comes in two distinct versions - MFM (Modified Frequency Modulation) and RLL (Run Length Limited). In principle there is no reason why other versions of the ST-506, or any of the other interfaces, shouldn't be introduced in the future. There is also a second and faster version of the SCSI interface, SCSI 2.

Before going into detail it is worth giving a brief outline of the characteristics of the different types of drive.

» ST-506 - this is the original hard disk interface introduced with the IBM PC/XT. It is slow and really only suitable for low capacity drives - 20-80 MBytes. It is rapidly being made obsolete by IDE drives.

» ESDI - a high speed replacement for ST-506. Still a good option for very high capacity - 500MByte and larger - drives.

» SCSI - this isn't a specialised disk interface but a general purpose way of connecting a range of devices. In practice it tends to be idiosyncratic to the point where you cannot rely on a SCSI controller board to work with any given SCSI device. This situation is slowly improving. A good choice for very high capacity - 500MByte and larger - drives.

» IDE - a fast interface suitable for use with almost all drive capacities up to 500MByte. The IDE drive has so many advantages that it is the first choice for all but the largest storage applications. Its only disadvantages are that you can only have a maximum of two IDE drives connected to one machine and it is only available for the ISA bus.

Drive specifications

The first component in the chain is the disk drive itself and its characteristics determine the best that can be achieved by the whole system. A hard disk works in more or less the same way as a floppy disk: a magnetic disk spins at high speed and a read/write head moves over the surface reading and writing data in concentric tracks. The difference between a floppy disk and a hard disk is that a hard disk is composed of a number of rigid disks or platters of magnetic material; it spins a lot faster and in a special enclosure that excludes dust and other contaminants. These differences allow a hard disk to pack more data onto the surface of the disk and read and write it faster.

As all of the heads move together, and so are all positioned over the same track on each platter, the collection of tracks under the heads is often referred to as a *cylinder*. The size of a cylinder in terms of the number of bytes it will store is important because it represents the largest amount of data

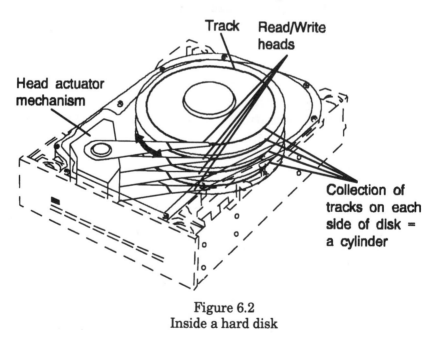

Figure 6.2
Inside a hard disk

that can be read without the time penalty of moving the heads to a new track. Each track is divided up into small chunks of data called *sectors* and the drive can only read or write whole sectors at a time.

In other words, a sector is the smallest unit of data on which a disk can operate. Disk drives respond to commands from the disk controller to position their heads at a particular track and sector number and how fast they can do this is one of the factors that determines how quickly a file can be processed. There are a number of ways of specifying how fast the heads can be positioned, but the most useful is the *average access time*, which is the time taken to move the heads across half of the disk. The longest you will wait for the heads to reach the desired track is when they move the entire radius of the disk. The shortest is when they are already correctly positioned and they don't have to move at all, so the average access time is a reasonable way to characterise the time that it takes to get the heads into position. Track-to-track access time, i.e. the time it takes to move the head from its current position to the next track, is an alternative measure of disk speed but it doesn't take into account the number of cylinders that the disk has.

Once the heads are in position the waiting may still not be over. As the disk rotates there is no guarantee that the particular sector that is needed is under the head. If it has just been missed the drive may have to wait one complete revolution before the sector comes round again. The average wait or *average latency* is usually taken to be half a revolution of the disk. As nearly all hard disks for the PC spin at 3600rpm the average latency is uniformly 8.33ms (milliseconds, 1ms=.001 seconds or one thousandth of a second.)

Now we are in a position to put together all the factors that influence disk speed. There are four factors:

» Cylinder size - the larger the cylinder the more data that can be read without moving the heads.

» Average access time - the smaller this time the quicker the heads can be moved to the desired position.

» Average latency - the time it takes for a sector to reach a correctly positioned head which is directly related to the speed of rotation of the disk.

» Transfer rate - the rate at which data can be read from the disk and transferred through the disk controller to the computer memory.

Of the four, average access time and transfer rate have the most effect. Average access time for modern disks ranges from over 40ms to 16ms or less. *Transfer rate* is a much more difficult quantity to characterise. Any particular disk drive has a maximum transfer rate, but whether or not this transfer rate is realised depends on the type of disk controller, the speed of the processor, and the way that disk is configured.

ST-506 MFM and RLL

Although the ST-506 drive is no longer the first choice for even moderate capacity single-user systems there are a great many in use and it still represents a well tried standard. Indeed, the real problem with the ST-506 is that its interface with the controller is so well defined that there is little scope for improvement. If you were to try to increase the data transfer rate say then the result wouldn't be an ST-506 drive and it wouldn't work with any of the many ST-506 disk controllers!

There are two slightly different types of ST-506 drives - MFM and RLL. Indeed these two designations are often used as alternative names for ST-506 drives. The difference between the two types is to do with the way that data is coded onto the disk as magnetic pulses or flux reversals. MFM (Modified Frequency Modulation) uses an average of .75 flux reversals per bit whereas RLL (Run Length Limited) coding uses an average of .25 flux reversals. This means that an RLL drive/controller combination will store more data in the same space. Strangely enough this increase in storage capacity isn't of much interest to an end user (it is to a disk drive manufacturer however!) The reason being that if I offer you two drives that store 100 MBytes, does it really matter how this is achieved? What is really important about RLL drives is that they offer a potentially faster data transfer rate to MFM drives. (There is a subsidiary issue of reliability. It is often said that RLL drives are less reliable than MFM drives because they store data at a greater recorded-bit density. In practice this difference seems not to matter as long as the drive is indeed an RLL certified drive and not an MFM drive that has been pressed into service as a cheap way of gaining 50% more storage.)

The reason that RLL drives are faster is that a cylinder represents the amount of data that can be read in one revolution of the drive, i.e. the amount of data that can be read in roughly 16ms in the case of most PC hard disks. Thus the larger the capacity of a cylinder or track the faster the potential data transfer and RLL coding crams more data into each track. The maximum data transfer rates achievable with MFM and RLL are 0.6 and 0.9 MByte/s respectively.

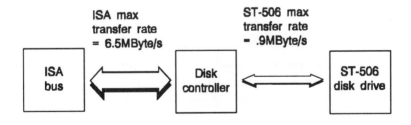

Figure 6.3
The ST-506 interface

IDE

Although the ST-506 drive has a low data transfer rate it only takes a minor modification to free it from this restriction. Originally the IDE drive was invented as a way of making disk systems cheaper by incorporating the disk controller within the drive itself. This effectively produced a drive that could plug more or less directly into the ISA bus. By combining the controller and drive electronics on one printed circuit board the interface between the two could be simplified. At this stage in the IDE's development it was thought of just as a way of packaging the standard ST-506 drive and doing away with the need to have a controller. Many mainboards were designed with 40-way IDE connectors that allowed the drive to be directly connected. This freed an adapter slot and even allowed the manufacturer to claim that the machine had a hard disk controller built into the mainboard!

The importance of the IDE interface was slow to dawn but in retrospect it is obvious. Once you have combined the disk controller with the disk there is no need to keep to any

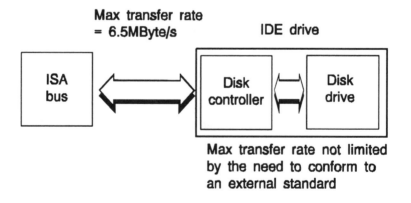

Figure 6.4
The IDE interface

standard. The drive manufacturer is free to modify the way the drive works in any way as long as the final interface connects to the ISA bus. In this sense the IDE drive's interface with the outside world is the ISA bus and so data can be transferred at any speed up to the limit of the ISA bus! This puts the upper limit on the data transfer rate of around 6.5MByte/s. Most IDE drives do not achieve this high rate of data transfer and 1-2MByte/s is more typical.

IDE drives achieve their higher data transfer rate by a range of methods. Some rotate faster than the standard 3600 rpm and some pack in more than the standard 17 sectors per track. This change in the number of sectors per track can be something of a problem in that the BIOS setup program usually only recognises standard 17 sector drives. When a drive is installed in a machine, the BIOS setup program has to be run to set the number of cylinders, heads and sectors per track. In most systems you do this by selecting a drive type number from a table - each drive type number corresponds to a given number of cylinders, heads and sectors per track. This isn't a problem as long as you can find a drive type number that corresponds to the drive being installed. If not then some BIOS setup routines will allow you to enter a user-defined drive type and this involves typing in the actual number of cylinders, heads and sectors per track that the drive has. If the BIOS setup doesn't support a user-defined type then most IDE drives will emulate a different drive drive geometries - i.e. they will pretend to have a different number of cylinders, heads and sectors per track. The only problem that the user has is to select a supported drive type that has a total storage capacity as close to, but not bigger than, the actual capacity of the IDE drive. This ability to emulate almost any drive geometry is often referred to as translation mode as opposed to the drive's native mode.

You can fit an IDE drive to most machines even if they don't have an IDE connector built into the mainboard. In this case you have to use an IDE controller card but as this is mainly a simple connector it is possible to combine it with other facilities. For example, you can buy an IDE controller card which also incorporates a floppy disk controller, serial port, parallel port and games port. There are some minor problems in using an IDE drive. Some early BIOS ROMs do not fully support IDE drives. The following is a list of dates and revision numbers of BIOS ROMs that do:

AMI	dated 4/9/90 or later
Award	version 3.04 or higher
Quadtel	any version supports a single IDE drive but only 3.04 or later supports dual IDE drives
Phoenix	Plus 386 version 1.10 or higher
PhoenixBIOS	version 1.00 or higher

Another minor incompatibly is that IDE drives are low-level, or physically, formatted at the factory. This means that to install them all you have to do is partition the drive and then use the standard FORMAT command to perform a logical format. This makes life much simpler for the user but it makes it impossible to use some advanced disk diagnostic and maintenance programs such as SpinRite (see later).

In spite of these minor problems, IDE drives are the most cost-effective choice for all single-user systems. The only situation in which it is necessary to consider other types of drive is when you need to extend drive performance beyond the data transfer rate offered by the ISA bus. If you want to make full use of the EISA or MCA bus then SCSI and ESDI are your only reasonable choices.

ESDI

The ESDI interface, like IDE, is also a modification of the ST-506 interface but in this case the controller is still a separate entity. This means that you can buy ISA, MCA and EISA ESDI controllers and so take full advantage of whatever type of external bus your machine has. ESDI drives and controllers use the same cabling as ST-506 drives and controllers, making them physically almost indistinguishable. Indeed, they are also similar internally and this means that no special software is needed to run ESDI drives - they are installed and configured in exactly the same way that ST-506 drives are. This means that ESDI drives can offer large storage capacities - up to 1 GByte - with fast data transfer rates without the need to use any special software drivers and without the fear of incompatibility. The data transfer rate for an ESDI drive can be as high as 4MByte/s but 1.25MByte/s is more typical.

High capacity ESDI drives have to use the translation mode feature as described in the section on IDE drives. This enables them to conform to the MS-DOS limitation that a drive must have fewer than 1024 cylinders by pretending to have more heads or more sectors per track. In this case the translation is performed by the ESDI controller. Because translation wasn't necessary in the early days of ESDI this may make it impossible to use the larger ESDI drives with older controllers.

SCSI

The SCSI interface is quite different from the other disk interfaces described here, because it isn't just a disk interface. The SCSI interface can be used to connect up to seven different peripherals to a machine - disks, tape drives, printers, optical drives, and so on. The SCSI interface is in reality a standardised bus to which peripherals can be connected. Within the machine the concessions are usually made by 50-way ribbon cables but it is also possible to use external connecting cables to plug together a chain of external modules. There are two types of external connector in common use; the 50-pin connector popularised by Hewlett Packard and the 25-pin connector used by Apple.

There are a number of slightly different implementations of the SCSI bus - SCSI 1, Fast SCSI, Wide SCSI and SCSI 2. Each of these is an attempt to increase the speed of operation of the bus in some way or another.

Each device connected to the SCSI bus is identified by a unique ID number, 0 to 6, and each device may be further subdivided into Logical Unit Numbers, or LUNs. For example, an optical disk may be configured to be device ID 5 but different partitions of the drive may be allocated at LUN 0, LUN 1 etc.. In most cases devices only make use of a LUN 0. So for example, the first SCSI hard disk may be ID 0 LUN 0 and the second ID 1 LUN 0 and so on.

The problem with SCSI is that while the interface between the SCSI devices is reasonably well defined, the interface between the SCSI controller and the machine isn't. The problem is that while it is clear how an ISA, MCA or EISA SCSI controller should be built from the hardware point of view, there is no standard for the way software should treat it. For example, a standard ST-506, IDE or ESDI hard disk

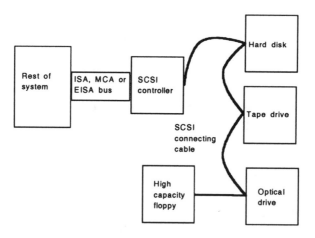

Figure 6.5
The SCSI interface

will be used to boot i.e. start, the machine because the software that deals with it is defined as part of the standard BIOS found in every machine. However, there is no standard software that automatically boots from a device connected to a SCSI controller. After all, how can the standard BIOS know that the device is a disk drive - it might be a tape drive, CD-ROM or a printer!

The most common solution to this problem is to include a special SCSI BIOS ROM on the controller itself. This will usually contain the software that identifies the device connected to the SCSI interface as a disk drive and will even boot the system from the drive. In this case the usual system BIOS has no part to play in handling the disk drive and the usual setup procedure should be used to set the drive type to "none". If an ST-506, IDE or ESDI drive is used at the same time as a SCSI drive then it is usual for it not to be used to boot the system. The SCSI BIOS usually scans the SCSI bus when the machine is first switched on by sending messages asking each device ID in turn to identify itself. There is usually a limit on the number of hard disks supported - typically two. If you need more then you have to make use of additional software drivers. The devices are scanned in order of ID number, 0 to 6 and the first device to identify itself as a hard disk is used to boot the system. After this SCSI hard disks behave like normal hard disks but low level formatting and advanced diagnostic programs generally don't work unless you obtain a version specifically written for SCSI drives.

The great attraction of SCSI is the idea of being able to connect other devices to the same controller. In practice this is more difficult than you would imagine, again because of the lack of a standard software interface. You may be able to connect a SCSI tape drive to the system without any fear of hardware incompatibilities, but you also need a device driver to allow MS-DOS, or whatever operating system, to make use of the device. The trouble is that this driver needs to be written specifically for the device and the controller combination. Device manufacturers have often overcome this difficulty by bundling a SCSI controller and software drivers with their device. So you get a SCSI controller when you buy a hard disk, another when you buy a CD-ROM and another when you buy a tape drive and so on. You can't say "no thanks" to the extra controller because you have already got one because the one you already have probably doesn't work with the driver that the manufacturer is also providing! The only sure route to compatibility is to use the controller, software drive and device supplied as a single package from one manufacturer. This situation is improving as SCSI controller manufacturers are attempting to supply a range of generic drivers with their controller cards. For example, Future Domain are attempting to establish a "plug and play" approach to SCSI by supplying a single controller card and a range of drivers that will work with common hardware and operating systems. In this case as long as you are careful in selecting devices you could achieve the goal of a single SCSI controller working with a number of devices.

The advantage of SCSI disk drives is simply their large capacity and potentially high transfer rates. In theory SCSI devices can achieve 5 to 10MBytes/s and they are available in capacities over 1 GByte. Of course in practice SCSI controllers tend to turn in performances only just a little better than ESDI but they have the potential for the future where ESDI cannot change without becoming a different standard! A second advantage of SCSI is the way that it can control multiple storage devices and overlap requests for data to each one. In other words, the controller can ask for data from one drive and then read data from other drive while waiting for the first request to be made ready. This makes it ideal for use in network file servers where the total throughput of data can be much higher than a single drive can support. SCSI also tends to be used to interface large capacity - 20-120MByte floppy disks and removable hard disks such as Bernoulli and SysQuest drives.

Which drive?

In order to summarise the arguments for and against each of the drive types it is worthwhile collecting them together into a table. The basic conclusion is that IDE is the best choice for any single-user machine up to 500 MBytes. For network servers over 500 MBytes ESDI and SCSI are both viable choices with ESDI having the advantage of simplicity and standardisation and SCSI that of sophistication but without good standardisation. SCSI is clearly the drive type for the future.

Drive type	ST-506	IDE	ESDI	SCSI
Sub-types	MFM - RLL	None	None	Fast SCSI, wide SCSI and SCSI 2
Storage range (MByte)	10-100	40 - 500	100 - 1000	100 - 2000
Transfer rate MByte/s	0.6 (MFM) to 0.9 (RLL)	1 - 2	1.25 - 2	1.25 - 10
Software drivers	AT BIOS	AT BIOS	AT BIOS	SCSI BIOS
Bus	ISA/ EISA/ MCA	ISA	ISA/ EISA/ MCA	ISA/ EISA/ MCA

Interleave

One of the main reasons why a disk drive/controller combination may not deliver its promised data transfer rate is that the processor may not be able to deal with it fast enough. For example, the fastest data transfer occurs when a file consisting of neighbouring, or contiguous sectors is read or written. In this case the data can in theory be read from the disk one sector after another with no delays due to excessive head movement. The only problem is that the processor may not be able to accept the data from the drive fast enough to allow the next sector to be read immediately after the current one.

If the processor needs longer to transfer a sector than it takes to read a sector then the next sector will be missed and the disk will have to make a whole revolution before it comes back under the read/write head again. Thus a high disk data transfer rate may actually swamp the processor and result in a very low actual transfer rate. For example, if a file is stored in each of 17 sectors in a track, the sequence of events might be:- read sector 1, miss sector 2 so wait while the disk revolves to bring it back under the head, read sector 2, miss sector 3 so wait while the disk revolves to bring it back under the head... Clearly it takes 17 complete revolutions of the disk to read the track, which should in principle be possible in just 1 revolution!

The solution to this problem is to introduce sector interleave to slow down the data transfer rate to match it more accurately to the processor's maximum transfer rate. Interleave is a technique of using non-contiguous sectors to store data. For example, a 2:1 interleave uses every other sector to store data.

To see how this might improve the actual data transfer, consider the previous example. If the processor can deal with a sector of data quickly enough to be ready to read not the very next sector but the one after that, then a 2:1 interleave provides the optimum actual transfer rate. The sequence of events is now - read sector 1, next unwanted sector passes under head while first sector is processed, read sector 2, next unwanted sector passes under head while second sector is processed, read sector 3... Now it only takes 2 complete revolutions of the disk to read 17 sectors which is a great

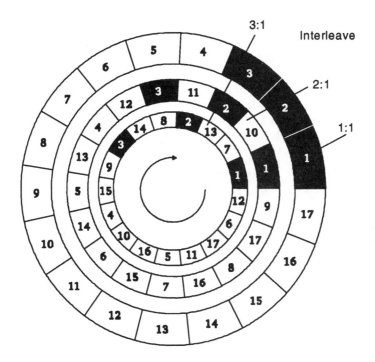

Figure 6.6
Layout of 1:1, 2:1 and 3:1 interleave

improvement over the 17 revolutions needed with a 1:1 interleave (i.e. no interleave.) The time required to read a track using different interleaves is:

Interleave	revolutions	time(at 3600rpm)	transfer rate (for an MFM ST-506)
1:1	1	16.66ms	0.50MByte/s
2:1	2	33.33ms	0.25MByte/s
3:1	3	50.00ms	0.17MByte/s
4:1	4	66.66ms	0.12MByte/s

which should be compared to the 266.66ms (which corresponds to a transfer rate of .03 MByte/s) to read the same track if the interleave factor is just wrong!

From this table you can see that getting the interleave factor just right is important and if in doubt it is better to use a larger interleave than risk getting it wrong. The interleave factor is established when the disk drive is low level formatted - i.e. not using just the DOS FORMAT command. Changing the interleave factor can be a traumatic experience because you have to back up your entire disk before reformatting. However, an easier solution is to use one of the available disk utilities such as SpinRite. This can be used to analyse a disk to discover if the best interleave has been used and if the answer is no then it can change the interleave factor without reformatting. Some BIOS setup programs also have a utility to analyse and set the interleave correctly but these destroy any data already stored on the drive. Notice that IDE drives are low-level formatted at the factory and you shouldn't attempt to low-level format this type of drive.

You may think that with a fast 386/486 a 1:1 interleave would be the norm. This isn't the case due to the way that many disk controllers are designed. Older AT disk controllers read a sector into a buffer (an area of memory on the disk controller board) and the processor had to wait to begin reading this until it was full. This was fine apart from the fact that the disk controller couldn't read the next sector until it was empty. This gave the processor only the time between sectors to move the data - a very short time. Thus many disk controllers made it more or less impossible for a processor to support a 1:1 interleave no matter how fast they were.

The solution is to use a more modern controller that contains either multiple sector buffers or a complete track buffer. A track buffer allows the disk controller to read a complete track into memory which is located on the disk controller. Once in the track buffer the processor can read the data at its own rate. Thus a 1:1 interleave using a track buffer results in a transfer rate determined almost solely by the speed of the processor - which is how things should be. You can think of both interleave and the use of a track buffer as a way of matching the disk transfer rate to the maximum that the processor can manage.

Interleave, or rather a bad choice of interleave factor, is the main reason why ST-506 and ESDI drives on particular systems perform worse than one might expect. For example, an RLL drive with an inappropriate interleave factor for the machine in which it is installed can turn in a performance far below that of an MFM drive with a correctly chosen interleave.

Drive performance

Figure 6.7 shows the relative importance of access time, latency and transfer rate. It also demonstrates what a powerful effect sector interleaving has - particularly when

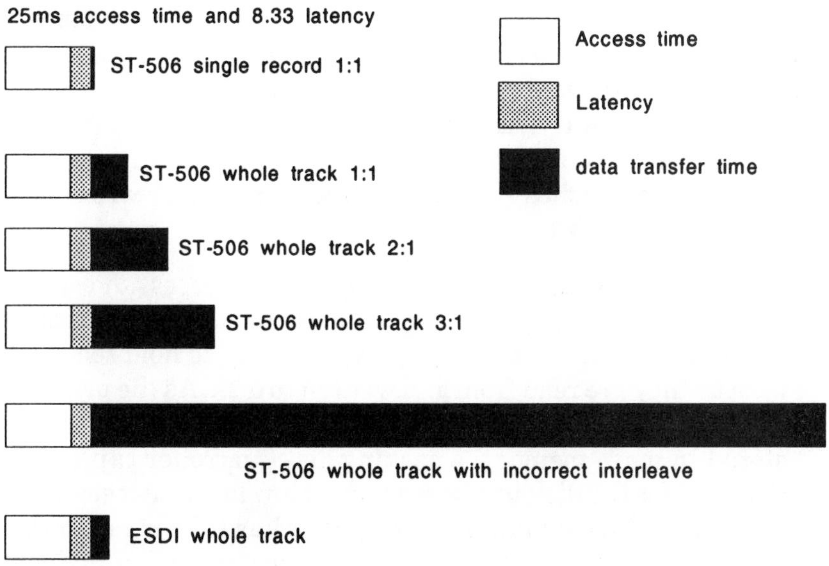

25ms access time and 8.33 latency

ST-506 single record 1:1

Access time

Latency

ST-506 whole track 1:1

data transfer time

ST-506 whole track 2:1

ST-506 whole track 3:1

ST-506 whole track with incorrect interleave

ESDI whole track

Figure 6.7
Drive performance

incorrectly set. The time to read a single sector or record is dominated by the access time and latency. This is because once the head is in the correct position, the time needed to read the comparatively small amount of data is negligible no matter what the transfer rate is. The time to read a whole track, 8.5 KBytes, is more influenced by the transfer rate. Once the head is in position and the first sector has rotated under it ready for reading all that matters is how fast the data can be transferred from the disk. You can see that in this case ESDI is noticeably faster than ST-506 using 1:1 interleave and appreciably faster than 1:2 or 1:3 interleave. Finally, notice once again the considerable time penalty in setting the interleave incorrectly.

Caching controllers

If the idea of using memory, in the form of a track buffer, on the disk controller board to speed transfer rates sounds like a good idea then you will welcome a caching disk controller. The idea of using a cache to speed processor access to slow memory has already been introduced in Chapter 4. The basic idea is to transfer to fast memory any data that needs to be used so that it is available   the next time it is needed. Because of the principle of locality - that is the idea that if you use a memory location then you are very likely to need it again in the very near future - caches reduce the need to read and write main memory to 2% or less.

The same trick can be used to speed up disk access. A caching disk controller contains a large amount of additional memory - 4 MBytes or more is typical - which is used to hold sectors of data as they are read from and written to disk. As the principle of locality holds for data stored on disk just as well as for data stored in main memory, a caching disk controller can reduce the need for the disk to be used to very low levels. Access times as low as 0.3ms are often quoted, but it has to be recalled that this is only an average assuming some proportion of cache hits. While the processor is working some controllers will perform 'read ahead' operations on sectors that are likely to be required to try to increase the probability of cache hits.

The presence of a large quantity of cache memory also allows a disk controller to implement sophisticated disk management principles usually only found on mainframes. For example, any sectors written to the cache can be accepted as quickly as the processor can write them and then the processor is free to get on with something else. The controller has the problem of writing the sectors in cache to disk at a later time. It may just write them out in the order in which they were received, or it may sort them into an order that minimises the travel of the disk head and so the time to write them out. This is the so-called 'elevator' algorithm because a lift or elevator answers calls on different floors in an order than minimises its movement rather than according to the times that the buttons were pressed. This sort of controller can be particularly effective in multi-user or network situations where a number of users are making demands on a single disk drive.

Some caching controllers can even include multiple disk drives in their scheduling methods. So for example, a request to read or write data from multiple users may be met in an order that best suits the current positions of the heads on a number of drives. Another important feature, especially for network situations, is mirroring. By attaching two drives to the same caching controller that supports mirroring, each sector can be written once to each drive. In other words, one drive acts as a mirror of the other. If there is a partial or total failure then the mirror drive is used to retrieve the lost data. This reduces the probability of data loss and keeps the system working even though a hard disk might fail.

Caching controllers are available for all types of disk drive including IDE.

Software caching

A lower cost alternative to using a caching disk controller is to use one of the many disk utilities that add a software cache to your operating system. A software cache simply uses standard memory to implement a set of sector or track buffers which it manages as efficiently as possible.

A software cache can speed up disk access if enough memory is allocated to that purpose. However, it is worth realising that a software cache cannot implement any of the sophisticated management strategies that are open to a caching controller. In particular, when a sector is written to disk there is no way that the processor can be released any sooner; it still has to take part in transferring data from the cache to the disk controller. However, when working with multi-tasking operating systems such as Windows, it is possible for software caches to put off using the processor to write data to disk until the processor isn't being used by another task. This may not relieve the processor of the task but by rescheduling it makes it look as if it has! The latest version of SmartDisk, the software cache that is supplied with Windows 3.1, uses this technique.

A hardware cache is certainly worth the investment in a network file server but for a single-user machine a software cache may be all that is required as long as it is big enough. For example, a disk system that reported a transfer rate of 0.5MByte/s jumped to 8MByte/s when a software cache was added. You will notice that this figure is larger than the theoretical transfer rate for the ISA bus! This is quite reasonable as the memory used for the cache was connected to the processor via a local bus and so quite capable of sustaining this high a rate of data transfer! For ISA bus machines this is another advantage in favour of software caching.

RAM disk

The idea of using main memory to store disk files has its full expression in the RAM disk. In this case memory isn't allocated to act as sector buffers, but as a simulated disk drive. In other words, a RAM disk behaves as if it was a disk drive. As this drive has no moving parts, access speed is high and data transfer rate is the same as for main memory. In practice the access speed isn't as high as you might expect from pure theory alone because of the overheads in finding where any given sector is stored in memory.

The disadvantage of a RAM disk is that it volatile. That is a RAM disk will only store files as long as the power is on and therefore it is blanked every time you switch your machine off. For this reason a RAM disk can only be used for temporary files or for the particular files on which you are working. In most cases you can configure applications software to use a particular drive as a scratch or temporary drive. If this scratch drive is arranged to be a RAM disk then the increased performance is often very noticeable.

You can try to increase performance even more by copying the files that you are going to work on to a RAM disk before activating an application but this is dangerous. If all you store back onto a RAM disk is the results of your work, this will be fast but very vulnerable to power cuts and fluctuations. Also you have to remember to transfer the files back to your hard disk after you have finished work for the day - if you happen to forget then all of your work will be lost.

Adding a RAM disk is fairly easy. It's just a matter of getting hold of the right piece of software - a RAM disk driver - and adding it to your operating system. Many versions of MS-DOS actually come complete with a RAM disk driver, see Chapter 11.

If you need the ultimate in hard disk operation then you can always invest in the hardware implementation of a RAM disk

- a silicon disk. This is generally a hard disk sized module that is crammed with RAM chips and electronics to make the chips act like a standard hard disk. There is usually some sort of battery backup option that makes the disk non-volatile, i.e. makes it keep its data even when the power to the rest of the machine is off. Silicon disks are fast, quiet and reliable but an expensive way of buying storage.

Cache or RAM disk

If you have some memory to dedicate to improving the performance of your machine's disk I/O, how should you use it - as a software cache or as a RAM disk? Surprisingly, this is a very easy question to answer. A software cache will only increase the speed of reading files whereas a RAM disk increases the speed of both reading and writing files. A RAM disk is volatile and has to be backed up but a disk cache writes changes to cached data back to hard disk and so requires no back up.

What all this means is that if you are using applications software that makes heavy use of temporary files then it is a good idea to use a RAM disk to speed it up. If you are using software that reads a particular file or parts of files repeatedly then use a software cache.

Another way to look at this is to notice that a software cache is a 'no-knowledge' approach. That is, you install a software cache and then forget it, knowing that it will speed up some software and do nothing for other software. A RAM disk, however, requires you to know something about the applications software that you are using and to select which items of software are directed to use it. Used selectively, a RAM disk can return the greater performance increase.

Which bus

In the discussion of data transfer rates little mention has been made of which type of expansion bus - ISA, EISA or MCA - is to be preferred. The reason for this is that at the moment the expansion bus has little effect on the overall performance of a disk system. Although in theory the EISA and MCA buses should out-perform ISA you can find lots of examples of ISA disk systems surpassing MCA and EISA disk systems. The point is that it is only the very fastest of SCSI drives that have the potential to saturate the ISA bus.

What all this means is that for simple single-user ST-506, IDE, ESDI and SCSI disk systems the ISA bus is adequate. The only time that an MCA or EISA bus becomes essential is when you need maximum performance from a caching disk controller where the speed of transfer from disk to processor is limited only by the maximum speed of transfer over the expansion bus. Buying a machine with an EISA or MCA bus simply to use a standard non-caching controller isn't worth it.

Keeping it fast

One phenomenon that many users of high performance computers notice is the gradual deterioration in the speed of access of their disk drives over time. Many think that this is a psychological effect, others think that it is to do with the disk being too full. Neither of these explanations is correct. The slowing of disk systems with use is due to *fragmentation*. When you start using a hard disk there is generally plenty of unused space available in large contiguous chunks. This allows the operating system to allocate storage to files, even large files, so that they are stored in one place on the disk. A file that is stored using sectors that are contiguous is fast to read and write.

However, as the disk is used free space is used up (and also created) by the deletion of files. Slowly but surely the free space becomes broken up across the disk's surface and eventually it isn't possible for the operating system to find chunks of free space large enough to store a file in one place. In this case the file will be stored using two or more chunks of free space - i.e. the file is stored using non-contiguous sectors. This makes the file slower to read and write because the drive's heads have to be moved across the surface of the disk to read the entire file. This is fragmentation and its effects can be a dramatic slow-down in the operation of a disk. You can often tell a badly fragmented disk by the sound of the head moving from track to track as a file that is scattered across the surface is retrieved. It gives the impression that the drive is working hard for simple file operations.

The solution to the problem is to reorganise the use of the disk so that fragmented files are stored using contiguous sectors and the free area of the disk is again composed of contiguous sectors. The reorganisation of the existing files results in an immediate improvement in the read time and the newly

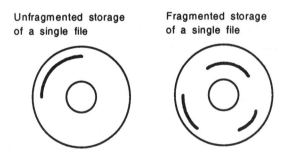

Figure 6.8
Disk fragmentation

contiguous area of free space means that fragmentation will not occur again when files are created. Thus defragmentation improves both read and write times back to the original performance of the disk as first delivered. Of course, as the disk is used and files are created and deleted fragmentation will slowly develop but another session of defragmentation soon cures that.

There are many disk utilities that will defragment a disk and perform other optimisations that are worthwhile but not quite so dramatic in their effect. The best known are Norton Utilities and Mace Gold.

Another reason why a disk drive sometimes slows down is because of slowly developing errors. All drives have built in error detection and correction facilities. When the operating system wants to read a sector, the drive attempts to read it but if an error is detected it will automatically re-read it 10 or more times. If it still cannot read the data then the error correction circuit attempts to repair the error. If this is successful the data is passed onto the operating system and the disk operation continues. This means that a disk can be on the point of failing and yet the only visible sign is the slowing down of disk operations. This can be negligible if only a few sectors are at fault or very noticeable if many sectors are involved. For example, if error correction has to be used on every sector of a file it can take minutes to read a file that previously loaded without a noticeable delay. You may also be able to hear the disk drive repeatedly seeking back to track 0 and then to the track where the difficult to read sector is located. The only solution to this problem is to make sure that there is a backup of the disk and then either replace the drive or low level format it. The subject of disk optimisation and maintenance is too large a topic to be dealt with in the detail it deserves in this book. If you are interested in this vital subject then see: *Data: A Power User's Guide to Data Storage, Optimisation and Protection* (ISBN 1-I871962-21-8) I/O Press, 1992.

Key points

» The disk controller interface governs the maximum data transfer rate. IDE, SCSI and ESDI are roughly twice as fast as the traditional ST-506 interface.

» The speed of a disk drive depends mainly on its access time. Drives with access times of 25ms or less are generally considered fast.

» IDE drives are good choices for all single-user machines that need disks up to 500 MBytes. Over 500 MBytes, and for network file servers, the choice is between ESDI or SCSI.

» ESDI drives are simple and standardised. SCSI drives are more sophisticated and so potentially higher performing but they are less standard.

» Sector interleave is used to match the data transfer rate of the controller and processor to the maximum transfer rate of the disk. Too little sector interleave is far worse than too much.

» A caching disk controller provides the ultimate in disk performance and it is the natural partner for MCA or EISA bus machines.

» Software disk caching, or the use of a RAM disk, provides useful speed gains in disk access but uses main memory.

» Disk fragmentation slows down disk operations but can be avoided by using a defragmentation utility. Incipient disk errors can also cause a disk to slow down.

Chapter 7
Video

In this chapter the video component of a system is examined in detail. Graphics performance is obviously important for applications such as DTP, CAD and commercial graphs and charts but, thanks to the introduction of graphics-based software such as Windows and Presentation Manager, it is becoming increasingly important to the general user.

In most cases the video part of a PC is provided by a plug-in card. This makes it possible to specify the graphics system independently from the rest of the machine. The only exception to this situation is where the graphics electronics is built onto the mainboard as standard - for example the IBM PS/2 range or most Amstrads. Even in these cases, you can usually add a graphics plug-in board to provide additional graphics modes to supplement or supersede those built in.

There are four types of graphics systems available at the moment:

» General purpose PC standards - e.g. CGA, EGA, VGA and HGA

» Super PC standards - e.g. super VGA

» Advanced or intelligent general purpose systems - e.g. TIGA or 8514/A

» Specialised displays - e.g. A4 monochrome for DTP

Before trying to work out what is the best type of graphics display for your system it is important to work out what your main application is going to be. If you have a single dominant application in mind then you need to choose between the lower cost but lower resolution standard or super standard boards, or pay more for a high resolution high speed intelligent system.

You will find a detailed discussion of each type of graphics board in the following sections.

The history

The history of IBM PC graphics standards is well known, although it is worth remembering that the first PC didn't have any graphics display capability at all because IBM claimed that a serious business machine didn't need any! The first PCs used a video adapter - MDA (Mono Display Adapter) - that provided nothing but 80x25 or 40x25 text.

This 'graphics are for games' mentality soon gave in under the pressure of very serious users and IBM introduced the CGA or Colour Graphics Adapter. This was a very low resolution colour graphics standard with an appallingly low quality text display but even so it served to get many applications off the ground.

CGA supports four modes - 80x25 text, 40x25 text, 320x200 four-colour graphics and 640x200 two-colour graphics.

The CGA text modes are superficially the same as MDA but each character is made up of a grid of only 8x8 dots as opposed to the 8x14 used by MDA. This reduces text quality to a point where it is now generally considered unacceptable for most uses. Initially CGA would only work with a colour monitor but other manufacturers later produced CGA hardware that would drive a monochrome monitor or LCD display.

As a reaction to the poor performance of CGA, the Hercules graphics standard was developed to allow users with mono-monitors to upgrade to graphics. The Hercules Graphics Adapter, or HGA, standard provides two text MDA compatible text modes and a single 720x348 mono graphics mode. The text modes use 8x14 character cells and so produce a display indistinguishable from MDA. Another advantage is that HGA works with very low cost monochrome monitors. Perhaps the most surprising fact about HGA is that it still offers the highest resolution of all of the standard graphics adapters - but only in two colours.

The next step for PC graphics was the introduction of the Enhanced Graphics Adapter - EGA. The EGA standard includes all of the CGA and MDA modes. The extra graphics modes improved on the number of colours that could be used and introduced one higher resolution mode. The two CGA resolutions, 320x200 and 640x200, were improved to give two extra 16-colour modes. The higher resolution modes increase the vertical resolution to 350 giving 640x350 in 16 colours. To make use of this higher resolution you need not only the EGA board but a special colour monitor. One little known problem with EGA is the fact that it is slow due to its memory refresh requirements (five out of six access cycles are dedicated to refresh).

VGA

With the introduction of the PS/2 range, IBM took the opportunity to upgrade the graphics performance of their machines yet again. The Multi-Colour Graphics Array (MCGA) used on models 30-002 and 30-021, not only changed the terminology from adapter to array but introduced a range of enhanced modes including CGA (but not EGA) compatibility. These days most people regard MCGA as a subset of the more powerful Video Graphics Array, or VGA, used on all other PS/2 models. VGA is compatible with both CGA and EGA, increases the resolution to 640x480 and includes text modes to 80 columns by 50 lines. Perhaps the most important change, however, is in the way colours are produced.

All the previous graphics adapters CGA, HGA and EGA had used a digital monitor. A digital monitor has three colour control lines, one each for Red, Green and Blue. Each of these lines can either be on or off so the maximum number of colours a digital monitor can display is eight. In practice an additional intensity control line is used to allow each of the colours to be displayed bright or dim giving a total of 16 on-screen colours.

VGA uses an analog colour signal which allows an almost infinite variety of colours to be displayed. As a consequence there are VGA modes that allow up to 256 colours to be displayed at the same time. You might think that increasing the resolution is more important in determining the quality of the display than increasing the number of colours but things aren't as simple as this. If you can display more colours then areas of the screen can merge into one another smoothly and this gives the impression of a higher resolution.

In addition to being able to display 256 colours these can be selected from a palette of over 250,000 colours. Compared to the palette of 16 colours made available by other adapters this is an incredible number and it makes it possible to produce very subtle colour changes.

If you find this discussion of video standards confusing then the following table provides a summary. What is important however is that VGA provides a standard that is backward compatible with all of the other video modes.

Resolution	Colours	Palette	Adapter
320 x 200	2	16	CGA-EGA-VGA
320 x 200	16	16	EGA-VGA
320 x 200	256	256K	VGA
640 x 200	2	16	CGA-EGA-VGA
640 x 200	16	16/256K	EGA-VGA
640 x 350	4	64/256K	EGA-VGA
640 x 350	16	64/256K	EGA-VGA
640 x 480	2	256	VGA
640 x 480	16	256	VGA
720 x 348	2	2	HGA-EGA-VGA

Beyond VGA - Super VGA

As VGA became the accepted new standard, board manufacturers first concentrated on building compatible boards, then they turned their attention to expanding on the capabilities of basic VGA. The highest resolution supported by a VGA board is 640x480 in 16 colours from a palette of 256. This is adequate for general work but still higher resolution is required for applications such as DTP, CAD and illustration. Even general applications working under Windows or OS/2 benefit from resolutions above 640x480.

The need for these higher resolutions has resulted in the adoption of three additional standard modes:

» 800 x 600 in 16 or 256 colours

» 640 x 480 in 256 colours

» 1024x768 in 16 or 256 colours

These modes have been agreed as standard by VESA, the Video Electronics Standards Association. However, the need for a standard has diminished greatly because of the use of Windows and OS/2. Now all that matters is whether or not you can obtain a suitable driver for Windows or OS/2. If you can then all of the applications running under these operating systems will make use of the enhanced modes. Most video card manufacturers supply drivers with their video cards and usually the only remaining worry concerns the quality of the drivers and the likelihood that updates will be issued to accommodate changes.

Super VGA, up to 1024x768, is rapidly becoming the accepted standard for new machines even if graphics isn't a main occupation. Standard VGA machines usually have an option to upgrade to Super VGA by adding some extra RAM chips to the video board. The big problem with VGA and Super VGA is that they are both based on very simple video hardware. All the work of drawing etc. has to be done by the processor. Even with a fast 386/486 this can involve moving very large quantities of data within the video memory. In other words, there comes a point where increasing the basic resolution of a VGA fails because of the burden this places on the processor. Most people consider that 1024x768 is about as far as VGA can go and many even feel that this is a little too far! For example, in most cases 1024x768 is half the speed of 800x600. In practice a Super VGA display is a reasonable choice unless you already know that your requirements are more demanding. (But see the comments on monitors and refresh rates.)

Monitors

One of the complications introduced by VGA is the range of different monitors that can be used with a typical VGA board. In principle VGA needs an analog monitor, but many manufacturers have realised the need occasionally to use VGA in lower resolution modes with cheaper digital monitors and so have provided RGB or TTL connectors. You can tell the difference in practice because the analog connector is a 15-pin D-type connector whereas the TTL connector is a 9-pin D-type.

If you use a TTL/RGB monitor then the VGA card will only work in a subset of its modes - roughly corresponding to EGA/HGA graphics. Notice, however, that not all VGA cards provide both types of connector and so some have to be used with a monitor specifically designed for VGA. A special VGA colour monitor will allow you to use all of the standard VGA modes, i.e. up to but not including any Super VGA modes.

There are also VGA monochrome monitors using the same 15-pin connectors. If you use a monochrome monitor then some VGA cards insist that you set switches to indicate that you aren't using a colour monitor and they will also stop you from using VGA modes that allow colour. This is often called AT mode because it was the method that IBM used to introduce VGA to its AT range. In the case of the PS/2, VGA can use either a monochrome display or a colour display without change.

To use Super VGA modes you need yet another type of monitor. You can either buy a special monitor that only works in the VGA and Super VGA modes or you can take the more usual route of using a *multi-sync monitor*. A multi-sync monitor can detect the type of VGA mode it is being used in and adjust itself accordingly.

VGA analog connector

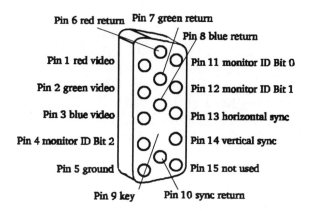

Digital TTL monochrome

Digital TTL colour

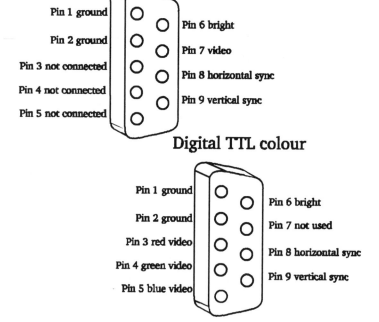

Figure 7.1
Standard video connectors

This complicated situation is best summarised as:

» Mono/Colour TTL/RGB - cannot be used with VGA card unless it has a 9-pin TTL output. Even then it isn't a recommended method of working as it only allows reduced resolution displays.

» Colour VGA (analog) - can produce all VGA colour modes and monochrome modes (automatically if the VGA card can support the PS/2 method of operation) but not Super VGA modes.

» Monochrome VGA (analog) - can produce all VGA monochrome modes and colour modes automatically if the VGA card can support the PS/2 method of operation but not Super VGA modes.

» Super VGA monitors - support the currently accepted VGA and Super VGA modes.

» Multi-sync Monitors - support all VGA and Super VGA modes and have the ability to support almost any mode up to some limit.

If you are buying a new system then the only sensible choice is between a Super VGA and a multi-sync monitor. The difference is often difficult to appreciate as both fully support all VGA and Super VGA modes, i.e. they are identical in operation! Each video mode requires a particular number of scan lines - the *horizontal scan rate* - and a particular number of frames per second - the *vertical scan rate*. The difference between a Super VGA monitor and a multi-sync monitor is that the Super VGA monitor is designed to work at the particular combinations of horizontal and vertical scan rates that VGA and Super VGA need, whereas a multi-sync monitor will work at a range of horizontal and vertical scan rates. This makes the multi-scan more flexible in principle but if you are only going to use it for Super VGA then this flexibility is wasted.

Interlaced or non-interlaced

There are a great many factors that influence the perceived quality of a video display. The sharpness of a display depends on the spacing of the dots that make up the screen, the type of tube and quality of the video electronics. However, it is extremely difficult to predict what one user will find acceptable and another unworkable. Even the same model can produce images of apparently different quality depending on how it is set up and how it has been treated.

One area where it is possible to be more definite about video quality is *flicker*. Flicker is caused in two ways. The first is by the vertical scan rate being too low. The human eye is fooled into seeing a steady image if it is presented with frames at

All the scan lines of an image
are shown in one frame in a
non-interlaced display

Using an interlaced display
the first frame shows the
odd lines of the image

The second frame shows
even lines and the eye
merges the two together

Figure 7.2
Non-interlaced v. interlaced display

around 40-50Hz, i.e. 40 to 50 frames per second. At low frame rates you can still see some flicker in bright light.

The second cause of flicker is due to the use of *interlace*. Monitors that can display more than 50 frames per second at high resolution are expensive. To make it possible to display resolutions such as 1024x768 on lower cost monitors each frame is split into two parts consisting of the odd and even lines from the complete image. The first half frame is displayed and then the second half frame is displayed shifted so that its lines fit between the lines of the first frame. This is called interlace and it succeeds in lowering the frame rate without increasing the flicker - it is used quite successfully, for example in broadcast TV pictures.

Unfortunately, as far as computer video goes its effects are very poor. Because of the way that computer graphics often use alternate lines, or patterns of lines to make intermediate shades or colours, this use of interlace often produces a strong and very noticeable flashing. It is possible to arrange a demonstration of interlaced video so that it looks acceptable by avoiding tones or colours that use regular odd/even line patterns. Equally, it is possible to find displays that make an interlaced display look like a fluorescent tube just before it fails! In practice, interlaced Super VGA is tolerable as long as you avoid even grey tones. Some applications packages are even altering their colour scheme to avoid flicker on interlaced systems - Ventura 4, for instance gives the user the option of changing the grey surround to an even colour to reduce flicker.

Some Super VGA boards support non-interlaced monitors and even increased vertical scan rates up to 70Hz. Changing to a non-interlaced monitor makes the biggest difference but a scan rate of 70Hz is also worthwhile. Notice that to make use of non-interlaced high scan rate modes you need a video card and a monitor that supports them.

Standards - video drivers

Once you leave the realm of CGA, EGA and VGA then you are outside the established standards. In most cases software will work with a VGA board no matter who it is made by without any trouble. This is a very satisfactory, if somewhat surprising, situation. The reason why it is surprising is that IBM haven't been entirely helpful in defining the VGA standard. As a result most of the graphics boards produced by other manufacturers aren't entirely compatible with the equivalent IBM products.

There are two levels of compatibility - BIOS and register. BIOS compatibility simply means that as long as the applications software doesn't try to use the graphics card directly, but only via the low-level BIOS routines, everything will work fine. The BIOS routines take account of any hardware differences between the adapter and the standard. Register compatibility implies that the adapter card is absolutely identical to the IBM hardware. Very few non-IBM adapter cards meet this stringent requirement and it is debatable whether if they did IBM would sue their manufacturer! However, most well known manufacturers - Paradise, ATI, Video Seven, Renaissance and Tseng Labs - all now produce VGA cards to a standard where compatibility isn't a real issue.

Once you go beyond the VGA standard actually making use of the increased resolution becomes a very real difficulty. There are so many possible non-standard modes that it is unreasonable to expect applications software to accommodate all of them. Instead, most applications packages take a different approach. They let hardware designers know the specification of the small piece of software that they use to drive the standard video boards. This is called a *video driver* and if you have one for the particular application and particular video card that you are using, then that application will be able to use that video card. Of course, if you don't have such a driver then you will not be able to use the graphics board in any of its non-standard modes with that applications program.

If the graphics board isn't a market leader then it is usually up to the manufacturer of the board to produce drivers for the leading applications packages. On the other hand, if the board is very nearly a standard in its own right then the manufacturer might support the well known applications packages but leave the smaller software houses to write their own drivers.

What this means is that if you want to use a particular applications package with a particular graphics board then it is essential that you check that a driver is available. If you have drivers available for some applications and not for others then it is important that the graphics adapter supports at least one standard graphics mode so that unsupported software can be used at a lower resolution. For example, if you are using a VGA card that supports a Super VGA mode then you would start using it in one of the standard VGA modes. If you then switch to an application, Ventura, PageMaker, AutoCAD, etc., for which you do have a driver then the application will make use of the Super VGA resolution, only to switch back to a standard VGA mode when the application finishes.

An alternative to this 'start-stop' approach to supplying drivers is to use a graphics operating system or Graphical User Interface (GUI) such as Windows, Geoworks, Presentation Manager (PM) or GEM. In this case all you need is a driver for the operating environment for the graphics board in question and then you can use any application that runs under it with the graphics board. As already mentioned the success of Windows and Windows applications has almost made compatibility problems a thing of the past. The availability of a Windows 3 driver allows a video card to work with a huge range of applications software without the need for any other software or configuration.

Intelligent video adapters - 24-bit colour

As graphics resolution increases, the amount of graphics memory needed to store a screen also increases. Once the limiting factor was the cost of memory, but now that memory is cheaper the limiting factor is the need to use the processor to move data into the video memory. Even a fast 386/486 processor has difficulty in updating the 256 KBytes, 512 KBytes or 1 MByte of video memory needed for VGA or Super VGA in a reasonable time. (There is also the problem of addressing 256/512 KBytes of RAM in the 64KByte window allocated to VGA cards.) As already mentioned, the maximum resolution possible with a VGA style card is 1024x768 and this is only reasonable with a fast 386/486. To go beyond this resolution different and more sophisticated techniques need to be used.

The solution is to use a special graphics processor - i.e. a graphics co-processor - complete with its own memory. The graphics co-processor relieves the burden of the main processor by receiving commands from it to draw standard shapes. So instead of having to calculate all the positions and colours of all the pixels within a circle say, and then transferring appropriate data to the graphics memory, the processor can simply ask the graphics co-processor to draw a filled circle. Once the command has been passed to the graphics co-processor it gets on with the job and leaves the main processor free to do something else. Because the graphics co-processor is specially designed to carry out graphics operations, and has high speed direct access to the video RAM graphics operations should be fast. Such graphics co-processor boards are often called *intelligent graphics adapters* and they tend to offer resolution in the 'mega-pixel' range, that is a resolution of 1024x1024. After this there is little point in extending resolution because the display resolution exceeds the perception of the human eye.

As well as increasing resolution, graphics co-processors are also capable of working with more colours. VGA and Super VGA boards, and most other common video boards, are limited to 256 colours chosen from a palette of 16.8 million. They are 8-bit colour boards. The newer intelligent graphics boards work with full 24-bit colour and can display all 16.8 million colours on the screen at the same time. The difference between 8- and 24-bit colour is considerable. Even at lower resolutions a 24-bit colour image can look like a colour photograph. The reason is simply that smoothly graduated colour can be used to mask the jagged edges normally seen in digital images. At higher resolutions 24-bit colour really does produce photographic quality images.

The problem with 24-bit colour is that it uses a great deal of video memory and processing power. Some manufacturers are of the opinion that it is so demanding that it can really only be properly supported on the MCA or EISA bus. Fortunately it is only needed for applications such as full process colour DTP or illustration.

There are many different types of intelligent graphics adapters, but most are based on either IBM's 8514/A design or TIGA from Texas Instruments. There are also a great many graphics "accelerators" which, while they fall short of being intelligent graphics cards, have hardware to specifically speed up particular operations common in GUI operating systems such as Windows. Indeed, these cards are so specific that they are often called Windows accelerators. The best known Windows accelerator is IBM's XGA.

8514/A

The first intelligent graphics adapter was the IBM PGA - Professional Graphics Adapter. This was based on an 8-bit 8088 general purpose processor and provided a resolution of:

» 640 x 480 in 256 colours from a palette of 4096.

The PGA controller was unpopular due to its higher cost for the performance offered. However, it did introduce a standard software interface, PGL - Professional Graphics Language, that is still supported by more modern graphics boards and it did establish IBM's approach to high level graphics.

IBM introduced the 8514/A in 1987 as a closed hardware product for use in its own machines. (The 8514 is in fact an IBM monitor that comes bundled with the AFDA - Advanced Functions Display Adapter - graphics card but the two have come to be known as the 8514/A.) IBM never published details of the product, which would have established an industry-wide standard, but nevertheless other manufacturers - notably Western Digital - have produced 8514/A hardware. As no standard was published the only way compatibility with the real IBM product can be assured is by making the hardware an exact copy - this is known as *register level compatibility*.

The 8514/A chip accepts graphics commands from the main processor via specific registers, much in the same way as the VGA hardware does. The difference is that each command is more sophisticated and achieves more. The 8514/A isn't as sophisticated as a typical TIGA board and it achieves its standardisation by not allowing any hardware variations. This once again is more in the spirit of earlier graphics standards, i.e. a board either was or was not VGA hardware compatible. Even though 8514/A is an IBM product, it isn't even slightly compatible with IBM's earlier graphics standards, although it can work with a VGA board to provide additional graphics modes on the same monitor. The resolutions available on the current version of 8514/A are :

» 640x480 in 256 colours from a palette of 262,144

and

» 1024x768 in 256 colours from a palette of 262,144.

Other manufacturers have extended the standard by using more than one 8514/A chip to include higher resolutions up to:

» 1280x1024 with 24-bit colour.

Another problem with 8514/A is that it uses an interlaced display and so is prone to flicker. Other manufacturers have ignored this part of the standard and there are 8514/A compatible graphics cards and monitors that are non-interlaced.

Instead of expecting the programmer to use the hardware directly, recall that the hardware specification hasn't been made public, IBM have introduced a software interface - the Applications Interface or AI. At the moment only Microsoft have deviated from using the AI. They have obtained the hardware specification from IBM under licence so that they can write drivers for Windows that go direct to the hardware. The AI provides a software standard that can be used by other graphics boards to provide a measure of 8514/A compatibility. It also allows IBM to change their hardware any time they need to leave the competition behind.

TIGA

By contrast with IBM's 8514/A, TIGA is a software standard produced by Texas Instruments (hence Texas Instruments Graphics Architecture or TIGA) that can be used by any manufacturer to produce an intelligent graphics board.

Although TIGA is an open standard, it is specifically designed to work with boards designed around Texas's graphics co-processor chips, the 34010 and 34020. Each of these chips is a full and powerful microprocessor in its own right. The 34010 is a 16-bit version of the 32-bit 34020. Most TIGA boards are based on the 34010 but the more expensive 34020 has the advantage of being roughly five times faster.

TIGA is best regarded as a graphics programming language designed to run on the 34010 or the 34020. In principle any software that has a TIGA driver can use any TIGA board irrespective of its exact design or manufacturer. TIGA is also resolution independent. What this means is that if graphics hardware improves to offer increased resolution this can be taken advantage of by the existing software. The reason is that TIGA commands take the form of 'draw a circle of radius r centred at x,y' and make no mention of how accurately this will be done - the higher the resolution the smoother the circle. Because of this resolution independence it doesn't make sense to talk of the resolution offered by TIGA but currently boards are available that work at:

»   1024x768 in 256 colours from a palette of up to 16 million colours.

»   1280x1024 in 256 colours from a palette of up to 16 million colours.

»   1024x768 in 24-bit colour

Windows accelerators -XGA

Windows is so popular an environment that graphics card manufacturers find it worthwhile to design hardware that provides Super VGA resolutions at higher speeds. These cards are usually not quite full co-processor designs but achieve their speed by implementing some of the more common Windows graphics operations in hardware. For example,

Windows spends most of its time during screen updates in *BitBlt operations* - Bit BLock Transfers - which involve moving a rectangular section of the image to another location. In standard video cards this involves the use of the processor to transfer the data. An obvious way of speeding Windows up is to implement a BitBlt operation in hardware. Coupled with a suitable Windows driver this can increase the screen update speed of Windows by 10 to 20 times. The amount of speed increase realised depends on the speed of the processor with which the accelerator is being used. Obviously, if you add an accelerator card to a machine that is already powerful enough to perform BitBlt operations very fast, then the addition will make little difference. On the other hand, if the processor is too slow to perform reasonably fast BitBlt operations then adding an accelerator card may make Windows usable without having to upgrade the processor.

Most Windows accelerators are ad-hoc designs supported by Windows drivers supplied by the manufacturers. The notable exception is IBM's XGA standard. This adds the 8514/A resolutions to the existing VGA resolutions in a single card. The XGA hardware isn't compatible with VGA or the 8514/A standard but its applications interface (AI) is a superset of the 8514/A AI. This means that applications that can use the 8514/A can also use XGA as long as they don't try to use the hardware directly - but of course most do!

XGA is optimised for Windows by supporting hardware BitBlt operations and a suitable Windows driver is available from IBM. Of course, once you are working within Windows, standards or lack of them matter much less. The big problem with XGA is that it is very closely associated with the MCA bus and makes use of the 32-bit transfers that it supports. While it may be possible that a non-MCA bus version of XGA may appear in the near future, it is arguable that it wouldn't be close enough to the original to warrant the name XGA. In addition, IBM have to modify the standard to allow it to work on the 16-bit MCA so perhaps the XGA standard is something of a misnomer.

It seems unlikely that XGA will be adopted as a wider standard but it is still important if you are committed to IBM hardware and want to run Windows. If you are using an ISA or EISA machine then almost any Windows accelerator will give you a performance that at least matches XGA.

Other standards

As well as 8514/A and TIGA there are also graphics boards based on other graphics co-processors. Notable among the competition is Intel's own 82786 graphics co-processor which directly supports windowing operations, making it especially suitable for operating systems such as Presentation Manager and Windows. You can also find graphics boards based on the NEC-7220, the Hitachi 63484 and even the Transputer. There is no real problem in buying or using a board based on these devices as long as a software driver is provided for the board and applications program that you need to use and you have confidence that new drivers will be forthcoming when needed.

There is also a range of alternative graphics software interface standards. For example, PGL - Professional Graphics Language (for PGA displays), DGIS and CGI. In all of these cases the only thing that matters is that the applications software that you want to use has a driver for the standard that your graphics board uses.

VGA feedthrough

The VGA hardware built into the PS/2 mainboard was designed with the idea that it might be supplemented by other graphics hardware to achieve higher resolutions. The MCA bus, see Chapter 3, contains a video extension that allows MCA video boards, such as the 8514/A, to connect to the VGA

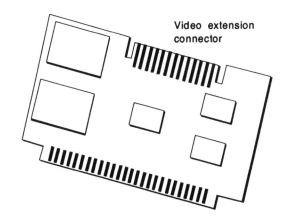

Figure 7.3
VGA card showing video extension connector

monitor via the VGA hardware. This means that when software selects a VGA display mode the VGA hardware is selected, but when the 8514/A is working the VGA hardware automatically switches off. This is a very simple way of extending the range of video modes available without using more than one monitor.

VGA cards designed for the ISA and EISA buses generally have a video feedthrough connector as a special edge connector on the top of the board. This performs the same task as the MCA video extension in that it allows other video boards to connect to the VGA monitor via the VGA hardware. Some intelligent graphics cards, including both 8514/A and TIGA, have the ability to connect to the standard VGA feedthrough connector by way of a ribbon cable. This allows the intelligent card to take over the display whenever the software selects it. Otherwise the system behaves like a standard VGA machine.

A4/A3 displays

As well as the move towards higher resolution general purpose graphics standards, there have always been graphics cards aimed at particular applications. The most common is the A4 or A3 monochrome monitor designed for either DTP or CAD applications. The reason for such graphics systems is obvious - if you are laying out an A4 or A3 page or drawing then being able to see the whole image in one go without panning speeds things up enormously.

The resolution offered by A4/A3 displays is very variable because the only real criterion that has to be met is that they display a full A4/A3 image - there is no mention of how high the quality of that image has to be. If you wanted to, there is nothing stopping you from displaying an A4 page using a 640x200 CGA display - you would be able to see the full page but definitely not what was written on it! For example, some A4/A3 displays are based on Super VGA offering a resolution of only 800x600. These really don't deserve consideration for true A4/A3 display status. A specially designed A4/A3 display usually involves a graphics co-processor. This offers high resolution but at a reasonable speed. Resolutions for A4/A3 displays are anything from 1024x768 to 2048x1536, although 1024x1024 is more typical.

The resolution used doesn't increase much in going from an A4 to a double sized A3 display. The key factor that changes is the size of the monitor. A large monitor (20" diagonal) can display an A3 or a pair of A4 pages in a readable fashion, even though the dot resolution is only 70 dots per inch, i.e. about the same as a low quality dot matrix printer. To find out how high a quality image you can expect, simply divide the number of dots across the screen by the screen width to give the dots per inch. Anything in the 100 dots per inch range is good.

There are other factors that affect perceived quality that are not so easy to measure. For example, image stability - how much wobble and flicker - and the sharpness of each dot is important. Many displays also offer between 2 and 64 grey levels and this can be used to provide smoother corners to the curves that make up a character. All of these factors make it very difficult to choose a monitor from a paper specification alone. If you are going to have to spend a long period of time working with an A4/A3 monitor then the best advice is to find a way of trying out a number of different models.

As A4/A3 displays are usually non-standard they are often used in a dual display mode. That is a standard display adapter, usually VGA, and monitor is used in conjunction with an A4/A3 display. The operating system and unsupported applications use the standard monitor and applications for which drivers are supplied use the big monitor. Many users find having two monitors on their desk more than they can cope with. A better solution is to use an A4/A3 graphics card that supports at least one standard graphics mode. For example, many offer either CGA (with improved text quality) or HGA emulation as well as a high resolution mode. In this case a single monitor can be used for all software but only in high resolution for software for which a driver is available.

As you might expect A4/A3 monitors generally come complete with drivers for the best selling DTP and CAD packages. The packages that are most often directly supported are: Ventura, PageMaker and AutoCAD. It is also usual for Windows and GEM drivers to be included. Other programs that are often supported include: Lotus 1-2-3, WordPerfect, WordStar and Publisher's Paintbrush. One important point is to make sure that the drivers supplied actually work with the latest version of the applications programs in which you are interested.

Landscape or portrait

The one problem with 1024x1024 resolution colour monitors and graphics adapters is their cost. A 1024x768 Super VGA display may not seem that far away from the desired resolution and it is much cheaper. The trouble is that for an A4 page the aspect ratio is wrong - that is a Super VGA monitor is a landscape monitor with 1024 pixels across the screen. This makes it suitable for full page illustration work or even for viewing spreadsheets, but it isn't much good for DTP work which nearly always works with pages that are longer than they are wide. There are a number of solutions to this problem. The first is the obvious hardware solution of turning the monitor on its side so converting it to a portrait monitor. This isn't quite as easy as it sounds because you not only need to alter the way that the monitor is mounted, but you also need special video drivers that turn the image through the same right angle! There are a number of VGA adapter cards that support a rotated display, the best known example of which is the Radius Pivot. This consists of a specially designed Super VGA card and a monitor which pivots. The driver can detect the orientation of the monitor and so automatically switch the display from landscape to portrait interactively. This is an ideal display if you need to work in both landscape and portrait mode.

An alternative software-only solution is to use a driver that creates a large virtual screen using RAM. The actual video display is then used as a window onto this larger display. The advantage of this is that the driver can also automatically detect when the mouse pointer is about to be moved off the edge of the screen and can move the window to show another portion of the screen. The best known examples of this approach are SoftKicker for Ventura GEM and More Windows which works with any Windows 3 application. These products only work with standard and not Super VGA but they still do a good job of simulating a full A4 display in monochrome and in colour.

Does the bus matter?

Many graphics boards are available in MCA (both 16 and 32 bit), ISA (both 8 and 16 bit) and EISA, and this raises the question of the effect the bus standard has on graphics performance. This question is a very difficult one. On the face of it, a graphics board requires a large amount of data to be transferred at high speed and therefore a 32-bit MCA or EISA bus should offer a big advantage over 16-bit MCA and ISA bus designs. For simple graphics cards, such as VGA, this advantage isn't very great because graphics data, as opposed to text data, tends to be transferred in 8-bit chunks. As a result, although a 16-bit ISA VGA card is usually to be preferred to an 8-bit ISA card, the difference in performance isn't as great as you might expect.

When it comes to intelligent and high resolution A4/A3 cards the difference is once again not as great as you might expect. The reason is simply that the intelligence built into these cards reduces the amount of data that has to be transferred to achieve the same results.

If you look at the benchmarks for a range of video cards you can find MCA and 16-bit ISA cards that are no faster and even slower than 8-bit ISA cards. In other words, there appear to be factors other than type of bus that influence graphics performance. It is widely agreed that the most generally important factor is the quality of the software driver supplied with a graphics board. A bad driver can lose any advantage that a faster bus might promise.

At the moment there seems to be no reason to prefer systems based on the 32-bit MCA or EISA bus until you reach 24-bit colour at high resolution, i.e. 1024x768. In this case the amount of data to be moved is such that the MCA or EISA bus does present an advantage.

The demands of multimedia may also be such that neither advanced bus, MCA or EISA, is sufficient in the future. For example, if you need high resolution moving graphics then the data transfer rate will have to be more than 30 MBytes/s (30 frames per second each one needing 1 MByte of data) which is at the limits of the EISA and MCA buses.

Some manufacturers, Hewlett-Packard and NEC for example, are already responding to this by designing special high speed video buses for Super VGA type systems. VESA and Intel have proposed a standard for such internal local video buses but at the time of writing standards are few and far between and manufacturers prefer to use their own proprietary designs.

Which video?

After all the discussion of the available standard, intelligent and non-standard video systems you would be correct in concluding that the overall situation is complex and changing. However, if you are using a 386/486 machine it is certain that you need a reasonably high performance graphics system and your choices are much reduced.

If you want to stay with a standard system and don't need any exceptionally high resolution graphics for DTP or CAD say, then only two graphics standards are worth considering - VGA or Super VGA. If you opt for VGA then make sure that Super VGA is available as an upgrade option, preferably as a non-interlaced display.

If you are planning to run Windows most of the time then a graphics accelerator card is a good choice, especially if you have a machine at the lower end of the power spectrum - a 20MHz 386SX say.

If you do need the increased resolution, i.e. beyond 1024x768 in 256 colours, for applications such as DTP, CAD or any graphics-dependent task, then your choice is between an intelligent controller or a specialised A4/A3 monitor. Which you choose depends on your budget and your need for colour.

For many DTP and some CAD applications colour is a luxury and so an A4/A3 monitor is cheaper and more suitable. If you need 24-bit colour then an EISA or MCA based machine is preferable.

Exactly which model of graphics adapter you should choose will obviously depend on how much you can afford to spend, but the most crucial issue is the existence of a working and up-to-date driver for the applications that you want to use. Without a software driver all of the super features, speed and excellence of a graphics board are pointless because you can't use them.

Key points

» Of the existing graphics standards - CGA, EGA, HGA and VGA - only VGA and Super VGA are good choices for a high performance 386/486.

» Super VGA increases resolution up to 1024x768 in 256 colours but it places a heavy burden on the processor.

» Graphics accelerators are designed to speed particularly common operations used by operating systems such as Windows and OS/2. IBM's XGA is a graphics accelerator for Windows that uses the MCA bus.

» Intelligent graphics adapters, complete with on-board memory and processors, are the key to higher performance graphics. Two common standards for such adapters exist, IBM's 8514/A and Texas Instrument's TIGA.

» 24-bit colour displays produce photographic quality images but to work at a reasonable speed they need an EISA based machine.

» For non-standard graphics adapters and non-standard modes a software driver is needed for each applications program that makes use of them, unless an operating system such as Windows is used, when all applications can make use of the same driver.

» Non-standard A4 monochrome monitors are often more suitable for DTP applications than full colour Super VGA displays. An alternative is to use a portrait-orientation Super VGA display.

Chapter 8
Communications

The simple communications ports, i.e. parallel printer ports and serial modem ports, are non-critical components in a single-user system. However, in a multi-user system the speed and power of such ports can determine the number of users that can reasonably be supported. In the same way the type and quality of network adapter affects the performance of a network server.

There are two types of simple communications port found on personal computers - parallel and serial. From the user's point of view the difference between the way the two types work is largely irrelevant.

Essentially a *parallel port* permits high speed communication usually in one direction only - transporting data from the computer to the connected device. Parallel ports are used mainly to connect printers but occasionally other types of output device use them.

A *serial port* is a lower speed communications port but it is generally bi-directional. That is, data can be transmitted and received over a serial port. Serial ports are most often used to connect modems for the transmission and reception of data over the public telephone system or over private lines. However, it is possible to find printers and plotters equipped with serial ports and you can even find small low cost local area networks based on their bi-directional capabilities. The most common type of printer that uses a serial port is the laser printer. Most laser printers have both serial and parallel interfaces. If you have a choice such as this then you should always use the parallel interface as it is faster and simpler to use.

Another less obvious use for a serial port is to connect a mouse (generally referred to as a serial mouse) or other pointing device such as a trackball or a bitpad. Serial ports can also be used for data collection devices such as bar code readers and similar pocket data collection computers.

Although there is no well-defined standard for parallel and serial ports, the IBM style connectors have become the de facto standard. Most IBM machines and clones use a 25-pin D-type female connector which is marked either "parallel port" or "printer port". On PC-style machines a 25-pin D-type male connector is used for serial ports and is marked "serial port" or "modem port". On AT-style machines a 9-pin D-type male connector is often used instead. You can even find a mixture of the two types of connector used on a single machine - the

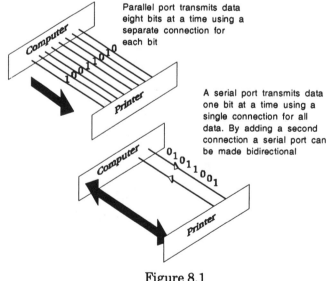

Figure 8.1
Serial and parallel ports

first port a 25-pin connector, and the second and subsequent ports as 9-pin connectors. Simple 9-pin to 25-pin connectors are available to solve any incompatibilities that may arise.

It is important to realise that the implementation of the parallel and serial ports on many devices including PCs isn't entirely standard. While it is rare these days to encounter any problems with incompatible parallel devices, it is not so uncommon to find incompatible serial devices. Such difficulties are usually cleared up by using a special cable to connect the two devices together - but making up such a cable is often a job for an expert or someone who has done the job before.

A minimum configuration for a single-user system is one parallel port to connect a printer and one serial port for use by a modem or a mouse. If you need both a serial mouse and a modem then two serial ports are advisable. Notice though that many internal modems come with their own built-in serial port which often requires any additional port you might have fitted to be disabled.

Parallel and serial ports are such simple devices that it hardly seems worth designing an extra add-in card for them. As a result many manufacturers provide a small number of ports on the main board, so reducing overall system cost and freeing one or two expansion slots. However, if your system doesn't have enough parallel or serial ports then you can usually add more by way of expansion cards. Parallel, serial and a combination of both are available as plug-in cards for the ISA/EISA bus and the MCA bus. As serial and parallel ports work with data at such a slow rate there is no reason to prefer a sophisticated bus interface such as MCA over ISA. Indeed most ISA parallel/serial cards use a lower cost 8-bit interface without any adverse effect on performance.

Installing parallel and serial cards for the ISA bus is just a matter of setting dip switches or jumpers to give the required port address and interrupt number. The AT supports as standard up to two parallel ports and eight serial ports. As with all EISA and MCA cards, no hardware configuration should be necessary.

There is some problem in using Windows 3.0 with more than two serial ports. This is due to the allocation of the same interrupts to the additional ports. Windows 3.1 doesn't share this difficulty and handles all four ports perfectly correctly.

Both serial and parallel ports have become much more important recently because of the increasing use of data transfer programs. To reduce their weight many portables do not have any sort of floppy disk, only a light weight hard disk. Data transfer between the portable and desktop is accomplished via a serial or parallel link using a program such as LapLink or FastLynx. The user is presented with a list of files on both machines and transfer is just a matter of selecting source and destination. Of course, for large files speed of data transfer matters. Most serial interfaces can work at 115,200 baud (i.e. roughly 14KByte/s) and this results in a reasonable transfer rate as long as you are not trying to copy a complete hard disk! Not all serial interfaces will work this fast but it is always possible to achieve file transfer by configuring the software to use a lower rate. Not all parallel ports can be used to transfer data in this way. You can also find software that uses a serial port to construct a low speed LAN. In this case the limitations are speed and the restriction to cables less than 50 feet.

Multi-user and personal?

Most PCs, even powerful 386/486 systems, are single-user systems as befits a 'personal' computer but increasingly even personal computers are being connected together to form networks and being used with multi-user operating systems such as Unix (see Chapter 14). Indeed many experts are of the opinion that the only good reason for buying a machine as powerful as a 386/486 is to share its power between a number of users via a multi-user operating system. Any user who has ever had to wait while a DTP, CAD, database or any sophisticated applications program performed some routine task will know that this isn't the case. I believe that a personal computer is the best sort of computer and if there is a need to share data or programs then a network is the only acceptable solution. Multi-user operating systems are suitable only for very specific and undemanding applications - such as a multi-user database based on character rather than graphics screens.

Serial cards for multi-user systems

The 386/486 is certainly powerful enough to allow more than one user to run a program at a time. A system where the power of a single processor is shared by a number of users is called a multi-user system. Most PCs are single-user systems because MS-DOS and OS/2 are single-user operating systems and only cater for one user at a time. If you want to switch to multi-user then you have only to adopt a multi-user operating system such as Concurrent DOS/386 or Unix. The only hardware changes needed are some way of providing each user with a screen and keyboard. This is generally achieved by using VDUs connected to the main machine via serial links. A VDU looks superficially like a computer - it has a keyboard and screen - but it isn't. All a VDU can do is send the data typed at the keyboard over a serial connection and display the data received over that connection on the screen. As a VDU isn't integrated into the PC in the same way as a video card you can't expect the same level of graphics support. Indeed, in most cases multi-user systems use text-only applications or ones that restrict themselves to simple character-based graphics.

The way that multi-user works is that the processor divides its attention between each user. One moment it will be dealing with user one, then user two, and so on. This switching is so fast that it gives each user the impression that they are being served by the machine on a continuous basis. As each user is connected to the machine via a serial port the way that the serial port works is important to the efficiency of the machine. If you only want to add a small number of users, two or three say, then it doesn't really matter very much what sort of serial port you use. If you want to add from four to eight users then it is important that you use a special multi-port serial card.

When a user types on the keyboard the character is transferred via the serial cable to the serial port. Before another character can be accepted by the serial port the main processor has to retrieve the data from the serial port and store it in main memory. This means that even though the data transfer rate from a serial port is low, the data must be cleared as soon as it arrives and so has to be given a high priority. In the same way, data that is sent from the processor to the serial port has to be sent a character at a time. Receiving and transmitting data in this way can involve the processor in a great deal of forced task switching which can waste a great deal of its time.

A better solution is to use an intelligent multi-port serial card that contains its own buffer memory and perhaps even its own processor to deal with communications. Using such a card the main processor isn't troubled about dealing with every single character that the user types. What happens is that the character is transferred from the serial port to the local buffer memory by the intelligent serial card's own processor. The input from each user is built up in the card's own memory until the main processor either needs or wants to deal with it. In the same way output to the user can be dealt with in block mode. The main processor can send a large chunk of output to the intelligent serial board where it is again stored in the local memory and passed out to the user one character at a time by the local processor.

This means that with the help of an intelligent serial port the main processor can send and receive blocks of data to and from each user without having to be concerned with communication at the character by character level. This frees the processor so that it can spend more of its time in running useful programs rather than dealing with low level communications.

Intelligent serial ports are available for all of the standard external buses. Notice that the only time it is necessary to use an intelligent serial card is when a large number of serial ports have to be used simultaneously. Apart from multi-user systems the only other application where this situation arises is in multi-modem bulletin boards. If you want to allow dial-up access by more than three or four remote users then an intelligent serial card is advisable, but a better option is an intelligent modem card that contains the requisite number of modems built in.

Networks

Local area networks or LANs are the best way of connecting machines together so that data can be shared. A network is formed by using an appropriate network adapter in each machine, connecting them by a suitable cable and using a network operating system (NOS) extension to your existing operating system. There are many different hardware standards for networks - Ethernet, Cheapernet, Token Ring, StarLan, etc. - all differing in their speed of transmitting data ranging from less than 1MBit/s up to 10MBit/s.

The main limitation on the speed of data transmission is the quality of cabling used. A simple twisted pair, much like a telephone cable, can manage 1MBit/s and a coaxial cable can work at up to 10MBit/s. At these speeds a network adapter doesn't really tax the resources of the ISA bus, so there seems little reason to look to more sophisticated bus interfaces such as 32-bit EISA or 32-bit MCA. However, a new generation of network cabling based on fibre optics promises to increase the data rate to 100MBit/s. In this case the EISA or 32-bit MCA bus would offer the sort of performance required.

In most networks it is possible to distinguish two types of machine - workstations and servers. A *workstation* is a machine that makes use of resources, disk drives, printers etc., offered for sharing by another machine, the *server*. The most common example of a server is a dedicated disk server. This is a machine that exists on the network for the sole purpose of sharing its, usually high capacity, disk drive, with a large number of workstations.

The requirements for a workstation aren't stringent - almost any machine can be used and will run at the same sort of efficiency on the network as off the network. However, a server is more critical. As it is likely to be in use by a large number of workstations, the volume of data that it sends and receives over the network is likely to be very high as is its use of its hard disk. Clearly this means that the hard disk installed in a server needs to be a high performance unit and this has been discussed in Chapter 6.

The network card in a server also has to offer a high performance, but not in the straightforward way of

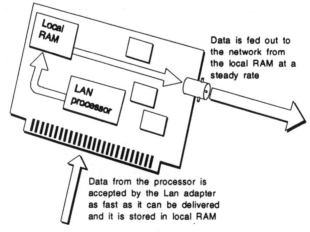

Figure 8.2
An intelligent network card buffers data

maximising the data transfer rate as you might expect. The argument is very much the same as the case for the intelligent serial card. If a network adapter has a large amount of on-board buffer memory, then the processor can concentrate on sending and receiving blocks of data to and from the network adapter's local memory. The network adapter can then get on with the task of transmitting or receiving the data, so freeing the processor to do something else. In the case of a server this usually means reading or writing to the hard disk to get ready to send or receive the next block of data from the network adapter.

By overlapping communications and disk access in this way the server can deal with more network requests before becoming overloaded. Notice that this argument also applies to a certain extent to a workstation that is transferring data to and from its own local hard disk. Notice also that the amount of memory on a network adapter card and the way that it is used has more effect on overall efficiency than the type of bus (ISA/EISA/MCA) being used. Indeed it is possible to find well designed 8-bit ISA network adapters that out-perform simple 16-bit ISA network adapters when fitted to a workstation. However, in the case of a server what matters is the combination of data transfer rate and the ability for devices to deal with their own data transfer without the need to involve the processor. The reason for this is that even in the case of the ISA bus it generally isn't the bus that reaches saturation, it is the processor. Using a bus that allows multiple bus masters such as EISA or MCA lets each adapter card deal with its own data transfer no matter how heavily loaded the processor is. Notice that this implies not only the use of an EISA/MCA bus machine but an EISA/MCA disk controller and network adapter cards. Of course, moving to an EISA/MCA based machine will not solve a performance problem caused by workstations overloading the capacity of the network itself, or anything else not related to the movement of data within the server.

Key points

» There are two types of basic communications ports on most PCs. Parallel ports are simple, fast and used mainly for connecting printers. Serial ports are more complex and bi-directional and so are used to connect modems and terminals.

» A reasonably equipped machine should have at least one parallel port and two serial ports (only one serial port is required if there is a dedicated mouse port).

» An intelligent serial card in a multi-user system frees the processor to get on with other tasks by buffering incoming and outgoing data and by dealing with many trivial tasks that would otherwise occupy the processor.

» The performance of a network server is critical to the operation of a network. Workstations, on the other hand, can be selected according to the tasks they are to perform.

» The ISA bus is quite powerful enough for use in network workstations unless it is subject to some other demand that makes an EISA or MCA bus necessary.

» A EISA or MCA based network server can handle more workstations before saturating if the disk controller and the network adapters are full EISA or MCA cards.

Chapter 9
Numeric Co-processors

If you make extensive use of applications that are concerned mainly with calculation then a numeric co-processor is essential. In this chapter we examine which co-processor is best and which applications really benefit from one.

We have encountered the idea of a co-processors of a number of types in earlier chapters of this book, but historically the numeric co-processor was the earliest important and common example of a co-processor. A numeric co-processor takes over from the main processor whenever an arithmetic operation is needed. To be strictly accurate, numeric co-processors generally only take over when a floating point arithmetic operation is need. A floating point operation can be thought of as one that involves fractional numbers or results - but this isn't entirely true because there is a way of handling fractional numbers that isn't based on floating point numbers, called fixed point arithmetic. What all of this means to the user is that a numeric co-processor really only helps when you are doing arithmetic that involves something other than whole numbers, and usually only when multiplication, division or some complicated trigonometric or transcendental function is part of the calculation.

Standards

In the early days of personal computers there was no particular standard for how numbers should be represented; now there is the IEEE 754 floating point standard. Software or hardware that conforms to this standard should always produce the same result. If this sounds like a reasonable enough expectation, it is worth saying that before the IEEE standard, different programs and different computers would give very different results for some calculations. Now it is generally sufficient to demand that any software or co-processor conforms to the IEEE standard.

The co-processor family

When Intel introduced the 8086 for the PC they also produced a numeric co-processor for it - the 8087 - and from that time on every 80x86 processor has been accompanied by its very own 80x87 co-processor. The 80286 has the 80287, the 80386 has the 80387, and the 80386SX has the 80387SX. The only exception to this regularity is the 80486, but as this is just an 80386 plus an 80387 on the same chip it isn't really different. The 486 gets rid of the co-processor problem by including one whether you want it or not. If you want to, you can add a more powerful external numeric co-processor than the 387 to the 486 but at the moment the only sensible alternative is the Weitek Abacus, 3167 or 4167- see later.

The only other complication is that the 386 can make use of the 287 or the 387. As the 387 is so much more powerful than the 287 the only reason for using a 386/287 combination is to save money. However, many early 386 machines were designed before the 387 was available and these only have provision for a 287. In this case it is important to realise that the 287 is a less powerful co-processor than the 387 even when used with the same processor. The 387SX also out-performs the 287, even when used at the same clock speed.

IEEE 754

Before 1985 there was no standard governing how computers should perform arithmetic. As a result programs would produce different answers depending on which machine they ran on and in extreme cases would refuse to work. IEEE standard 754 brought an end to this chaos by establishing a set of numeric formats and precisions. Fortunately many manufacturers adopted the standard many years before it was finalised.

Sign bit   Single precision - 32 bits in total

	Exponent 8 bits	Significand 23 bits

Double precision - 64 bits in total

	Exponent 11 bits	Significand 53 bits

Extended precision - 80 bits in total

	Exponent 15 bits		Significand 63 bits

Explicit integer bit

The IEEE 754 standard defines two basic formats - single precision and double precision - and an extended precision.

The 80387 uses the extended format using 80 bits of storage per number for all calculations. Any lower precision format number is converted as it is loaded into the co-processor and rounds off the result on the way out.

The IEEE 754 numeric formats are also used by programming languages and applications packages. The range of values that each format can represent on each type is:

Format	size	range	
single precision	4 bytes	$1.2\text{x}10^{-38}$	$<\text{x}<$ $3.4\text{x}10^{38}$
double precision	8 bytes	$2.3\text{x}10^{-308}$	$<\text{x}<$ $1.7\text{x}10^{308}$
extended precision	10 bytes	$3.4\text{x}10^{-4932}$	$<\text{x}<$ $1.1\text{x}10^{4932}$

Although the IEEE standard doesn't include trigonometric and other transcendental functions, the 387 does support a full range of functions.

Recently other chip manufacturers have seen the potential in the add-on co-processor market and have produced alternatives to the Intel range. Of course, being competitors with the Intel range these co-processors have to be better or cheaper or both. There are two sorts of competing co-processor, the incompatible types such as the Weitek Abacus (3167) and the compatible types such as those from Cyrix and IIT technology. The incompatible co-processors promise the highest performance, but as they are not Intel compatible software has to be re-written to make use of them. Although there are many specialised packages that can make use of them, the great bulk of applications still only recognise the Intel range and compatibles.

The current situation is best summarised by the table below:

	Source	**Processor**	**Notes**
8087	Intel	8088/8086	Designed before any standards.
80287	Intel	80286/80386	Not as powerful as 387.
80387	Intel/Cyrix/ IIT /ULSI	80386DX	Standard 386 co-processor. Other manufacturers claim their chips are faster and cheaper than Intel's.
80387SX	Intel/Cyrix/ IIT/ULSI	80386SX	Standard 386SX co-processor. Other manufacturers claim their chips are faster and cheaper than Intel's.
EMC 387	Cyrix	80386DX	Faster but not entirely compatible version of the 387.
Abacus 3167/4167	Weitek	80386/80486	Not compatible with 387 and only sensible upgrade to 486. Can be used with 387 installed. 4167 is faster than 3167.

Which applications?

One of the difficult things about trying to quantify the effect of adding a numeric co-processor is that not only do different applications use numeric co-processors to different extents, but a single application will vary in its use of a co-processor depending on the job it is tackling. For example, it is generally held that spreadsheet programs are heavy co-processor users but it isn't difficult to find examples of spreadsheets that do virtually no floating point arithmetic! For example, a spreadsheet that has been constructed to act as a database is very unlikely to perform any arithmetic worth installing a co-processor for.

To find out the likely impact of a numeric co-processor, estimate how much time your program spends in floating point calculation. Even in situations where the application appears to do nothing but arithmetic the estimation can be much more difficult than you might expect. For example, suppose you have a spreadsheet consisting of numeric data and formulae and it takes 30 minutes to recalculate. A simple minded approach would suggest that if you add a numeric co-processor that does floating point calculations five times faster than software the calculation would only take six minutes. If you try this out you will usually be disappointed. The reason is that the 30 minutes to do the calculation isn't occupied solely by floating point calculations - data has to found and results returned to the correct locations. In all probability no more than 75% of the 30 minutes is spent in performing floating point calculations and this is the only portion of the calculation time that can be reduced by the addition of a co-processor. In this case the calculation time would go down to only 12 minutes instead of the promised six.

The situation is so complex that apart from specialised number crunching applications such as statistics and engineering which clearly need one, it is possible to give only very broad guidelines about when a co-processor might be useful or not. To decide about the 'sometimes' applications in the following table you need to look carefully at the way that they actually work. For example, the DTP package Ventura makes specific mention of the fact that it doesn't need, or indeed make any use of a numeric co-processor.

Application	Co-processor needed?
Word processing	No
Database	No
Spreadsheet	Sometimes
Graphics	Sometimes
CAD/CAM	Yes
DTP	Sometimes

In the case of spreadsheets the important questions are how long you are left waiting during a recalculation and whether the majority of the formulae are numeric. If the formulae that your spreadsheet uses are mainly text or logical formulae then a numeric co-processor will have no effect. It also won't help improve the speed of slash commands or that of macros (apart from any numeric calculations that may be also be involved).

When it comes to graphics and DTP the role of the co-processor is more or less the same. It enables a program to do complex calculations concerning the positioning of points in much less time. However, in most graphics applications (unless a special graphics co-processor is used) more time is spent in moving pixels from one place to another than working out where they should go. In other words, if you are running a standard VGA or Super VGA system then the chances are that a numeric co-processor won't do very much good. One important exception is the generation of fonts or any shape based on spline or Bezier curves. In this case the number crunching required is extremely large and repetitive - this is the reason why PostScript laser printers have to be equipped with such powerful processors. So if you are using GoScript, UtraScript or any of the other PostScript emulators, or an internal PostScript upgrade card such as the WinJet card, then a numeric co-processor is a very good idea and roughly halves the time it takes to print a page.

Installing a co-processor

Installing a co-processor is easy as long as your computer has the correct socket on the main board - without one it's impossible! The socket for a 287, which is sometimes found on early 386 mainboards, is a long 40-pin socket.

A 387 socket is a square and comes in at least three different forms. In each the notch on the chip has to be lined up with the notch on the socket. In the case of the socket with three rows of holes the chip is inserted into the inner two rows of holes.

The 387SX socket is quite different from the standard 387 socket because it doesn't have holes for pins. Instead it has spring loaded metal strips that press against the edge of the chip. Inserting a 387SX chip is easy, and the only thing that you have to remember is to make sure that the notch on the chip is aligned with the notch on the socket. Don't make the mistake of trying to insert a 387 in a 387SX socket or vice versa.

The Weitek Abacus can be installed in the same way. Many main boards have sockets for both the 387 and the Weitek Abacus. An earlier version of the Abacus needed more than one chip and in this case it was a matter of using a small printed circuit board that would fit in place of the 387. You

8087/80287

Figure 9.1
40-pin socket for 80287

can still find add-in boards for machines that do not have sockets for the Weitek chip.

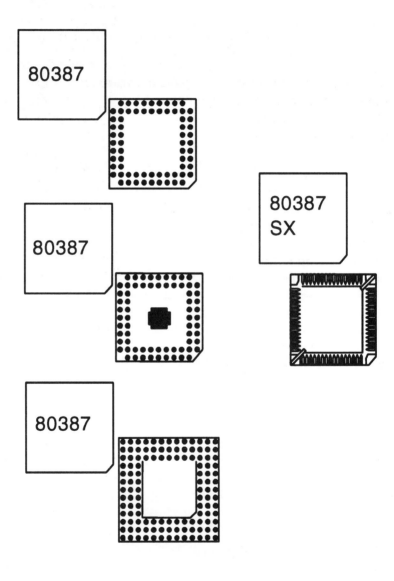

Figure 9.2
Three types of 387 socket and the 387SX socket

When buying a co-processor it is important to make sure that it can run at the same speed as the main processor. For example, if the processor is a 25MHz 386 then you need to buy a 25MHz 387. Some main boards can be set to use a slower co-processor than the main processor - this may save money but loses speed. You can of course always buy a co-processor faster than is needed - this just costs more without any increase in speed!

In most cases installing a co-processor chip is just a matter of removing the case and plugging the chip into the socket. The only thing you have to get right for everything to work is inserting the chip the correct way round into the socket - see diagrams. Also be very careful not to bend the pins as you insert the chip and make sure that all of the pins are in place. The most common cause of a co-processor chip not working is a pin bent up underneath the chip. The best method is to place the chip partially into the socket, then check that all pins are in place (a dental inspection mirror can help in awkward corners) and finally push the chip home firmly and evenly. Removing a co-processor chip without bending the pins can be very difficult without a proper removal tool, but it can be done with care. Whether you are inserting or removing a co-processor chip you should take precautions against static damaging the device. For more information see the technical box in Chapter 5 concerning static precautions.

How fast?

If you haven't got a co-processor fitted then any program running has to perform floating point arithmetic the soft way. That is, every multiplication, division, addition and subtraction has to be performed by a suitable subroutine. These days software that supports numeric co-processors generally uses routines to simulate a co-processor if one isn't fitted. In this case the only noticeable difference between using or not using a co-processor is speed. A co-processor will complete in a few clock cycles an arithmetic operation that might take tens or even hundreds of clock cycles using software.

The two measures of floating point speed are the Whetstone - 1 Whetstone is one Fortran floating point operation per second and the FLOP/s - 1 FLOP/s is one Floating Point Operation per second, see Chapter 2. The table below lists typical benchmark results for a range of co-processors running at 25MHz. As numeric performance is linear with clock frequency you can obtain figures for other clock rates by scaling the results. For example, if you halve the clock rate to 12.5MHz then you roughly halve the Whetstones and MFLOP/s.

Co-processor performance at 25MHz

	KWhetstones	MFLOP/s
80386 without co-processor	100	.01
8087	400*	.05
80287	800*	.1
80387	2500	.33
80387SX	2031	.28
IIT 387 clone	3000	.34
Abacus	5267	.87

*Note that the fastest 287 available at the time of writing is 12.5MHz and the fastest 8087 is 8MHz so the performance shown is theoretically what could be achieved by 25MHz versions if they existed. To obtain approximate figures for other clock speeds divide the rating by 25 and multiply the result by the desired clock speed. All performance figures are for single precision calculations.

The conclusion is that for the fastest possible calculations you should use the Weitek Abacus as long as the software in which you are interested can use it. The clones of the 387 are only marginally faster in general use, despite what the specification sheets claim. In this case price is the only feature worth taking into account. However, some of the clone 387 chips do have special additional operations that can speed up particular types of operation as long as the software is written to make use of them. It is also worth noting that the 387 implements trigonometric functions whereas the 287 does not.

The reality

Whetstones serve to compare co-processors but it is difficult to translate them into anything meaningful in terms of how much faster a program would run with a co-processor. Of course, this is an impossible question to answer with any generality but in an effort to provide some guidelines various benchmark spreadsheets based on Lotus 1-2-3 Release 3 and SuperCalc 5 were timed with and without a co-processor.

With an 8086 PC/XT, adding an 8087 halved the time that the calculation took. This 50% decrease isn't as impressive as the 17 times improvement the raw Whetstone figures would suggest but is still not bad. For the 286 system the calculation time went down by a quarter, i.e. a 25% decrease. For a 386 system the calculation time went down by close to 40%. Repeating the benchmarks with the clone 387 chips produced almost identical results.

The 40% speed up in calculation-intensive parts of applications is, in my opinion, typical of the effect of adding a numeric co-processor. Obviously some applications are more affected than this, for example, PostScript interpreters such as GoScript or UltraScript run 100% faster with a co-processor.

Software for co-processors

It is not enough just to install a numeric co-processor to speed up applications; it is also essential that the application can make use of the co-processor. Intel make available a list of popular products that support the 387 but in general any sufficiently well developed product that can benefit from using a 387 co-processor does make use of one.

If you are programming numerical applications then most compilers will generate code for the 387. If you need Weitek support, or even more efficient 387 support, then NDP Fortran 386, NDP C 386 and NDP Pascal 386 are worth examining. They all produce code for the 386/486 and support the 80287, 80387 and the Weitek. They are available from MicroWay (see the *Useful Addresses* at the end of this book) as are a wide range of 387 and Weitek subroutine libraries NDP-NAG, 87FFT etc. and support tools.

Ultra power

There are a range of PC add-on products that raise the performance of the 386/486 into the mainframe, if not super computer, bracket when it comes to calculations. These add-ons all share the characteristics of being expensive and non-standard. If your budget stretches to them and if you can buy or write the software to make use of them then they will allow you to solve problems on a PC that traditionally needed a large allocation of mainframe time.

Perhaps the best known advanced numeric boards are based on arrays of Transputers. The Transputer is an advanced general purpose processor that includes its own numeric co-processor (or more exactly the T800 Transputer does). The Transputer is fast but its main advantage is that it can be used in intercommunicating groups to speed up computation beyond what is achievable by any single processor. For example, the MicroWay Quadputer has four Transputers and can be linked together with other Quadputers to form even bigger parallel processing networks.

An alternative to the Transputer that is gaining in popularity is the Intel i860. There are mainboards (for example the Haupauge 4860) that have an i860 built in as a standard co-processor to help with tasks such as graphics and arithmetic. You can also buy an i860 add-on card from MicroWay which claims to reach 11MFlops in a 40MHz machine. As you might expect, such add-ons are not cheap and there is the additional problem of obtaining software that makes use of them. If you have the ability to develop your own programs then this is not such a problem as MicroWay supply a number of parallel languages that enable you to write programs for a range of co-processors including the 387, the Weitek range, the Cyrix EMC and the i860.

Key points

» A numeric co-processor will speed up only those parts of an application that involve arithmetic.

» Not all applications will make use of a numeric co-processor, and not all of those that do make good use of one.

» The 387 co-processor is markedly more powerful than the 287 co-processor.

» The 486 includes a 387 on the same chip.

» Installing a co-processor is easy as long as you take the necessary precautions against static and avoid misinserting the chip into its socket.

» The most powerful co-processors for the 386/486 family are those in the Weitek Abacus range, but they are not compatible with the 387 and not all software can make use of them.

» More powerful co-processors are available but they are generally very non-standard and have very little general software support.

The Software

At this point all the necessary hardware topics have been discussed and it is time to turn our attention to the software aspects of 386/486 systems. This division into hardware and software isn't clear cut because what the software can do depends on the hardware it has at its disposal - there is an interaction between the two. If you have skipped hardware topics in the first part of this book then you may find that you have to go back to clarify points raised in this part of the book. You cannot be a software expert without knowing about the underlying hardware.

The biggest problem in using a 386/486 system to the full is that MS-DOS treats all machines as if they were 8088/86 systems. Thus under MS-DOS most of the power of the 386/486 is ignored. Changing to OS/2, Unix or any other operating system designed for the 386/486 solves this problem completely. However, there are more applications packages for MS-DOS than for any alternative operating system, it has more users and there is over ten years' experience of its strengths and weaknesses. As a result there is a great deal of inertia in the MS-DOS using community and alternative operating systems are only slowly being adopted.

Because of this inertia many ingenious ways have been found to extend the way that MS-DOS works to take account of the increased power of the 386/486. In the main these methods work and they are very effective but from a user's point of view they can appear complex. Indeed, because of the proliferation of standards and possible approaches they can appear complex, even from an expert's point of view!

The following five chapters attempt to untangle this complex web of ideas.

Chapter 10 describes the memory management abilities of the 386 family. It discusses real mode, protected mode, extended memory, expanded memory, the HMA, upper memory blocks, virtual memory, and shadow RAM. All of these are described in very general terms to enable the user to understand the principles and ideas. In later chapters the topics are discussed again but with reference to real software and real systems.

Chapter 11 deals with the use of a 386/486 under MS-DOS. The major topics are how memory managers can be used to provide expanded memory, DOS extenders and DOS multi-taskers.

Chapter 12 is about how you can stay with MS-DOS and yet have many of the advantages of a protected mode operating system. Specifically it deals with Windows 3.0 and 3.1. It also briefly examines how Windows can develop into a full protected mode 32-bit operating system - i.e. Windows NT.

Chapter 13 looks at the main alternative to staying with MS-DOS, i.e. OS/2. Version 2.0 will run MS-DOS, Windows and native OS/2 application so there seems to be little to lose in using it, but is there anything to gain?

Chapter 14 closes the section on software with an examination of Unix and its potential to change the way we use the 386. Unix has a long history of being the main challenger to MS-DOS but a proliferation of standards and versions makes it difficult to see exactly why.

Chapter 10
Memory Management

In this chapter we look at the way that the 386 family manages memory. The ideas of conventional, expanded, extended and virtual memory are explained in detail along with the more general memory management capabilities of the 386/486.

All of the processors in the 386/486 family have the power to work with memory in sophisticated ways. This is as important as their ability to run programs faster. Much of the increased processing power of the 386/486 is, however, ignored by applications software that treats it as if it were merely an 8088/86 or 286. Even in these situations the memory management facilities of the 386/486 can still be used to gain increased performance or flexibility.

A 16MHz 286 and a 16MHz 386SX actually run MS-DOS, and many other applications, at more or less the same speed. Many benchmarks even turn in slightly slower times for the 386SX. The reason is that most of the time both processors are being used as if they were 8088/86 machines. However, the 386SX has memory management facilities that can be used to completely reconfigure the machine using nothing but software. It can be used to run multiple programs with a much reduced danger of one program affecting another and it can do it more efficiently. It can also make use of disk storage to extend the amount of memory available in a simple and efficient way. What is more, it can do all of this without needing any of the applications to be modified in any way. This is the real reason why a 386SX is to be preferred to a 286 that apparently provides the same performance.

Of course, if you make use of software that is specially written to make use of the 386/486 then the difference is even more marked. The 386/486 processor has a range of 32-bit instructions that, when used, make applications much faster. It also has a number of technical advantages in handling memory and multi-tasking that currently most software simply ignores. Software that is specially written for the 386 is often referred to as 32-bit software - and it has the potential to be much superior to the 16-bit software that is so prevalent at the moment. Estimates of performance gain are difficult but in some situations 32-bit software could be more than twice as fast as 16-bit software.

The current memory management situation is very complicated. The need to be compatible with earlier processors and their original ways of doing things has produced a confusingly wide range of jargon and a lack of standards. It is almost true to say that you need to understand the whole topic before you can comprehend any of it! There is also the interplay between what the 386/486 processor is capable of and how it is actually used in practice due to the need to be compatible with earlier machines. Often its powers are used to solve problems, created by this earlier generation of processors and their programs, that simply would not exist if we agreed to wipe the slate clean and start again. This means that it isn't enough to just look at what the 386/486 can do with memory in isolation, you also have to see how this relates to the shortcomings of the earlier processors.

The memory map

When considering memory configuration it is common to think in terms of the processor's *memory map*. A memory map is a diagram showing how the different address ranges are used. The processor has at its disposal a fixed number of address lines and this determines the maximum amount of memory with which it can work. However, not all of this memory capacity has to be used. For example, the 386SX has a total addressing range of 16 MBytes. This means that you could fit up to 16 MBytes of memory and the processor would be able to select which byte it wanted to read or write using its address bus. However, if only 8 MBytes of memory was installed the processor could still attempt to address the full 16 MBytes, but it would find that half of the addresses were unoccupied and unresponsive. If the processor attempted to store data at an unoccupied address there is nothing to stop it but it would fail. The range of addresses that a processor can use is referred to as its *address space*.

In general there are four possibilities for any given address. It can be occupied by RAM, ROM, hardware or it can be unused. If it is occupied by RAM (Random Access Memory) then data can be read and written. If it is occupied by ROM (Read Only Memory) then data can only be read from the location. Hardware such as video adapters, networks cards etc. often occupy areas of memory, and in this case how the allocated addresses behave varies greatly. Sometimes a location that is occupied by hardware can be read and written, sometimes just read and sometimes just written.

Now you should be able to see that a memory map, in the form of a diagram or table showing how the various areas of the address space are allocated to different types of memory or even different types of uses, can tell you a great deal about a system. Memory maps will be used throughout this chapter to explain how the 386/486 manages memory. Also see the box, *Hex addressing and memory maps* at the end of this chapter.

Real mode

The early PCs based on the 8088/86 processor could access up to 1 MByte of memory. As this seemed like a great deal of memory at the time IBM decided that only 640 KBytes would be allocated for the use of applications and the remaining 384 KBytes would be used for system ROMs, graphics memory and other purposes.

When the 80286 was introduced it increased the amount of memory that could be used to 16 MBytes and the 386

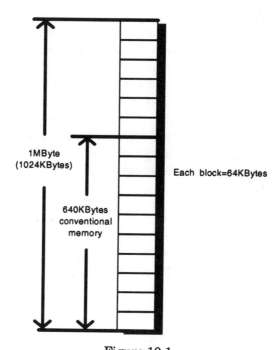

Figure 10.1
The real mode memory space. The diagram is drawn to scale and each division corresponds to a 64KByte block of memory.

increased it yet further to 4 GBytes. Unfortunately under MS-DOS both processors are made to pretend that they are the 8088/86, i.e. they emulate the 8088/86, and in this mode they can only access 1 MByte of memory, no matter how much is actually available.

A 386/486 emulating an 8088/86 is said to be in *real mode* and the terminology is also used for software that operates in this mode, hence - *real mode software*. When a 386/486 system is 'being itself' it is said to be in *protected mode* and in the same way software that operates in this mode is *protected mode software*. For example, MS-DOS is a real mode operating system whereas OS/2 is a protected mode operating system. Also notice that protected mode is available on both the 286 and the 386/486 processor so this is not a source of difference between the 286 and 386.

Real and protected mode

When the 386/486 (or the 286) are first switched on they operate in *real mode*. In this mode the processor pretends to be a more powerful version of the 8088/86 processor. The natural mode, that is one in which both processors can be themselves, of both the 286 and the 386/486 is *protected mode*. Real mode ensures downward compatibility with earlier processors but it severely restricts the use of the 386/486. In particular it cannot access any memory above the first 1 MByte. Although the 1MByte limitation is the more obvious to a user, the additional restriction that memory has to be treated in 64KByte segments is more serious to a programmer. The 286 has this limitation even in its protected mode but the 386/486 can work with memory segments up to the full 4GBtye total memory limit. This unrestricted segment size makes it much easier for a programmer to create sophisticated programs.

As well as not being able to use more than 1 MByte of memory in real mode, the 386/486 cannot make use of its advanced page addressing facilities which allow it to move 4KByte blocks of memory around by an almost instantaneous remapping of their addresses. Page management is used to implement expanded memory in 386/486 based systems - see later.

In addition to providing advantages with regard to the maximum amount of memory that can be used and how it can be used, protected mode also offers a range of facilities for multi-tasking. The biggest problem with multi-tasking, that is having more than one program in memory at a time, is stopping a badly behaved program from interfering with other programs or even crashing the whole system. Protected mode provides a range of privilege levels and checks on which regions of memory can be used by any particular program. These 'protection mechanisms' are, of course, why protected mode is called 'protected mode'.

What limits memory?

Many users find the 1MByte limit very difficult to believe. How can a 386/486 system have 4 or 8 MBytes of RAM installed and yet be unable to make use of it? The answer is that in real mode the processor only has access to 20 of its addressing lines and only the memory that can be selected using just these that is usable. You can quickly work out that if one address line allows you to select one of two memory locations, then two address lines select one of four, three one of eight and so on up to ten which select one of 1024 memory locations, i.e. 1 KByte of memory. (Notice that this is the reason that 1K is defined as 1024 and not 1000.) If ten address lines can select 1 KByte you should be able to see, by the same sort of reasoning, that 20 address lines can select 1024 KBytes i.e. 1MByte. (In general n address lines can select one of 2^n memory locations.)

If you change to protected mode then the 386SX (and the 286) have 24 addressing lines available, making it possible to select one location in 16 MBytes of memory and the 386DX/486 have 32 address lines making it possible to select one location in 4 GBytes i.e. 4x1024 MBytes.

When you first switch on a 386/486 processor the BIOS self test will often count the amount of memory installed in protected mode, so showing the true figure, only to change back to real mode before starting any programs. Hence you can have a machine that reports the correct amount of memory during the self test only for this memory to vanish when you start using the machine under MS-DOS.

The 640KByte limit

If real mode is restricted to accessing only 1 MByte of memory, why is this reduced to the 640KByte limit under MS-DOS? The answer to this question is simply that this is what IBM decided when they built the first PC. There is no actual barrier to software using the whole 1 MByte, and there have been variations on the basic design of the PC that have made as much as 720 KBytes or more available to programs.

The 640KByte limit is in fact just the area that is normally available to programs. In some cases, see later, this can be increased even in a standard PC design. Above 640 KBytes is reserved for special use by BIOS ROMs, video and other hardware. Some of the address space above 640 KBytes is empty, some filled with RAM that is used by video adapters etc. and some is filled with ROMs that contain the low level drivers for devices such as hard disk controllers, LAN adapters and video adapters.

The area of memory above 640 KBytes is often referred to as *Upper Memory Area* or UMA and the area up to 640 KBytes is called *conventional memory* but it is important to realise that the distinction really is the result of a 'convention' rather than anything to do with hardware constraints. On the other hand there has to be some space allocated to BIOS ROMs, video RAM, etc..

The problem of extended memory

The memory beyond 1MByte that is only accessible when the 386 is in protected mode is generally referred to as *extended memory*. However, from the preceding discussion you should be already aware of the fact that it isn't any different from conventional or upper memory - apart from only being accessible from protected mode.

In principle, making use of extended memory is just a matter of changing to a protected mode operating system such as OS/2 or Unix, but many users simply have too much invested in MS-DOS applications to make this a realistic course of action. As a result various ways of extending MS-DOS to allow applications that run under it to make use of extended memory have been implemented. In general these achieve their objective but at the cost of making the situation much more complicated. Perhaps the most confusing factor is the issue of *expanded memory* - a type of memory specifically designed to allow MS-DOS programs to go beyond the

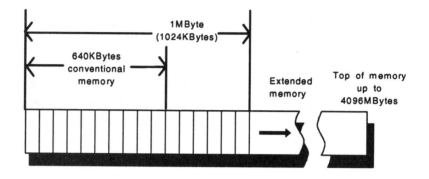

Figure 10.2
Protected mode memory

640KByte barrier without the need to leave real mode.
Expanded memory is discussed later in this chapter.

DOS extenders

A DOS extender is a piece of software that enables an MS-DOS
application to run in protected mode while still making use of
MS-DOS. What happens is that the application starts working
in real mode in the usual way and then when it is ready it calls
the DOS extender to change into protected mode. While in
protected mode it has access to however much extended
memory the system has, but it doesn't have access to MS-DOS.
When the application needs to make an MS-DOS call, to save
a file say, it calls the DOS extender again with the details of
what it wants MS-DOS to do. The DOS extender then switches
the processor back into real mode and calls MS-DOS on the
application's behalf. (In practice the DOS extender has rather
more to do than this because it also has to cope with interrupts

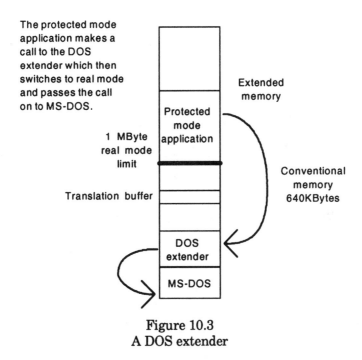

The protected mode
application makes a
call to the DOS
extender which then
switches to real mode
and passes the call
on to MS-DOS.

Extended
memory

Protected
mode
application

1 MByte
real mode
limit

Conventional
memory
640KBytes

Translation buffer

DOS
extender

MS-DOS

Figure 10.3
A DOS extender

generated by hardware and software while in protected mode
that need to be directed to real mode interrupt handlers.)

Another interesting question is how data can be passed from
real mode to protected mode and vice versa. After all, in real
mode none of the extended memory is accessible. The answer
is that an area of conventional memory has to be set aside to
be used to hold data in transit between real and protected
mode. This is usually called a *translation buffer*.

The need for standards

As well as DOS extenders, a number of other programs
managed to find their own ways of using extended memory.
For example, RAMdisk drivers, disk caches and network
drivers all succeeded in accessing extended memory. How
these programs do this is of little consequence unless they
have to work together. For example, if you have a machine
with 4 MBytes of extended memory running under MS-DOS,

only the first 640 KBytes of memory are usable, so adding a RAMdisk or a disk cache that uses extended memory is an excellent idea. As it is the only program that makes use of extended memory it might as well make use of all of it! In this case the method that the program uses to allocate the extended memory to itself is irrelevant but if you decide to use another program that requires extended memory there could be a conflict if they both allocate the same area of extended memory for their own exclusive use. Clearly there has to be some co-operation in the way that extended memory is allocated.

There are four commonly used standards for extended memory allocation - INT 15 or *top down allocation*, XMS, VCPI and DPMI - and each has different characteristics.

Top down allocation

The first method of allocating extended memory was invented and re-invented by many programmers. It doesn't even need an agreed standard because it takes advantage of the machine's hardware. To allow for extended memory a new function, INT 15, was added to the AT BIOS which returned the current amount of extended RAM installed. The idea was that a program could use INT 15 to discover the largest amount of extended RAM that it could use. However, INT 15 can be altered by the program to report a different amount of extended memory, reflecting the amount claimed for use by the program. The next program that tries to use extended memory discovers the lower limit set by the earlier program and so doesn't use the same area of memory. You should be able to see that this results in extended memory being allocated from the top of memory down to the 1MByte limit.

A similar scheme was used by early versions of VDISK, the IBM RAMdisk driver, only it allocated extended memory from the bottom up. In practice the VDISK method proved to be less stable than the top down, INT 15, method and so it has largely been abandoned.

This sort of extended memory allocation works reasonably well in practice when used with device drivers that are loaded at the same time or before the operating system (by being named in the CONFIG.SYS file in the case of MS-DOS). Each driver claims its portion of memory which is then in a sense removed from the sight of the rest of the system. The portion of memory that is reserved depends only on the amount of memory required and the order in which the drivers are loaded - they each carve a chunk off the top of the memory remaining. This is the reason why conflicts in extended memory allocation between MS-DOS device drivers can sometimes be resolved by altering the order in which the drivers are listed in the CONFIG.SYS file. However, you can tell from this comment that this sort of low level memory allocation isn't ideal. In particular, there is no way of dynamically allocating extended memory. If one of the drivers wanted to give up its portion of extended memory there would be no way for it to be returned to a pool of available memory. Clearly something more sophisticated is needed.

Notice that INT 15 (top down) extended memory allocation is still in use by many device drivers and in the majority of cases it will co-exist with the more sophisticated allocation methods described below.

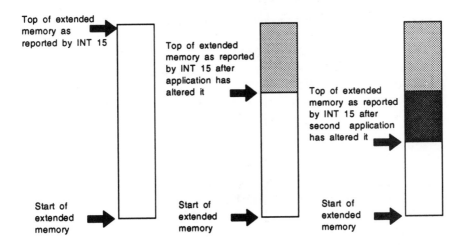

Figure 10.4
Top down allocation

XMS and HIMEM.SYS

Although historically not the first extended memory standard, XMS is currently the most important. Originally XMS started life as a specification for allowing real mode software to access just the first 64KBytes of extended memory. The reason behind this singling out of the first 64KBytes, the so-called *High Memory Area* or HMA, is worth examining in a little more detail.

When Intel designed the 286 they allowed a tiny portion of the protected mode memory to show through into real mode. It turns out that by an accident of the way that memory is addressed it was possible to access the first 64KByte block of extended memory without leaving real mode. The first twenty address lines that are used to access the first 1 MByte of memory are numbered A0 to A19 and these should be the only address lines used in real mode. The very next address line A20 is the first to come into play when memory above 1MByte is accessed in protected mode and in theory it shouldn't be possible for a real mode program to alter the state of the A20 line - but in practice they can. This isn't the case with the real 8088/86 processor that the 386 is trying to look like when it is running in real mode, and so some extra hardware was added to 'gate' the A20. When running in real mode, the A20 is normally disabled but programs that know about it can enable the A20 to gain access to an extra 64KBytes - the HMA.

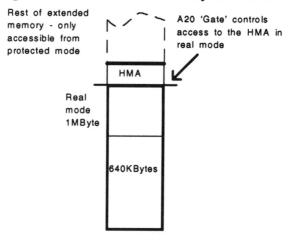

Figure 10.5
The HMA

To control access to the HMA, Microsoft introduced the XMS standard and implemented this in the HIMEM.SYS extended memory driver. With this early version of HIMEM.SYS any real mode program could gain access to the HMA without fear of conflicting with other programs' usage. In this form XMA wasn't particularly popular or common. Real mode applications tended to ignore the HMA as a small amount of memory whose use wasn't worth the effort of being XMA compatible.

The change came about when Microsoft extended XMS in Version 2 into a complete extended memory manager. This turned it into the basis for other more sophisticated memory managers to build upon. Real mode programs still can make use of HIMEM.SYS to gain access to the HMA but it is also used by real mode device drivers to allocate extended memory in preference to the INT 15 method. For example, SuperCalc 5.1 added 64 KBytes of working memory by making use of the HMA via HIMEM.SYS. MS-DOS 5.0 and DR-DOS are both capable of loading 64KByte sections of themselves into the HMA, so freeing an additional 64 KBytes of conventional memory for applications programs. Most of the device drivers that are supplied with MS-DOS can also make use of XMS memory for data buffers etc.. Windows 3 also makes use of HIMEM.SYS to allocate extended memory to real mode programs that run under it and so on.

XMS and the HMA have now become so important that nearly all CONFIG.SYS files now start with the line:

DEVICE=HIMEM.SYS

Only after this line can you load device drivers such as RAMDRIVE.SYS, SMARTDRV.SYS and EMM386.EXE that make use of XMS extended memory. If you also want to make use of device drivers that use the older INT 15 extended memory allocation method then you have to add:

int15=*size*

to the HIMEM.SYS line where *size* is the number of KBytes that is reserved for this purpose. In nearly all cases it is advisable to try to replace these older programs by improved versions that make use of XMS extended memory.

Expanded Memory

Before going on with the account of extended memory it is necessary to take a detour into the subject of expanded memory. Expanded memory isn't a difficult idea but because it sounds so much like extended memory, the major danger is simply getting the two confused!

The 640KByte limit became a problem before the 286, let alone the 386, came on the scene. To make more memory available to applications running on 8088/86 based systems, Lotus, Intel and Microsoft got together in 1985 to define the Lotus, Intel, Microsoft or LIM expanded memory standard. This made use of a page swapping technique to expand the

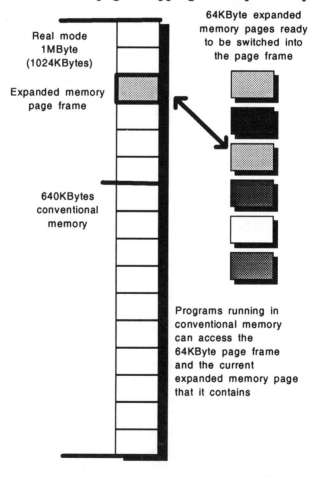

Figure 10.6
Expanded memory

address space of the 8088/86 processor. This may sound complicated, but in practice it is something with which every user is familiar in the form of the floppy disk drive and its diskettes. A single floppy drive may be limited to the storage capacity of a single diskette, 720 KBytes say, but by inserting different diskettes it has an effectively infinite capacity. In the case of expanded memory it isn't a diskette that is swapped in and out of a drive but a page of memory in and out a page frame.

In the first version of LIM, a 64KByte area of the address space is allocated as a page frame into which any of a number of 64KByte pages of expanded memory can be inserted. An application program that has been written to take advantage of LIM expanded memory can read and write data into a page and when it is full it can simply switch to another page. You can see that LIM provides a way of breaking the 640KByte barrier without actually removing it! A LIM application can make use of much more than 640 KBytes of memory but at any one time it can only access the standard 640 KBytes, plus of course the 64KByte page that is currently in the page frame.

LIM expanded memory has been redefined and improved a number of times - see the technical box *LIM / EMS standards* - but the version described above using a 64KByte page size, LIM 3.2, is ideal for applications that need to store more data than 640 KBytes can cope with. There is a more sophisticated version, LIM 4.0, that allows the page size to be as large as the application chooses and this can be used to run more than one program at a time. Programs such as DESQview often use LIM 4.0 on PC/XT machines to make multi-tasking more efficient.

Expanded or extended?

In the case of the 8088/86 processor, supporting expanded memory involves adding extra hardware in the form of an expanded memory card. You could add RAM in the usual way to bring the machine up to the 640KByte limit. After this any memory that you add has to be expanded memory because the entire address space has already been allocated. In later

The problem of the page frame

For expanded memory to work there has to be a 64KByte area above conventional memory that can be used as a page frame. In many cases you can leave the automatic installation routine of the EMM that you have chosen to pick the location of the page frame for you. If your system is fairly standard then this should work without any problems. However, if your system is even slightly non-standard the automatic location method is likely to fail. In this case it is up to you to find a free 64 KByte area and enter its address as a parameter in the line that loads the EMM in the CONFIG.SYS file. There are two main problems with doing this. The first is that you have to use hexadecimal notation to specify the address and this frightens many users. The second is actually finding a free area. The first problem can be solved by reading the technical box on *Hex addressing* later in this chapter. The second problem can be solved by either reading your machine's manual, or using a memory mapping utility (for example the one included with System Sleuth) or, if all else fails, a trial and error procedure testing each possible 64KByte block in turn.

If you can't find a 64KByte page frame in high memory then many EMMs will allocate a 64KByte area in conventional memory to be used as a page frame. The main disadvantage of this is the loss of 64 KBytes of valuable conventional memory. A true LIM 4.0 application can manage without a page frame by simply swapping any section of conventional memory with expanded memory blocks. In this case you can set the LIMulator not to allocate a page frame and so avoid the loss of conventional memory.

The IBM PS/2 386 machines (models 70 and 80) are particularly awkward to set up when it comes to finding a page frame. The reason is partly that larger BIOS ROMs are installed but is mainly because the adapter cards take larger amounts of address space. The solution is to reconfigure the machine using the setup disk so as to move the adapter cards to free a 64KByte region of memory. The LIMulator 386MAX includes copious instructions about how this can be achieved for a range of systems, but sometimes it is simply impossible.

PC/XT designs the expanded memory hardware was often built into the mainboard and so the user wasn't quite so aware of the distinction between the two types of memory and the lengths to which the system had to go in supporting expanded memory.

In the case of 286 and 386 machines, there is a choice of how to add memory once you move beyond the first 640 KBytes. As the address space in protected mode extends to at least 16 MBytes you could add memory beyond 640 KBytes in the form of extended memory. However, as already discussed, this extended memory would be inaccessible to all real mode programs. Alternatively, you could use the same sort of hardware found on PC/XT machines to add expanded memory. This would work in exactly the same way as expanded memory on a PC/XT - that is real mode programs that had been modified to make use of it could break the 640KByte barrier - but it wouldn't be used as extended memory in protected mode.

So which type of memory should you use to add memory beyond 640 KBytes - expanded or extended? This is a very real problem because if you opt for expanded memory then protected mode applications will ignore it but if you opt for extended memory then real mode applications will ignore it!

In other words

» expanded memory can be used by real mode programs but is ignored by protected mode programs

» extended memory can be used by protected mode programs but is ignored by real mode programs

This difficulty was partially helped by the appearance of memory cards for the ISA bus that allowed the extra memory to be configured to be either expanded or extended memory. This ability to configure additional memory as either expanded or extended memory was also included on many 286 and some 386 mainboards. In the case of the 286 this is a reasonable way of going about things but in the case of the 386 it isn't. The reason is that the 386 can convert extended memory into expanded memory without the need for any additional hardware.

Virtual 8086 mode

So far, most of what has been written applies more or less equally to the 386 family and the earlier 286 both of which can operate in real or protected mode. However, the 386 has an additional operating mode all of its own - *virtual 8086 mode*. This allows it to emulate multiple 8086 processors by moving different blocks of extended memory into the first 1MByte to create *virtual machines* or VMs. Each virtual machine is isolated from the rest and by swapping the blocks of memory very rapidly each one can be given a turn at running. That is virtual 8086 mode makes it look as if there are a number of separate 8086 processors each one capable of running an application.

Virtual 8086 mode is clearly an ideal way of implementing a multi-tasking system that can run multiple real mode applications in a way that is secure. However, its first common use was for something much simpler in principle, much more complex in practice. While operating in Virtual 8086 mode

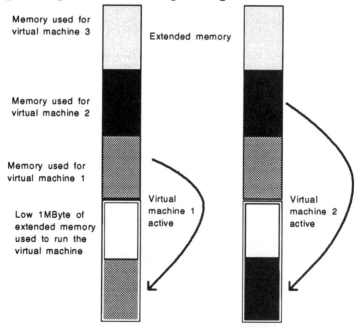

Figure 10.7
Virtual 8086 mode as a multi-tasker

real mode programs can be run, but the full flexibility of the 386's memory management is also available. In particular, it can map any 4KByte page of memory from one location to another - see the box on *Paging* at the end of this chapter. This means that it is possible for a 386 to completely rearrange its memory map quickly and efficiently. This is an ideal mechanism for converting extended memory to expanded memory.

All you need is a specially written piece of software that changes the processor from real mode to virtual 8086 mode, which is itself a variety of protected mode. Next, the software re-configures the memory map to produce a single virtual machine complete with expanded memory page frame. The

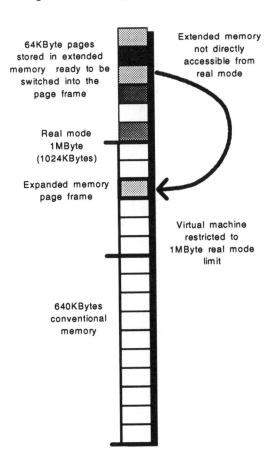

Figure 10.8
Virtual 8086 mode used to create expanded memory

remainder of the extended memory is left outside the virtual machine's address space but it can be swapped into the page frame very rapidly whenever an applications program makes a request for expanded memory. You can see that this effectively converts extended memory into expanded. Notice that from the user's point of view the machine appears to be a perfectly normal 386 system in real mode running MS-DOS and all of the familiar real mode applications. In fact it is actually operating in protected mode as a virtual 8086. In most cases the difference between these two operating modes isn't important but just occasionally it becomes crucially important.

Software that will convert extended memory into expanded memory is generally called a LIMulator or an Expanded Memory Manager (EMM) - 386MAX or QEMM 386 were early examples of this type of software. (See the next chapter for more information on real EMM software.)

So although virtual 8086 mode was designed as a way of allowing multi-taskers to run more than one real mode application at a time, it turned out to be just as useful in the creation of expanded memory to be used by a single real mode application.

The first conflict - VCPI

The ease of creating expanded memory resulted in many 386 machines being run in virtual 386 mode under the control of an EMM. From the application software's point of view the machine looks like an entirely standard 8086/88 processor with expanded memory installed. The truth is that the machine is actually a 386 running in a form of protected mode, i.e. virtual 8086 mode, and every time an expanded memory operation is carried out the EMM takes over and makes use of the protected mode facilities that are ignored by the real mode application.

This setup works quite happily until the user attempts to run an MS-DOS application that makes use of a DOS extender to work in protected mode or any application that makes use of protected mode. At this point the illusion fails because there is already a program in control of the machine in protected mode i.e. the EMM. This situation really did occur in the early days of the 386 when programs such as Lotus 1-2-3 Release 3.0 would refuse to work while an EMM such as 386MAX was loaded.

To make it possible for DOS extenders and EMMs to work together, the VCPI (Virtual Control Program Interface) standard was produced. This defined a protocol for a DOS extender to discover if an EMM was already installed and if it was how they should work together to manage the extended memory in protected mode. In this situation the EMM was usually in charge of allocating memory and played the role of the VCPI server while the DOS extender or any other program that wanted to make use of extended memory played the role of a VCPI client.

At the time it was introduced VCPI solved many of the problems of compatibility between different applications seeking to make full use of the 386 - but it had serious shortcomings that would only become clear later.

DPMI and VCPI

XMS is a reasonable standard for allocating the HMA and extended memory in general to real mode programs and drivers but it isn't a DOS extender. A DOS extender allows an entire application to run in protected mode and allows it to make use of all of the facilities of protected mode. This raises more complex issues of how conflicts can be avoided. In the early days of the 386/486, VCPI seemed to be the obvious candidate for a standard for protected mode programs to share extended memory and other resources. However, VCPI was designed to work well in a very particular situation where a protected mode DOS extender needed to co-operate with a protected mode EMM. That is, it didn't deal with the situation of more than a pair of protected mode programs running at the same time.

LIM/EMS standards

The LIM/EMS standard was introduced in 1985 as a way of allowing software to swap data in and out of the 640 KBytes conventional memory. The original EMS 3.0 specification allowed up to 8 MBytes of expanded memory to be used. This was quickly superseded by EMS 3.2 which introduced the idea of using a free 64 KBytes of memory space above the 640KByte area. This 64KByte page frame was divided into four 16KByte sub-frames that any 16KByte block of expanded memory could be switched into. For many applications EMS 3.2 is all that is required as it provides everything needed for managing data in expanded memory.

The next step in the expanded memory story was taken by AST Research, Quadram Corp and Ashton Tate who introduced the Enhanced EMS or EEMS specification. The most important new feature added in EEMS was the support for 16KByte blocks of expanded memory to be swapped with any area of memory. This change meant that EEMS can not only be used store data but also programs operating in the 640KByte region. It also introduced two sets of mapping registers. The mapping registers are used to keep track of which expanded block is actually switched into any given portion of memory.

The EEMS specification operated as an upward compatible alternative to the LIM/EMS 3.2 specification. In 1987 it was incorporated into a new LIM 4.0 standard which also took the opportunity to extend the EEMS capability even further. In particular it added 32 sets of mapping registers and allowed up to 32 MBytes of expanded memory. Expanded memory hardware that didn't meet the new specification can be upgraded to LIM 4.0 by installing new software drivers that emulate the page mapping registers in memory. The only disadvantage of this method of upgrading to the new standard is loss of speed. Of course if you have a 386/486 system such problems do not arise as it is more reasonable to implement expanded memory using nothing but software anyway! Finally it is worth mentioning that the main reason for introducing LIM 4.0 was to allow multi-tasking on non-386 based systems.

VCPI is a good standard for DOS multi-taskers such as DESQview because in this situation there are many real mode programs being run but only two protected mode programs - the EMM and the multi-tasker, i.e. QEMM 386 and DESQview itself. However, VCPI fails when you move to the more complex requirements of a full protected mode multi-tasking system such as Windows 3. In this case it is possible for a number of real mode applications and a number of protected mode applications to be running at the same time and this goes beyond what VCPI was designed to control.

To solve these problems Microsoft introduced the DOS Protected Mode Interface or DPMI. The first version was included as part of Windows 3.0 and appeared isolated in the sense that Windows 3.0 was the only product to support it! DPMI isn't VCPI compatible and all VCPI DOS extenders and EMMs immediately refused to work with Windows 3.0. However, the success of Windows 3.0 was so complete that within a few months nearly all DOS extenders and EMMs were reissued in DPMI compatible versions. This change was made without removing the VCPI compatibility and now most EMMs claim to be VCPI, DPMI and XMS compliant.

DPMI was extended to produce version 1.0 and this was incorporated into Windows 3.1 to produce a standard that looks set to survive for some time.

Unfortunately the adoption of the DPMI standard has resulted in a confusing situation concerning what will work with what. The first thing to say is that Windows 3 will not work with any software that is only VCPI compliant but it will work with any software that is DPMI and VCPI compliant. For example, you cannot run an early version of Lotus 1-2-3 Release 3 under Windows or use early 386MAX or QEMM because they are only VCPI compliant, but you can run later versions that are both VCPI and DPMI compliant. In the same way any product that is both DPMI and VCPI compliant will work with software that is only VCPI compliant. In other words, the VCPI and DPMI standards are not compatible but neither are they mutually exclusive - a product can support both.

The final question to be answered is what the continuing existence of two standards - VCPI and DPMI - means for the user. If you only want to use EMMs, DOS extenders and DOS multi-taskers then the VCPI standard is quite sufficient and you can live with old versions of software. If, however, you move to a protected mode multi-tasker, such as Windows, then DPMI is essential and upgrading to a version that supports both VCPI and DPMI is necessary. In practice the dual standard is likely to continue for some time, but with DPMI being certain to be the long term winner.

Upper Memory Blocks

Even though a machine may have many megabytes of memory it is still possible for it not to be able to run particular real mode applications programs due to a shortage of conventional memory! The reason for this is that while a program may be able to make use of expanded or extended memory to increase its data storage, it generally needs a certain minimum amount of conventional memory to work at all. In most cases the 640 KBytes of conventional memory is a precious resource that needs to be used with care. For example, the 640 KBytes

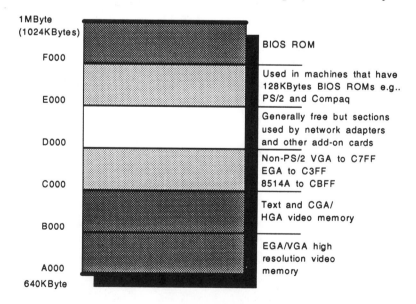

Figure 10.9
The Upper Memory Area

has to hold the operating system and all of the device drivers that it uses. If you are working with a network than the network device driver alone could add up to around 100 KBytes.

The first and most effective way of clearing more of the conventional memory area is make use of the HMA. Many device drivers can load themselves into the HMA. If you are using MS-DOS 5 then it can load a full 64 KBytes of itself into the HMA. Of course the problem is that it is a single 64KByte area and once it is used up that is it. In most cases you should reserve it for the software that can make the most use of it, i.e. load the largest into the HMA. The HIMEM.SYS driver can be set to deny access to any software that doesn't request sufficient of the HMA to make it worthwhile.

After the HMA has been used the only other possibility is to make use of free areas of the memory map above the 640KByte limit. If you recall, this 384KByte area, the Upper Memory Area or UMA, isn't any different from the first 640 KBytes of memory, it's just that it is used for a different purpose. If there is an area of the UMA that isn't being used for a ROM, video

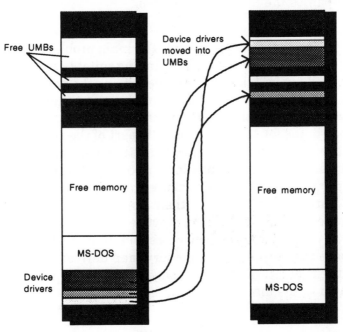

Figure 10.10
UMBs

RAM or other device then there is no reason why it shouldn't be used to store a device driver that would normally be stored down in conventional memory. In other words there is no reason why the 'holes' in the UMA shouldn't be used as island outposts of conventional memory. There are a number of problems to putting this scheme into practice though. The major problem is that the holes in the UMA are in fact unallocated regions of the memory map - that is they don't contain any RAM at all. In the case of the 8088/86 and the 286, to move memory into the holes in the UMA involves the use of special hardware, but in the case of the 386/486 the same memory paging that allows extended memory to be converted into expanded memory can be used to move memory in 4KByte pages into holes in the UMA. To do this you need some additional software - an Upper Memory Block (or UMB) provider or server. Nearly all of the Expanded Memory managers, such as 386MAX or QEMM, are also UMB providers and will move extended memory into the holes in the UMA as requested. The second problem is to move the device drivers into the UMBs, but this is usually solved by the use of a special high memory loader program that accompanies the memory managers.

The theory of making use of UMBs is easy enough, actually doing so is a little more involved. The main problem is finding out where the holes are and then finding suitably sized drivers to fill them up with least waste. Identifying the position of the holes is a matter of using a scanning utility that examines every memory location and reports back with a memory map of what it has found. This is usually part of the software that comes with a UMB provider. The scan isn't always 100% accurate because it can misidentify some areas of memory as being unoccupied - either because they correspond to 'write only' hardware, or because their use changes according to what the machine is doing. In practice such problems occur in only a small percentage of cases but it is still helpful to compare the output of the memory map derived by the scan with the theoretical memory usage based on the information supplied in the machine's manuals.

Once you have a reliable list of UMBs, the next step is to decide which drivers to move into which blocks. The problem is that you will have a list of UMBs of various sizes and drivers which occupy various amounts of memory to fit into them with minimum waste. This problem isn't as difficult as it sounds, but if you feel it too technical or too boring you can always use a UMB provider that includes an automatic allocation procedure.

The final question is how much memory a UMB provider can make available? The answer varies according to the type of machine and the efficiency of the UMB provider in locating holes and making use of them. In practice you can expect to add between 100 and 160 KBytes of memory and so potentially increase the conventional memory available to 610 KBytes, even with network drivers etc. loaded. The only cost of this technique is the 100 KBytes of extended memory that is paged down to form the UMBs and the time and trouble it takes to organise the system in this way. There is also the potential to generate system faults caused by moving drivers into UMBs that are in some way incapable of being run from a higher memory location. This risk is very low if you confine your attention to drivers that explicitly mention that they can be moved into UMBs and leave any that are vague or suspect in conventional memory. Another strange problem can be caused by being too successful at freeing conventional memory. Some applications programs, quite unreasonably, refuse to work if they are loaded into memory below the first 64KByte block. The solution to this problem is to use a special program loader that moves them above the first 64KByte block, even if it is partially free, so wasting some of the memory that you tried so hard to free! See Chapter 11 for practical details of using real UMB providers.

Backfilling

In the unlikely event that your 386/486 machine has less than the full complement of conventional memory, the same paging mechanism that was used to move extended memory into UMBs can also be used to fill conventional memory up to the

640KByte limit. In the case of the original PC this *backfilling* involved special hardware. Of course very few, if any, 386/486 machines need this facility but it can be used in some cases to increase conventional memory beyond the 640KByte limit. This is possible because the memory just above the 640KByte limit is allocated to video memory and, if for some reason it isn't used, extended memory can be paged into the same location and added to conventional memory. The amount of memory that can be reclaimed depends on the type of graphics adapter that is in use i.e. on the amount of video memory that isn't in use!

	MGA	HGA	CGA	EGA	VGA
Max conventional memory	704	704	736	640	640

Unfortunately, most 386 systems will be using VGA graphics and in this case no gain is possible. However if you are prepared temporarily to disable EGA or VGA graphics, i.e. work in text-only mode, you can still increase the size of conventional memory to 736 KBytes. This sort of backfilling is supported by many 386 memory managers - see Chapter 11 for more details.

Shadow RAM

Yet another use of the 386's ability to move pages of memory around is Shadow RAM. A great deal of the system software controlling all aspects of the machine's hardware is stored in the ROM BIOS and any extension ROMs that are found on video cards and other adapters. ROM has the great advantage that it doesn't have to be loaded from disk and it cannot be corrupted by being overwritten. Its great disadvantage is that it is very slow. Whenever ROM is accessed, the system automatically puts in multiple wait states to give it time to keep up with the processor. As ROM only accounts for as little as 64KBytes of the total memory you may not think that this slow down represents a big problem. It does, because the BIOS routines are among the most commonly used sections of software - applications and the operating system call on them to do a great many standard tasks. As a result the slowness of the ROM BIOS can have a large impact on the overall performance of the machine.

One solution to this problem is to convert slow ROMs into reasonably fast RAM. The method involves copying the contents of the ROMs temporarily into a free area of memory, mapping a section of extended memory into the area that the ROMs occupied, and then copying the ROM programs into the RAM. The exact details of how all this is achieved vary slightly but the effect at the end of the operation is to have replaced ROM by RAM containing the same software. This is called *shadow RAM*.

Shadow RAM is very effective in speeding up a machine and well worth the loss of the extended memory that it uses. However, there can be problems with shadow RAM. In particular if you are only working with a 1MByte machine then shadow RAM can use up the entire 348 KBytes of extended memory that are left over when you take away the 640 KBytes of conventional memory. In this case it may well be better to disable the shadow RAM and claim back the relatively small but valuable extended memory. It may also be better to simply add more memory to the machine to make it a more reasonable overall configuration! If you opt to disable the shadow RAM then you may find this isn't possible.

Some early machines implemented shadow RAM using special electronics to supplement the 386's ability to move

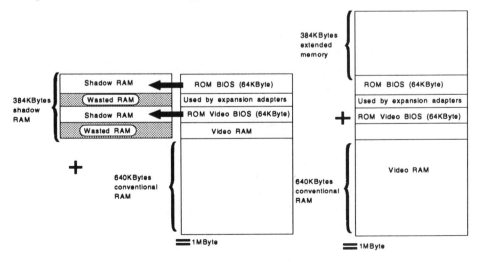

Figure 10.11
1 MByte system with and without shadow RAM

blocks of memory. This was intended to make the process of using shadow RAM simpler and more transparent to applications software. For example, if applications software accidentally writes to a ROM location nothing happens, but if it writes to the same location implemented using shadow RAM then what was the ROM contents are changed and the system could crash. To stop this happening electronics was added to disable writes to the shadow RAM region. In addition the electronics made it possible to use shadow RAM without having to change to virtual 8086 mode, i.e. while still in real mode. Of course the 386 can do all of this without the extra electronics and most memory managers will create shadow RAM, even in a machine that doesn't support it via extra hardware. They will even attempt to turn off any shadow RAM hardware that is actually fitted to a machine but sometimes this isn't possible. Thus shadow RAM can sometimes account for the fact that a machine that claims to have 1 MByte of RAM only seems to have 640 KBytes of conventional memory and no extended memory at all.

Virtual Memory

So far the 386's ability to move pages of memory around in the memory map has been used to create expanded memory and shadow RAM, but its most important use and the one that it was designed for is to allow *virtual memory* to be implemented. Virtual memory is just the creation of additional RAM by using disk storage. On machines based on the 286 this can still be achieved to a limited extent by using application swap files. If a multi-tasker is trying to run more programs than will actually fit into memory then part, or possibly all, of the application that isn't currently active can be written out to disk as a swap file. If the user activates the application that is stored on disk then obviously it has to be read back into RAM and another application swapped out to disk. This slows task swapping down to a point where the delay is very noticeable - perhaps of the order of 5 seconds or more per task swap.

The 386/486 can handle the same problem in a much more efficient way. All of the memory in the system is divided into

4KByte *pages*. These can be relocated anywhere within the memory map and do not even have to be kept in memory. When an application starts running it is allocated the number of 4KByte pages that it needs and these are placed in the memory map to form an area that it can use. If at a later time another application starts and claims more 4KByte pages than there are available, then some of the pages belonging to the first application will be written out to disk and the space reused. Thus, using page mode not all of an application needs to actually be in memory while it is running. If the software tries to use a page that isn't in memory a page fault is automatically generated and the processor passes control to the operating system which reads in the page that is required after writing out another page to free some memory. In principle an application could claim as much as 64 TBytes (or 16,381x4 GBytes) of virtual memory, but in most cases a few megabytes is more typical!

Notice that this *page mode virtual memory* is implemented in a fairly automatic way. The only tasks that the operating system has to perform are the initial allocation of memory and the processing of page faults. The processor keeps track of whether or not a page is in memory. Thus page mode virtual memory is relatively fast and efficient. On the other hand, after going to so much trouble to improve the performance of a machine by using cache, fast hard disks etc. it seems almost perverse to then reduce efficiency by using virtual memory which is at least 100 to 1000 times slower than the real thing!

In practice virtual memory is a useful way of extending a machine's memory capacity when running a rare combination of applications or when loading is unusually high. It shouldn't be used as a way of avoiding adding the real memory that a system requires to do its everyday jobs at a reasonable speed. Typical 386 systems use two or three times the amount of real RAM fitted in virtual memory. For example, a 10MByte virtual memory allocation would be reasonable for a 4MByte machine.

Hex addressing and memory maps

One of the biggest problems with working with memory is that locations are usually specified in terms of *hexadecimal* or hex. Although it looks intimidating hex is a much more natural way of specifying memory locations than decimal. For example, 1 KByte is 1024 in decimal but it is exactly 400 in hex notation.

Hex is simply counting to base 16 instead of base 10. In the decimal system there are 10 digits (0 to 9) in the hexadecimal system there are 16 digits (perhaps hexits is better?), 0 to 9 and then A, B, C, D, E and F. Counting in hex works in exactly the same way as in decimal but instead of using 10s, 100s and 1000s you use 16s, 256s (16*16), 4096s (16*16*16) and so on. This makes it sound more complicated than it is because in computing numbers such as 16, 256 and 4096 are natural and occur with monotonous regularity and in hex they are simply 10, 100 and 1000 respectively. To count in hex you start off in the usual way 0, 1, 2 .. until you reach 9 and then you carry on with A, B, etc. until you reach F. Then you start again with 10, 11, 12 and so on to 1F, then 20 to 2F and so on until you reach FF when the next value is 100 and so on. Each time you reach F you add one to the column to the left.

In practice you don't even have to be able to count in hex to use hex notation. It is enough to know that 64 KByte is 10000, 640 KByte is A0000 and 1 MByte is 100000. Using these figures you should be able to navigate your way around your computer's memory. Notice that if you start numbering memory from 0, as all computer systems do, a block of memory stops one short of the sizes given above. For example, the memory locations from 0 to 0FFFF make up the first 64 KBytes (one more than 0FFFF is 10000).

The memory map for a typical 386/AT system complete with hex addresses can be seen opposite. In any given system the actual memory usage will be slightly different but it should follow the general usage pattern given. The area between C0000 and EFFFF is the most likely to provide a free 64 KBytes for an expanded memory page frame and you can see a detailed view of the three possible 64 KByte frames. If you have problems installing a LIMulator then you should try each of these possible page frames in turn.

The final complication is the use of segment addresses. In the 286 a segment is a 64 KByte block of memory. A segment can be any 64 KByte block of memory that has a starting address that ends in 0. For example, C1230 can be the start of a segment but C1234 cannot. As the final digit in a segment address has to be zero it is customary not actually to quote it. So segment C123 is a 64KByte block starting at memory location C1230. Many memory utilities use segment addresses to specify 64KByte blocks. For example the three possible page frames are segments C000, D000 and E000. It is important to be clear about the difference between simple hex addresses and segment addresses.

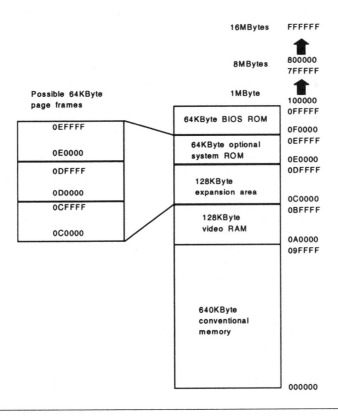

DMA problems - VDS

As you can appreciate, the memory in a typical 386/486-based system is on the move for much of the time! Memory managers will remap pages of extended memory to produce expanded memory, move expanded memory into UMBs and, as described in the previous section, a page of memory may not even be resident in RAM! This causes few problems because the operating system knows about all of the changes to the memory map at any given time and makes the correct adjustments. However, things can go wrong when a hardware device takes control of the expansion bus, ISA, EISA or MCA, to transfer data from or to memory. For example, many SCSI and other advanced controllers offer bus mastering, that is they can take over control of the external bus and transfer data directly into memory as a way of increasing data transfer speed. The problem is that a bus mastering controller doesn't necessarily know how the memory in the system has been moved by the 386's memory management facilities and yet it will attempt to address memory directly. It is quite possible for it to transfer data into an area of memory that it thinks of as its own when in fact the 386 has allocated it for some other purpose and moved it to a different location in the memory map.

In the early days this movement of data transfer buffers proved to be a very real problem as many memory managers simply did not allow for such behaviour. Slowly they incorporated facilities to allow the user to allocate special fixed areas of memory that would not be used but it was still very much up to the user to realise that there was a problem with bus mastering DMA controllers in the first place. For example, QEMM 386 version 5 included a command, DISKBUF=, that allowed it to work with some, but not all, bus mastering SCSI controllers. The basic idea in all of these attempts to allow bus mastering to work is to ensure that the disk buffer has the same logical and physical address - i.e. the 386's memory manager must not have moved it to a new location. Often the safest solution was to disable the bus mastering aspect of the controller and allow it to work at a slower, but reliable, speed. It is in this sense that ST-506, IDE and ESDI drives were described as standard and SCSI as non-standard in Chapter 6.

There is now a standard for the treatment of bus mastering controllers-*Virtual DMA Services* or VDS. Bus mastering controllers that have VDS compatible drivers need no special attention. Older controllers that do not support VDS have to be treated specially by the operating system or memory management software. For example, Windows 3.1 supports non-VDS disk controllers by using double buffering as part of the SmartDrive disk cache - see Chapter 12.

A technical overview

This chapter has described many complex ideas concerning the way that the 386 can manage memory and it seems worth bringing together some of the main points. The first thing to say is that while the 286 and the 386 both share the ability to run in protected mode, and so access memory beyond the 1MByte real mode limit, the 386 can do more. It alone has 8086 virtual mode and memory paging. The 8086 virtual mode makes multi-tasking more secure and more efficient. Memory paging can be used to change the memory map dynamically to provide expanded memory, shadow RAM, UMBs and virtual memory - using nothing but software. What all of this means to users is that they can forget having to decide how to configure their machines in hardware terms. All memory on a 386-based system should be configured in hardware as simple ordinary extended memory - anything strange or exotic such as expanded memory can be implemented using software!

You will find a number of technical boxes at the close of this chapter. Reading and understanding them certainly isn't necessary to making the best use of a 386 machine, nor is it essential to the understanding of the rest of this book. However, they do provide a deeper insight into the way that the 386 actually performs the miracles of memory management that are so important.

Glossary of memory terms

16-bit software - programs that make use of either the 8088/86 or the 286.

32-bit software - programs that make use of the instructions unique to the 386 family.

Bus Master - in simple systems only the processor can access memory and control the bus. In more sophisticated systems it is possible for other components to take over control of the bus, i.e. become a bus master, and transfer data between themselves and memory.

Conventional memory - the first 640 KBytes of real mode or protected mode memory space.

DOS extender - a program that allows a specially written application to run in protected mode while still making use of MS-DOS in real mode.

DMA, Direct Memory Access - a method whereby some other component of the system can access memory without involving the processor.

DPMI, DOS Protected Mode Interface - a standard that allows real mode and protected mode programs to share extended memory. Supersedes but is not compatible with VCPI.

Extended memory - protected mode memory above 1MByte. Extended memory is only accessible to protected mode programs.

Expanded memory - a system of paging memory within conventional memory. Expanded memory is only used by real mode programs. Extended memory can be used to simulate expanded memory.

EMM, Expanded Memory Manager - see memory manager.

EMS, Expanded Memory Specification - alternative definition of the LIM standard.

HMA, High Memory Area - the first 64KBytes of protected mode address space above 1MByte. The HMA is the only portion of extended memory that can be accessed by a real mode program.

LIM, Lotus Intel Microsoft - a set of standards that define the way that expanded memory should be implemented. Currently LIM 3.2 and LIM 4.0 are the most commonly supported standards.

Memory manager - a program that makes use of the 386's memory management facilities to create any of expanded memory, UMBs and shadow RAM.

Page frame - an area of the memory map where expanded memory pages can be switched in and out.

Protected mode - the mode only available on the 286 and 386 which gives access to extended memory. It also has additional facilities to control the access that particular programs have to memory and other machine facilities.

Protected mode program - a program that runs in protected mode and has access to the complete memory space of the 286/386.

Real mode - the only mode available for an 8088/86 processor. The 286 or 386 in real mode is effectively pretending to be an 8088/86 processor.

Real mode program - a program that can only run in real mode.

Shadow RAM - the replacement of slow ROM by fast RAM that contains the same programs.

UMA, Upper Memory area -the 384 KBytes of real mode or protected mode memory space above conventional memory. Also called high memory.

UMB, Upper Memory Block - an unused area of the UMA that can be filled by RAM and used as an extension of conventional memory.

VCPI, Virtual Control Program Interface - the first standard designed to allow protected mode programs to share extended memory. It has been superseded by DPMI.

VM, Virtual Machine - an 8088/86 processor simulated in virtual 8086 mode.

Virtual memory - memory that is simulated by using disk storage.

Virtual 8086 mode - an extension of protected mode only available on the 386/486 processor in which multiple 8088/86 machines are simulated. This can be used to multi-task real mode programs or to make use of the memory mapping facilities of protected mode to create expanded memory, UMBs etc..

XMS, eXtended Memory Specification - a standard for allocating the HMA and extended memory in general to real mode programs.

Segment addressing

Although it isn't necessary to know anything about how the 386/486 actually makes use of memory, it is interesting. The addressing methods of the 386/486 are described in this box and in the following box on *Paging*. The details presented are technical and there is certainly no need for you to master them fully to gain some idea of just how sophisticated and powerful a processor the 386 is.

The idea of using memory in segments is an old one. In a simple system the address contained within a program determines directly which memory location will be used. In a segmented system there are two parts to every address - a base and an offset. The base address marks the start of a block or segment of memory and the offset indicates exactly which memory location within the segment is to be used. The base address is stored in a segment register and the program contains the offset.

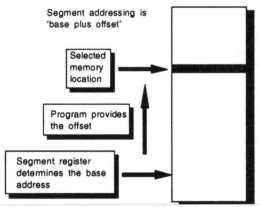

Segment addressing is 'base plus offset'

Selected memory location

Program provides the offset

Segment register determines the base address

The advantage of segment addressing is that a program can be run anywhere in memory simply by changing the base address stored in the segment register. Relocating a program that doesn't use segmented addressing is a complex and time-consuming process. The second advantage of segment addressing is that a number of segment registers can be used to establish segments for different purposes. For example, a code segment, a data segment and so on. These logical segments make writing programs that manage large amounts of memory easier and less error prone.

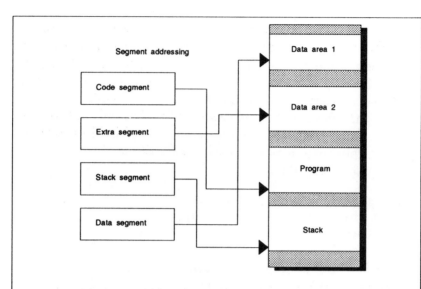

When the 386/486 is in real mode the type of segmentation that can be used is very limited because of the need to be compatible with the 16-bit 8088/86. The contents of a 16-bit segment register are added to the 16-bit offset contained in an instruction to give a 20-bit physical address. The only complication is that the contents of the segment register are padded with four zero bits to make a 20-bit segment address before the 16-bit offset is added.

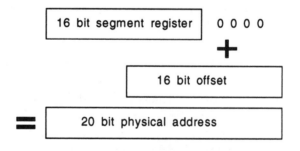

The fact that the final physical address is 20 bits long limits the addressing capability to 1 MByte - which is of course where the 1MByte real mode limit originates.

In protected mode segmented addressing is much more sophisticated. In this case the 16-bit segment register is used to select an entry in a segment descriptor table. The segment descriptor table contains the full 32-bit base address of the segment that has been selected by the contents of the register. The final physical address is obtained by adding a 32-bit offset generated by the program to the base address obtained from the descriptor table.

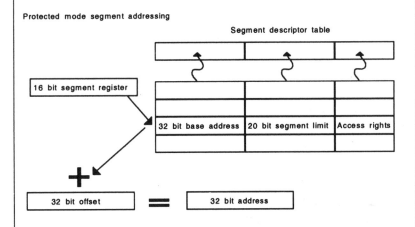

Protected mode segment addressing

As well as specifying where the segment starts in memory, the descriptor table also contains information on the total length of the segment so that any attempt to use memory outside of the segment can be detected and stopped. It also contains information on access rights that can be used to deny or control access to a segment. The ability to check the legality of access to a segment is what gives protected mode its name and enables the 386/486 to be used to implement multi-tasking reliably. The 286 has the same facilities but it is restricted to 16-bit offsets and so the largest segment it can work with is 64 KBytes. In the case of the 386 a segment can be as large as the available memory.

Paging

As well as supporting segmented addressing, the 386/486 also supports paging in protected mode. Paging is like segmentation but it works with fixed sized blocks of memory. In the case of the 386/486 each block or page is exactly 4 KBytes. When paging is activated the 32-bit address that would be applied to select the memory location to be used is used to index two tables - the page table directory and the page table. The page table directory is a list of base addresses of up to 1024 page tables. Each page table contains a list of the base addresses of up to 1024 4KByte pages. You can see that if there are 1024 page tables and each can keep track of 1024 4KByte pages, the total amount of memory that can be handled is 1024x1024x4 KBytes, or 4 GBytes.

32 bit address produced after
segment addressing

10 bit page directory offset	10 bit page table offset	12 bit offset

Page table directory

32 bit base address

Page table

32 bit base address

Page directory physical address (CR3)

32 bit physical address

The way that the 32-bit address is used to select the appropriate page is straightforward. The first 10 bits of the address are used to select which entry in the page table directory will be used to determine the base address of the page table. The next ten bits are used to select which entry in the page table will be used to determine the base address of the page. Finally the remaining 12 bits are used as an offset that selects the exact memory location in the 4KByte page.

You may think that paging is overly complex. Especially so when you recall that it can be used in conjunction with segmentation. In such instances the segmentation mechanism described earlier is first used to produce a 32-bit address which is then subjected to the paging mechanism just described. Only the 386/486 has the paging ability - the 286 has segment addressing but not page addressing - and paging is responsible for much of the 386/486's superiority. For example, by altering the entries in a page table, an address produced by segmentation can be made to refer to any physical memory location. This means that it is possible to make it seem as if any 4 KByte page can move its location in memory by changing the contents of a single location in a page table. This allows a 386/486 system to reorganise its memory by mapping any 4 KByte page anywhere it is needed.

A second advantage of paging is that it can be used to implement *virtual memory*. If a system has less than the 4 GByte of pages that the 386/486 can handle it is possible to use disk storage to provide additional pages. The way that this works is that the page table contains a bit that can be used to indicate that a page isn't in memory. In this case the page address can be used to indicate where on disk the page is stored. If a program makes reference to a page that is not in memory, then the operating system is automatically alerted to this and it can take steps to read the page into memory. If there isn't any available memory then a page can be selected and written out to disk to free a 4 KByte page. This mechanism is called virtual memory and it is supported by advanced operating systems such as OS/2 and Unix. As well as information to help with the implementation of a virtual memory system, the page table contains another layer of protection to supplement those provided by segment addressing.

Key points

» The 286 and the 386 can work in both real and protected modes. Real mode limits memory access to 1MByte but provides compatibility with the 8088/86 processor and MS-DOS applications.

» Extended memory is available beyond 1MByte but only in protected mode, i.e. real mode applications cannot use extended memory (with the exception of the HMA).

» The XMS standard allows protected mode software to allocate extended memory without conflict. It also controls access to the HMA - a 64KByte area of extended memory that real mode applications can make use of. It has replaced the older INT 15 or top down allocation method.

» A DOS extender is a way of allowing protected mode applications to use MS-DOS in real mode.

» Expanded memory is a way of adding memory beyond 1 MByte that is accessible by real mode applications.

» Extended memory can be converted into expanded memory using nothing but software.

» VCPI was the first standard controlling how protected mode applications should share extended memory. It has been superseded by the DPMI standard introduced with Windows 3.0.

» The 386's memory mangement can be used to create not only expanded memory from extended but also Upper Memory Blocks (UMBs) to increase conventional memory, shadow RAM to increase speed and virtual memory to increase the total memory.

» Advanced SCSI drives that make use of bus mastering need special treatment by protected mode operating systems.

Chapter 11

MS-DOS

Once the problem of utilising the additional memory found in most 386/486 systems has been solved, the next question is how to extend the capabilities of MS-DOS to make use of the additional processing power that is available.

To get the best from a 386/486 system you have to move beyond MS-DOS. However, there are still very good reasons why users stay with MS-DOS, particularly in the case of less powerful machines such as 386SX systems or machines with only 1 MByte of memory. To make use of the sophisticated software designed specially for the 386 you still need plenty of processing power, plenty of disk storage and RAM. In the case of a system that lacks any of these MS-DOS is a good basis for running a wide range of applications and you can take advantage of the memory management abilities of the 386.

Which MS-DOS?

There is no doubt that MS-DOS, starting with version 5, has finally been augmented to take some notice of the special capabilities of the 386 processor. MS-DOS 4.0 had some facilities that made it able to make use of extended memory and even a simple memory management program to convert extended to expanded memory. However, in MS-DOS 5 these have been improved and extended to include the use of Upper Memory Blocks (UMBs). There is no question that MS-DOS 5 and beyond represents the best choice for a 386 machine.

There are two other versions of MS-DOS that are still in common use with 386/486 systems - MS-DOS 3.3 and MS-DOS 4. MS-DOS 4 has a number of important advantages over 3.3 for 386/486 systems but it gained a poor reputation for reliability when it was first introduced by Microsoft. It contained a number of unfortunate bugs that caused it to lose data stored on disk when its more advanced options were used. This resulted in manufacturers and users tending to stay with MS-DOS 3.3 rather than using MS-DOS 4.

The evolution of MS-DOS to take account of the 386/486 was made artificially slow due to the initial attempt to make OS/2 its natural successor. The current situation is that Microsoft plans to build a series of operating environments suitable for the 386/486 starting with MS-DOS, moving on to MS-DOS plus Windows and finishing with Windows NT for the most powerful systems. IBM are still trying to promote OS/2 as the operating system of choice for the 386/486 and so make Windows and Windows NT obsolete. However, for the committed MS-DOS user what matters is that Microsoft have restarted work on MS-DOS and new versions that make increasingly good use of the 386 should appear over the next few years.

Before moving on to consider MS-DOS 5 it is worth considering how MS-DOS 3.3 and MS-DOS 4 can best take advantage of the 386. In practice, though, the better option is to upgrade to MS-DOS 5.

MS-DOS 3.3

The only problem with running MS-DOS 3.3 on a 386/486 system is that it doesn't on its own recognise the existence of extended or LIM expanded memory. You can install a 386/486 memory manager and even move some of its device drivers into high memory, but MS-DOS 3.3 will not make use of LIM expanded memory either to increase efficiency or to save memory in the 640KByte area of conventional memory.

The only exception to this is the RAM disk driver included with some MS-DOS 3.3 systems. The standard VDISK driver supplied before MS-DOS 4 will use only conventional memory but some customised versions of MS-DOS include an alternative such as RAMDRIVE.SYS. This can use either conventional memory, expanded memory or LIM expanded memory as long as it is available. A careful and selective use of a RAM disk can speed particular applications greatly. To install a RAM disk in LIM expanded memory use the command:

DEVICE=RAMDRIVE.SYS *size sector entries* /A

and to install a RAM disk in extended memory use the command:

DEVICE=RAMDRIVE.SYS *size sector entries* /E

where *size* is the size of the disk, *sector* is the sector size and *entries* is the number of directory entries to be allowed in the root directory of the disk. The default sector size is 512 and the default root directory capacity is 64 and these are reasonable values for most applications. For example:

DEVICE=C:\RAMDRIVE.SYS 1024 512 200 /E

installs a 1MByte (1024KByte) disk with 512Byte sectors, and 200 root directory entries in extended memory. Changing the /E to /A would install it in expanded memory. Notice that if you choose to use expanded memory then an EMM (Expanded Memory Manager) has to be installed before the RAM disk.

In other words, you can't use expanded memory before you have created it. In most cases it is better to use extended memory as this is the only version of the command that will work at all with Windows and reliably with non-VCPI/DPMI EMMs.

If your version of MS-DOS 3.3 didn't supply an improved RAM disk driver then you can buy one. You will also need a memory manager to make use of the RAM disk driver. For example, 386MAX comes with 386DISK.SYS. The 386MAX RAM disk driver is more sophisticated than most and is very reliable. The command to install it is very similar to the one used for RAMDRIVE.SYS:

DEVICE=C:\386DISK.SYS *size sector entries option*

option specifies the medium on which the disk data is stored: /EMS for expanded memory, /EXT for extended memory, or /XMS to use extended memory through the XMS driver. EMS is the default storage medium. Notice that you are unlikely to install an XMS extended memory driver under MS-DOS 3.3, unless it happens to be 386MAX or you are planning to run Windows 3.

Apart from RAM disks the only other ways that MS-DOS 3.3 can make use of extended memory is via disk caching, printer spooling or applications programs that use it. In short, under MS-DOS 3.3 it is advisable to install a VCPI/DPMI compatible EMM or move to Windows 3.

MS-DOS 4

MS-DOS 4 was the first version of MS-DOS that recognised the existence of expanded memory. Even so, its use of expanded memory was less than it should have been. A number of MS-DOS commands were changed so that various buffers could be placed in expanded memory, so reducing the amount of memory used in the 640KByte region and increasing the maximum number of buffers that could be allocated. However, it is very important that you read the paragraph at the end of this section concerning bugs in MS-DOS 4.

The command:

BUFFERS=*xx*

included in the CONFIG.SYS file allocates *xx* 512 byte buffers that are used to store disk data being read and written. The MS-DOS buffers provide a very simple form of disk caching - see Chapter 6. In MS-DOS 3.3 and earlier the number of buffers was restricted to a maximum of 99 and each buffer took roughly .5 KBytes from conventional memory. In other words, if you chose to speed up disk access by allocating 99 buffers this would cost you roughly 50 KBytes of RAM from conventional memory. In MS-DOS 4 you can allocate up to 10,000 buffers and place them in expanded memory. The command:

BUFFERS=*xx* /X

will create *xx* buffers in expanded memory. Various experiments have shown that allocating a very large number of buffers, 200 and greater, does increase the speed of disk access. Another modification made in MS-DOS 4 is the ability to allocate *look-ahead* buffers. The command:

BUFFERS=*xx*, *y* /X

will allocate *xx* buffers in expanded memory and *y* look-ahead buffers. A look-ahead buffer is used to read the next part of a file before it is required. Using this method is basically betting on the fact that if you ask for the first part of a file you will want the second part next, then the third part and so on. Of course if this isn't the case then the time spent reading ahead is wasted. Allocating three or four look-ahead buffers does reduce the time to read a sequential file.

The FASTOPEN command was available in MS-DOS 3.3 but in MS-DOS 4 it can make use of expanded memory to store its tables. FASTOPEN reduces the time it takes to find and open a file by storing directory information in RAM. In MS-DOS 3.3 the command:

> FASTOPEN C:=x

would set aside RAM to store x directory entries in RAM. In MS-DOS 4 the command:

> FASTOPEN C:=(x, y) /X

uses expanded memory to store x directory entries. Each directory entry takes 35 Bytes. The second number y specifies the number of sector buffers to allocate. Each sector buffer takes 16 Bytes. A sector buffer is used to keep track of where a file is stored on disk and can greatly speed up file access. Experiments suggest that a value of 15 to 20 directory entries should be stored in RAM and between 10 and 50 sector buffers should be allocated.

In addition to BUFFERS and FASTOPEN the IBM version of MS-DOS 4 also has a new version of VDISK that can make use of expanded memory. The equivalent in Microsoft versions of MS-DOS 4 is RAMDRIVE which has already been described in connection with MS-DOS 3.3.

Another extra utility supplied with MS-DOS 4 is SMARTDRV.SYS which is a disk caching program more commonly associated with Windows 3 - see Chapter 12. This can use either expanded or extended memory and it is recommended that you use extended unless this is impossible for some reason. The command to add to the CONFIG.SYS file is:

> DEVICE=SMARTDRV.SYS *size*

which will allocate *size* KBytes of extended memory for use as a disk cache. If you want to use expanded memory instead add /a to the end of the command.

Bugs in MS-DOS 4

All the features described above are valuable but it is important that you don't try to make use of them on version 4.00 of MS-DOS released on 17 June 1988 and 3 August 1988. The bugs are all in the way that MS-DOS 4 deals with expanded memory. If you use BUFFERS, FASTOPEN or VDISK without allowing them to use expanded memory they will work reliably. However, if you do configure them to use expanded memory eventually the system will crash with, in the worst cases, the result that directories on the hard disk are corrupted. Indeed, before the bug had been tracked down many users, and even manufacturers, thought that the problem was with their hard disks.

MS-DOS 4 - Limulators

Both the Microsoft and IBM versions of MS-DOS 4 include EMMs - the IBM version includes XMAEM.SYS and XMA2EMS.SYS and the Microsoft version includes EMM386.SYS. These are perfectly workable EMMs but notice that they are not VCPI compatible and the IBM version is not guaranteed to work on non-IBM machines.

The XMAEM.SYS driver converts extended memory to expanded. The command:

DEVICE=XMAEM.SYS *number*

included in the CONFIG.SYS file will convert *number* 16KByte pages into expanded memory. For example:

DEVICE=XMAEM.SYS 10

will convert 10x16KByte pages, i.e. 160 KBytes of extended memory, into expanded memory. If you don't specify an amount of memory then all of the extended memory will be converted. The XMAEM.SYS driver emulates an expanded memory board but it isn't a full expanded memory driver. If you had actually installed the expanded memory board then you would have to include the line:

DEVICE= XMA2EMS.SYS frame=*address* /x:*size*

in the CONFIG.SYS file to determine the page frame address and the number of 16KBytes chunks of expanded memory to be converted to LIM/EMS standard. If *size* is not specified then all of the expanded memory is used. You should specify *size* smaller than the total amount of expanded available if some of it is being used by FASTOPEN, BUFFERS, etc..

In a 386 system it is unlikely that a real expanded memory card would be installed because the hardware can be emulated using the XMAEM.SYS emulator. So in a 386 system the CONFIG.SYS file should contain the lines:

DEVICE=XMAEM.SYS
DEVICE=XMA2EMS.SYS frame=D000

The first line converts extended memory into an emulation of an expanded memory board and the second is the LIM driver. Notice that in this example all of the available memory is converted to LIM expanded memory, with a page frame positioned at D000. You can consider the combination of XMAEM.SYS and XMA2EMS.SYS as a LIMulator.

The biggest problem with using XMA2EMS.SYS is finding a suitable 64KByte location for the page frame. If an unused 64KByte region cannot be found, you can allocate each 16KByte sub-frame separately. (The standard 64KByte page frame is used as four 16KByte expanded memory blocks.) For example:

DEVICE=XMA2EMS.SYS P0=C000 P1=C400 P2=D000 P3=D400

places four 16KByte sub-frames at different locations. Notice that applications that conform to the LIM 3.2 specification need a single 64KByte page frame. Only true LIM 4.0 applications can make use of separate 16KByte page frames. The Microsoft driver is simpler to install. The line that has to be included in the CONFIG.SYS file is:

DEVICE=EMM386.SYS *size* X:*range* M*x*

where *size* is the amount of extended memory that you want converted to expanded (default 256KByte), *range* is any region of memory that should not be used for the page frame and M*x* is the location of the page frame. In most cases EMM386 will find any regions that should be excluded and find a suitable location for the page frame automatically. If this is true for your machine you can install EMM386 using the simple command:

DEVICE=EMM386.SYS *size*

As long as you don't need VCPI or DPMI compatibility and you only need to convert extended memory to expanded memory EMM386 is a reasonable choice.

MS-DOS 5

There are two important changes introduced with MS-DOS 5 that affect all 386/486 users. The first is that the XMS memory standard is fully supported and both an XMS driver, HIMEM.SYS, and a full DPMI EMM, in the form of EMM386.EXE, are included. The EMM is also an UMB provider, allowing drivers to be moved into the upper memory area. What this means is that for the first time there is no need to buy an EMM such as 386MAX or QEMM to get the best from a 386/486 system under MS-DOS. Of course there are some advantages to buying other EMMs, but for many users EMM386 will be more than sufficient.

You can also make use of expanded and extended memory with drivers such as RAMDRIVE, as described for earlier versions of MS-DOS. There is also a new disk caching program, SmartDrive which is of particular use with Windows and is therefore described in Chapter 12.

HIMEM.SYS

The key to all MS-DOS 5's memory management options is the XMS memory driver, HIMEM.SYS. This has to be loaded before any programs or drivers that use extended or expanded memory. Essentially it takes control of all the extended memory including the HMA in the machine and all other software has to ask it for permission to use it.

At its simplest the HIMEM.SYS driver is loaded by making

DEVICE=HIMEM.SYS

the very first line in the CONFIG.SYS file, but there are a few optional parameters that can be set to control the way that it works.

In most cases HIMEM.SYS will test exactly how the A20 gate, which gives access to the extended memory, has been implemented and will adjust itself accordingly. However, it is possible for it to misidentify the hardware that it is running on and in this case you may have to add:

/machine:*x*

where *x* is a number identifying the machine type to the end of the line. A list of machine types is given in the MS-DOS 5 manual and in the Windows manual. In most cases this is a problem that troubles 286 machines, and 386 machines should need no special attention - but there are exceptions, the Tulip 386SX being an example.

Two other parameters deal with the complexities of the A20 gate. The parameter:

/a20:*on*/*off*

specifies whether or not HIMEM.SYS is to take control of the A20 line, even if A20 was on when it was loaded. In principle the A20 line should be off when HIMEM.SYS starts up and finding it on is an indication that some other software is using A20 before HIMEM.SYS gets to it. This could mean that HIMEM.SYS shouldn't take control of A20 or that this is a peculiarity of the machine! In most cases HIMEM.SYS should always be allowed to take control of A20 and the default of A20:on should be used. The parameter:

/cpuclock:*on*/*off*

deals with a complication that affects mostly 286 machines. In some cases the A20 handler will accidentally alter the speed of the CPU clock. Setting /cpuclock:on should cure this fault.

If your machine uses shadow RAM and you are short of extended memory then you can try adding:

/shadowram:off

to the end of the line that loads HIMEM.SYS to turn it off. This only works on some machines.

The parameter:

/numhandles=n

allocates additional memory to keep track of extended memory allocation. In nearly all cases the default of 32, i.e. enough memory to track 32 separate XMS memory allocations, is sufficient. You only need to change this parameter if you start to get error messages relating to XMS memory allocation.

If you are using any programs that make use of extended memory via the old INT 15 top down allocation scheme then you should include the parameter:

/int15=x

to the end of the line where x is the number of KBytes of extended memory that HIMEM.SYS will not use. The amount reserved is rounded down to the nearest whole number of 64KByte pages. Always specify 64 KBytes more than your programs actually need. A better solution is to find a replacement for all INT 15 programs.

The final parameter controls access to the HMA. Only one real mode program can make use of the HMA and this implies allocating the whole 64KByte block of extended memory to any program that requests it even if it actually only uses 1 KByte of it! In an attempt to make sure that the HMA is allocated efficiently the parameter:

/hmamin=x

specifies the smallest amount of memory, in KBytes, that a program can request to be granted access to the HMA. In most cases you are unlikely to use this parameter because the obvious candidate to use the HMA is MS-DOS itself.

After HIMEM.SYS is loaded you can request that MS-DOS loads a chunk of itself into the HMA by adding the line:

DOS=HIGH

to the CONFIG.SYS file. If you are using MS-DOS 5 then this is by far the best use of the HMA because nearly all of its 64 KBytes is put to good use and all applications benefit from the increase of 64 KBytes in the conventional memory area.

If you are making use of HIMEM.SYS with versions of MS-DOS earlier than 5.0, and you can do this if you want to, then you should allow the driver or application that makes the most use of the HMA to have access to it. For example, in the case of SuperCalc 5.1 the HMA will be used automatically as long as HIMEM.SYS is loaded and the HMA isn't already in use.

EMM386

HIMEM.SYS provides XMS extended memory and EMM386 can make use of this to provide LIM 3.2 or 4.0 expanded memory and UMBs. Notice that the version of EMM386.EXE supplied with MS-DOS 5 is quite different to earlier versions which were called EMM386.SYS. A common mistake is to make use of EMM386.SYS which has been left behind from an earlier version of MS-DOS. Also notice that there are now two reasons for loading EMM386 - to provide expanded memory or to provide upper memory blocks.

In most cases adding the line:

DEVICE=EMM386.EXE

to the CONFIG.SYS file is all that is necessary to make use of EMM386 but as in the case of all memory managers you may have to manually configure it by adding parameters to the end of the line. The main problem is that there are a great many parameters and this is a common fault shared with all memory managers.

As long as you have a perfectly standard machine with no expansion cards over and above the usual VGA, floppy/hard disk controller, serial and parallel ports, then EMM386 should be able to discover enough about your machine's memory map to install itself automatically. If in addition you only want to make use of EMM386 as an expanded memory provider, and not as a UMB provider, then the only parameter worth setting is to specify the amount of extended memory it can use. For example:

DEVICE=EMM386.EXE 1024

makes use of 1 MByte of extended memory to produce 1 MByte of expanded memory. If you don't specify the amount of expanded memory you need, then 256 KBytes is allocated. In most cases real mode applications derive most benefit from about this small amount expanded memory. If you allocate much more than they need then they usually start to slow down because of the amount of data that they are working with. An alternative way of setting the size of the expanded memory that is available is to use:

L=*minxms*

where *minxms* is the smallest amount of extended memory that you want left unconverted to expanded memory.

There are two main groups of parameters that deal with two different types of problem that occur with expanded memory. The first group concerns the position of the page frame. As already discussed, expanded memory works by swapping blocks of memory in and out of a page frame. In the case of LIM 3.2 this page frame has to be a single 64KByte area and the problem is finding such a large free area in the memory map. It is always possible to place the page frame in conventional memory, but this results in a loss of 64 KBytes to applications. Normally it is preferable to find a free 64KByte region in the Upper Memory Area or UMA. If the machine is reasonably normal EMM386 will find such a free space automatically and simply report the address that it is using during system startup. However, it can get it wrong in two ways. It can fail to find a 64KByte area when one actually exists, and it can mistakenly use the first free area it finds only to discover that it isn't actually free. In both cases the solution is to specify the location òf the page frame manually. You can do this in two different, but entirely equivalent, ways by adding:

$$m x \quad \text{or} \quad \text{frame}=address$$

to the line that loads EMM386. In the first instance you have to specify x, a number between 1 and 14 and in the second an equivalent segment address. The values and addresses are:

1=C000	8=DC00
2=C400	9=E000
3=C800	10=8000
4=CC00	11=8400
5=D000	12=8800
6=D400	13=8C00
7=D800	14=9000

Notice that the values 10 to 14 place the page frame in conventional memory and should only be used as a last resort. For example, to place the page frame at CC00 you could use:

DEVICE=EMM386.EXE m4

or

DEVICE=EMM386.EXE frame=CC00

To discover the location of a potential page frame sized gap in the memory map you could use a utility that examines the memory to generate a memory map - but if the configuration is complicated enough to fool EMM386's automatic installation it will also fool simple memory mappers. One crude but effective way is to simply try each of the possible page frame locations in the UMA, i.e. from 1 to 9. When you do this, indeed whenever you alter the CONFIG.SYS file, it is important to make sure that you have a floppy that can be used to boot the machine in case the changes stop the machine booting from the hard disk.

It is worth mentioning that another reason for moving the location of the page frame is to optimise the available UMBs. It is possible for the page frame to split a free area into two smaller free areas. By moving the page frame the two small free areas can be made into one big and more useful free area. In the first instance, however, finding a page frame location that works is usually the first priority!

If you are using applications that make use of the LIM 4.0 expanded memory standard then in principle at least the requirement for a single 64KByte page frame is dropped. In practice many applications that claim to conform to LIM 4.0 still need a single 64KByte page frame. However, if you cannot find a suitable free area and you know that the applications will tolerate it, you can allocate four separate 16KByte page frames instead of a single 64KByte page frame using:

   p*n*=*address*

where *n* is in the range 0 to 3 and *address* gives the locations of the sub page frames. Going a step further with the LIM 4.0 specification, you can actually specify more than four 16KByte sub-frames and *n* can range from 0 to 255 but it is very rare that an application demands or can make use of this facility.

Rather than try out locations for the page frame manually it is also possible to exclude and include memory ranges during the automatic installation. For example, if you know that an adapter card uses memory locations C800 to CC00 and EMM386 is still allocating the page frame incorrectly, you can incorporate this information using:

   x=C800-CC00

which excludes the range from consideration in the automatic selection procedure. In general if you know that an area of memory is occupied and so should be excluded use:

   x=*start-stop*

and if you know that an area is definitely free then use:

   i=*start-stop*

where *start* and *stop* are the segment addresses of the region to be excluded or included. If the pair of ranges overlap then the excluded region takes precedence over the included region.

The second group of parameters are all concerned with the implementation of LIM 4.0 expanded memory as used in multi-tasking. These are only likely to be relevant if you are using DESQview or some other multi-tasker.

Swapping conventional memory with expanded memory pages is how real and standard mode multi-taskers change between applications. The lowest address that will be used as a LIM 4.0 page frame can be set using:

b=*address*

The lowest address simply gives the size of conventional memory that is not swapped because it holds the operating system which all of the applications want to use. The default for this is 4000 or 256 KBytes. You should only change this value if the multi-tasker that you are using tells you to do so.

When multi-tasking, each application has access to a different set of expanded memory control registers. You can set the number of registers, and so the maximum number of tasks, using:

a=*altregs*

In nearly all cases the default value of 7 is quite sufficient.

Each block of expanded memory that is allocated is identified by a number or 'handle' set by:

h=*handles*

This parameter controls the number of separate blocks that can be handled at the same time. Although it is possible to run out of handles with any application, it generally only happens with a multi-tasking system. Increase the default setting of 64 only if you see error messages concerning expanded memory allocation.

The remaining parameters are concerned with a range of different aspects of EMM386's operation.

If you are using a Weitek numeric co-processor then you have to include:

w=on

The reason is that the Weitek uses an area of memory within the UMA and therefore needs special treatment.

The problem with bus mastering DMA controllers described in the previous chapter can occur when using EMM386. If the machine has an advanced SCSI or ESDI disk controller then it might be necessary to add:

d=*size*

to allocate a fixed DMA buffer of the specified size - in KBytes from 16 to 256. You have to set the buffer size to the largest amount of data that will be transferred in one DMA session. This usually isn't easy to discover. Setting the buffer to a larger size than necessary doesn't cause difficulty other than wasting memory. You could attempt to find a suitable size by trial and error - start from a maximum size and slowly reduce the allocation until problems occur. If you are using Windows 3.1 then a better solution to the problem is to use SmartDrive's double buffering mode even when not running Windows.

If applications fail to work while EMM386 is loaded you can try the command:

EMM386 OFF

which switches off the memory management functions and returns the machine to a standard real mode environment. You can reactivate it using:

EMM386 ON

before running an application that needs expanded memory. You might also find that:

EMM386 AUTO

solves the problem and avoids the need to switch it back on manually. In this case the memory management functions are reactivated automatically when an application requests expanded memory. In most cases, though, when an application will not run with EMM386, or any other memory manager, the only option is to remove it from the CONFIG.SYS file altogether.

UMBs

So far all of the discussion of EMM386 has concerned its use as an expanded memory provider, but it can also provide UMBs. To activate EMM386 in this role all you have to do is add:

        DOS=UMB

or:

        DOS=HIGH,UMB

to the CONFIG.SYS file before the line that loads EMM386 and add either:

        RAM

or:

        NOEMS

to the EMM386 line. If you specify RAM then EMM386 will provide expanded memory and UMBs. If you specify NOEMS then only UMBs will be provided.

If you have set up EMM386 to create expanded memory correctly it is still possible that adding RAM or NOEMS to the command will cause the system to crash. The reason is that when providing expanded memory EMM386 only has to find a suitable location for the page frame, but when filling unused regions of the UMA it is possible for it to move a page of RAM into a region that is in fact in use by some adapter or other. This will not happen in an entirely standard system but it does happen. The solution is to exclude the area that is being incorrectly used to form a UMB by adding:

        x=*start-stop*

to the line that loads EMM386 where *start* and *stop* specify the region that shouldn't be used to form a UMB.

As long as no regions of the UMA are used incorrectly, the system should run as normal, but the amount of extended memory available will have decreased by the amount that has been used to create the UMBs. The next step is to make use of the UMBs by moving drivers into them. This involves discovering the number and size of the UMBs and the size of the drivers that could be moved to fill them. To find out about the drivers and the UMBs simply use the command:

MEM /C I MORE

This first lists the use of conventional memory, giving the name and size of each driver, and then lists the use of the UMA, giving the size of each free block. To load a driver into a UMB all you have to do is change DEVICE= in the CONFIG.SYS file to DEVICEHIGH=. To load other memory resident programs in a UMB you have to add LOADHIGH to the start of the command, usually in the AUTOEXEC.BAT file that normally loads the program. You may notice that in neither case is there any way of indicating which UMB will be used by the DEVICEHIGH= or the LOADHIGH command. The reason for this is that a very simple first-come-first-served allocation to UMBs is used. Each device driver is loaded into the largest UMB that is still available even if it would fit into a smaller UMB. For example, consider the effect of loading MOUSE.SYS (14.5 KBytes) and SmartDrive (22 KBytes) into UMBs in different orders. If there are two UMBs available of 15 KBytes and 23 KBytes respectively, then loading MOUSE.SYS first would use up 14.5 KBytes of the 23KByte UMB leaving two UMBs of 15 KBytes and 8.5 MBytes respectively. In this case it would be impossible to load SmartDrive into the remaining UMBs. However, if SmartDrive had been loaded first then it would have used up 22 KBytes of the 23KByte UMB leaving two UMBs of 15 KBytes and 1 KByte respectively and MOUSE.SYS could still be loaded into the 15KByte UMB. Clearly the order that drivers and memory resident programs are loaded is crucial to the efficient utilisation of UMBs.

In general you should load drivers and memory resident programs starting with the largest first. However, it is possible that a variation from this scheme would result in being able to fit more drivers in. It's a classical packing problem!

In most cases you should have sufficient UMBs of reasonable size to make the order of loading less critical than in the previous example, but an understanding of what is going on should enable you to manage the situation. One of the advantages of alternative memory managers is that they usually try to optimise the use of UMBs automatically by loading them to achieve a best fit.

It is important to realise that not all device drivers and memory resident programs will work properly when loaded into UMBs. You should take a step by step approach to moving programs out of conventional memory. Move a driver and then test the machine for a while. If everything works then move another and so on. Any problems can then be associated with the driver that has just been moved. Some drivers attempt to take up more memory after they have been loaded. Sometimes this works because there happens to be just enough free space in the UMB to accommodate this increase. Most of the time it causes the system to crash because there isn't any free space. Again the order in which drivers are loaded makes a difference to what happens. If you know that a driver needs more memory than its initial size would suggest, then add:

> size=*amount*

just following DEVICEHIGH= where *amount* is the amount of memory in hex.

Notice that EMM386.EXE itself uses 9 KBytes of conventional memory and 100 KBytes of extended memory.

A case study

As an example of making use of extended memory under MS-DOS 5, consider the steps involved in creating as large a conventional memory area as possible. Starting from a system with no memory optimisation applied, the conventional memory area was 524.8 KBytes in size. The first step is to install EMM386.EXE as an expanded memory manager. In this case no memory areas had to be excluded and the page frame was successfully allocated at C000 by the automatic procedure. Adding the line:

> DOS=HIGH,UMB

and the option:

> RAM

to the end of the line that loads the EMM386 in the CONFIG.SYS file results in MS-DOS moving into the HMA and UMBs being created. At this stage the command:

MEM /C | MORE

produces result shown below.

Conventional Memory :

Name	Size in Decimal		Size in Hex
MSDOS	18224	(17.8K)	4730
HIMEM	2896	(2.8K)	B50
SETVER	416	(0.4K)	1A0
EMM386	8400	(8.2K)	20D0
ANSI	4192	(4.1K)	1060
SMARTDRV	22992	(22.5K)	59D0
COMMAND	2880	(2.8K)	B40
TSENG	432	(0.4K)	1B0
KEYB	6208	(6.1K)	1840
SHARE	6192	(6.0K)	1830
FREE	64	(0.1K)	40
FREE	582144	(568.5K)	8E200
Total FREE :	582208	(568.6K)	

Upper Memory :

Name	Size in Decimal		Size in Hex
SYSTEM	172032	(168.0K)	2A000
FREE	24544	(24.0K)	5FE0
Total FREE :	24544	(24.0K)	

Total bytes available to programs (Conventional+Upper) : 606752 (592.5K)
Largest executable program size :   581968 (568.3K)
Largest available upper memory block : 24544 (24.0K)
2441216 bytes total EMS memory
2048000 bytes free EMS memory
3407872 bytes total contiguous extended memory
        0 bytes available contiguous extended memory
    8192 bytes available XMS memory
  MS-DOS resident in High Memory Area

If you study this you will discover a number of important facts. The first is that just by moving MS-DOS into the HMA, the size of the conventional memory area has increased to 568 KBytes. The second shock is that there is only a single 24KByte UMB available! The reason for this is that the version of EMM386 supplied with MS-DOS 5.0 doesn't use the area E000-EFFF because it is filled with an additional ROM BIOS in the case of the PS/2. As the machine in question isn't a PS/2 adding i=E000-EFFF to the EMM386 line in CONFIG.SYS marks this block as usable. After this change MEM /C produces the following UMBs:

```
Upper Memory :
Name            Size in Decimal        Size in Hex
SYSTEM          237600  (232.0K)       3A020
FREE            24512   (23.9K)        5FC0
FREE            65504   (64.0K)        FFE0
Total FREE :    90080   ( 88.0K)
Largest available upper memory block : 65504   (64.0K)
```

The UMB of 64KBytes makes it possible to load most of the device drivers and memory resident programs out of conventional memory without worrying about fragmentation. The resulting CONFIG.SYS file was:

```
DEVICE=C:\HIMEM.SYS
DOS=HIGH,UMB
DEVICE=C:\DOS\EMM386.EXE 256 i=E000-EFFF RAM
DEVICEHIGH=C:\DOS\SETVER.EXE
DEVICEHIGH=C:\DOS\ANSI.SYS
DEVICEHIGH=C:\DOS\SMARTDRV.SYS 2048 512
BREAK=ON
COUNTRY=44,,C:\DOS\COUNTRY.SYS
FILES=99
BUFFERS=15
LASTDRIVE=E
SHELL=C:\DOS\COMMAND.COM C:\DOS\ /E:512 /P
```

and the corresponding AUTOEXEC.BAT file was:

```
ECHO OFF
PROMPT $P$G
LOADHIGH C:\DOS\KEYB UK
LOADHIGH SHARE
\TSENG
PATH C:\DOS;C:\CALC;C:\CAD;C:\DESKSCAN;
```

Notice that in general it is safe to load all of MS-DOS's drivers and memory resident programs into UMBs, with the exception of HIMEM.SYS and EMM386.EXE. In this case for example, it didn't seem worth the risk of moving the \TSENG driver into a UMB (and saving 0.4 KByte) because it was supplied with graphics hardware rather than MS-DOS.

After making these changes to the CONFIG.SYS and AUTOEXEC.BAT files the conventional memory was 607.7 KBytes and there was still 48 KBytes of UMB to use up! If more UMB space was required then the page frame could be switched off by adding NOEMS to the end the EMM386 line. However in practice it would be better to keep the 64KByte page frame, and the possibility of using expanded memory.

MS-DOS and DR-DOS

The availability of memory management is an advantage of MS-DOS 5 unique to the 386/486. However, there are also a range of other advantages that are accessible to other types of machine. In particular:

» Disk partitions up to 2 GBytes

» A new Windows style GUI shell

» Task switching

» A new screen editor to replace EDLIN

» Improved command line editor including recall of previous commands and user defined shortcut keys

» On-line help for all commands

» Better disk management including undelete and unformat commands

» QBasic programming language as standard

If you would like to know more about MS-DOS 5 in general then see *MS-DOS 5: A Power User's Guide*; Harry Fairhead; I/O Press (1991).

Also notice that many of these advantages, including the memory management facilities, are available in DR-DOS which is an alternative to MS-DOS. It has its equivalent of HIMEM.SYS and EMM386, and can make use of UMBs and will even move various operating system buffers out of conventional memory that MS-DOS will not. In short, there are many ways in which DR-DOS out-performs MS-DOS but, despite the many vociferous arguments of its enthusiastic supporters, the are no compelling reasons for using it in preference to MS-DOS 5. Indeed, there is something to be said for losing some of the minor advantages to stay with the mainstream product. On the other hand, if you are currently using DR-DOS then, as long as you are not suffering compatibility problems, there is no reason to switch to MS-DOS in a hurry.

Other memory managers

Although MS-DOS 5 provides all the memory management software that most users need, there are a number of other memory managers. These offer various advantages over HIMEM.SYS and EMM386.EXE but perhaps their greatest attraction is their ease of use. Even if you know very little of extended and expanded memory, you can still use one of these alternatives which automatically install themselves and optimise the configuration, including moving drivers into UMBs. In addition most add-on memory managers offer a range of minor improvements in the largest conventional memory area that can be created, or in the size of UMBs. In practice these advantages often involve changes that are potentially damaging to either the stability or the performance of the entire system.

The memory management facilities supplied with MS-DOS 5 may be very conservative in their technology but they should work reliably. Memory optimisation, while important, is secondary to system stability. If you understand the memory management options describe in Chapter 10 and in this chapter then you should be able to achieve very similar levels of memory optimisation using nothing but HIMEM.SYS, EMM386 and your own intelligence. If you feel in need of help then an alternative memory manager will attempt an automatic optimisation of your system but even here they are far from foolproof and you might discover that you still have to sort out the most complex part of the problem manually!

One advantage that alternative memory managers have over HIMEM.SYS+EMM386 is that most can dynamically allocate XMS and expanded memory from a single pool of extended memory. In the case of EMM386 you have to state the amount of expanded memory you want. This is created when the machine next boots up and you cannot change this allocation unless you edit the CONFIG.SYS file and re-boot the machine. Both QEMM and 386MAX will dynamically allocate expanded memory without having to restart the machine.

However, if you are working with versions of MS-DOS before 5 then buying a memory manager is the only alternative to upgrading. The best known 386 memory managers are 386MAX and QEMM which provide more or less the same range of features in slightly different ways.

QEMM-386

The basic features of the Quarterdeck Expanded Memory Manager 386 usually referred to as QEMM-386 version 6 are:

» full LIM/EMS V4.0 implementation

» VCPI and XMS 2.0 compatible

» increases UMB size by reusing the space occupied by BIOS ROMs, a technique referred to as stealth

» automatically 'best fits' device drivers and memory resident programs into UMBs

» can increase conventional memory by adding unused video memory (up to 704 KBytes on MGA and 736 KBytes on CGA systems)

» automated setup and installation

» can load FILES, BUFFERS, FCBs and LASTDRIVE into UMBs

» remaps fast memory into the first 640 KBytes

» uses 3 KBytes of conventional and 160 KBytes of extended memory (plus 12 KBytes of UMB if using stealth)

QEMM will automatically install itself and configure your system to free as much conventional memory as possible. However, unless you make use of its more advanced features it will not give you any more conventional memory than HIMEM.SYS+EMM386 which it replaces. It uses three different techniques to free additional conventional memory. The first is that it will move extended memory into the address space of any unused video RAM. If you are using applications in text only or CGA mode only then it can increase conventional memory to over 700 KBytes, see Chapter 10 for an explanation of how this works.

The second method is that as well as moving device drivers and memory resident programs into UMBs, it can also move a number of MS-DOS internal buffers and other memory areas into UMBs. Specifically, you can move the memory used by the configuration commands FILES, BUFFERS, FCBs and LASTDRIVE into UMBs. In most cases this will work reliably but it isn't a recommended procedure. The third method is much more radical and has even been given a special name - *stealth*. There are a number of memory managers that will move unused ROMs out of upper memory so that they can be replaced by RAM. For example, the PS/2 range has a second 64KByte BIOS ROM that works only in protected mode and so can be removed in a real mode MS-DOS system. Stealth goes one step further by removing BIOS ROMs that are used!

The basic principle is that the BIOS ROMs are mapped into extended memory and the space that they free in upper memory is used to create UMBs into which drivers etc. can be loaded. QEMM places an additional driver into the UMB which detects any use of the, now missing, ROM and switches it back into place before allowing the program to proceed. Clearly this is a workable way of sharing a limited amount of address space and can add around 128 KBytes in UMBs. Obviously the cost of this procedure is the extra time it takes to switch the ROM BIOS in and out of the memory map. The actual degradation in performance varies according to the exact pattern of BIOS and driver access and how it results in switching of memory. In some cases it does slow down video and disk access, in others the effect is negligible.

The most important aspect of QEMM-386 is that it is tailored to Quarterdeck's DESQview 386 program and as such includes options to tailor LIM expanded memory to multi-tasking. If you plan to use DESQview then QEMM-386 is the natural memory manager to use at other times as well. However, notice that QEMM version 6 isn't DPMI compatible. There is also a version of QEMM specially designed for PS/2 series 50 and 60 - QEMM 50/60.

386MAX

The basic features of 386MAX are:

» full LIM/EMS V4.0 implementation

» VCPI, DPMI and XMS 2.0 compatible

» can increase conventional memory by adding unused video memory (up to 704 KBytes on MGA and 736 KBytes on CGA systems)

» can move TSRs and device drivers into hi memory

» remaps fast memory into the first 640 KBytes

» special Blue Max version for PS/2 machines

» uses 1 KByte of conventional and 220 KBytes of extended memory

386MAX has an automatic installation mode that will configure and optimise your machine's memory use in one step. It doesn't have the extras that QEMM 386 supports in the sense that it will not move the MS-DOS data areas into UMBs and it doesn't have stealth to move BIOS ROMs that are in use. It will, however, move BIOS ROMs that are not used! Its biggest single advantage is that it is DPMI compatible. At the moment there are only a few programs that demand DPMI, most will work with either DPMI or VCPI, but the number will probably grow.

The speed of expanded memory

In the main the speed of expanded memory isn't a critical issue for 386/486 systems because all memory managers produce an acceptably fast implementation. What is more interesting is how this simulated expanded memory compares to the real thing - i.e. hardware implemented expanded memory. Some 386 machines have the choice of implementing expanded memory using hardware built into the mainboard or simulating it in software using an EMM. The most important factor in evaluating LIM 3.2 expanded memory is simply data transfer rate, i.e. how fast data can be moved to and from expanded memory in KBytes/s.

The table below gives details of transfer rates for expanded memory implemented in a number of ways using the same 20 MHz 386DX system. The external hardware expanded memory was a medium quality ISA board - in practice you could do better by paying more. Notice that it isn't the absolute figures that matter but the relative differences.

Comparison of expanded memory transfer rates:

	Transfer rate (KByte/s)
External Hardware EMS ISA	328
Internal Hardware EMS	1372
EMM386	1267
386MAX	1323
QEMM	1450

The conclusion is clearly that using internal memory either via special hardware or via software simulation is better than trying to squeeze data though the ISA bus. Expanded memory hardware based on the EISA or MCA bus is likely to perform better, but in a 386/486 there hardly seems any point in going to these lengths when software expanded memory is so cheap and efficient.

DOS extenders

There was a time when it looked as if the way forward in making the best use of a 386/486 system under MS-DOS would be to change to products that incorporated DOS extenders. From a user's point of view a good DOS extender application runs as if it was a standard MS-DOS program - apart from the fact that it can use all of the machine's available extended memory. In fact what has happened is that most applications have made the change to running under either Windows or OS/2 rather than incorporate a DOS extender. The reason seems to be that, with only a few exceptions, the use of extended memory via a DOS extender can be avoided by using either expanded memory or by using conventional memory more efficiently. As a result most of the major applications have either stayed within MS-DOS real mode or moved to protected mode via Windows 3.

The few major applications that make use of DOS extenders - Lotus 1-2-3 Release 3, Interleaf Publisher and AutoCAD 386 for example, - are all VCPI/DPMI compatible. This means that they can be run while a VCPI/DPMI memory manager or Windows 3 is installed without fear of conflict.

DOS multi-tasking

As explained in Chapter 10 expanded memory and UMBs are created by 386 memory managers using virtual 8086 mode. Of course, once you have taken the plunge to using virtual 8086 mode to manage memory the next step is to use it to multi-task real mode programs. Many users don't see the point of a multi-tasking environment because they claim only to use one program at a time. The point of multi-tasking on a personal computer isn't so much being able to run more than one program apparently at the same time, it's more a way of switching between tasks very rapidly. For example, you might be running a spreadsheet and need to swap quickly to a word processor to make a few notes. A multi-tasking program is the best way of improving your productivity under MS-DOS.

There are a number of MS-DOS task switching programs, such as Back and Forth and Software Carousel, and there is even a limited task switching facility included as part of the MS-DOS 5 Shell. Using these you can load more than one program and switch between them with only a keypress. The MS-DOS 5 task switcher is particularly slow as it always makes use of the hard disk to store the applications that aren't running. In this case a task swap involves writing the current task out to disk and reading the new one back in.

When it comes to true MS-DOS multi-taskers the most popular is DESQview 386, but DR's Multiuser DOS is also capable of full multi-tasking as well as multi-user operation. The same Virtual 8086 mode is used to create virtual machines to give the illusion that more than one user, connected via serial ports, can actually use the same machine.

Of course the most popular of all MS-DOS multi-taskers is Windows 3 but this is just one side of its personality. As well as being able to run multiple real mode programs Windows 3 can multi-task a particular type of protected mode program. Windows is more like a memory manager, multi-tasker and DOS extender all rolled into one. It is described in full detail in the next chapter.

DESQview 386

DESQview 386 is a windowing multi-tasker - each DESQview window is a complete virtual MS-DOS environment with 640 KBytes of conventional memory and as much expanded memory as the application requires. It can multi-task almost any real mode application and some protected mode DOS extender programs, provided that they conform to the VCPI specification. It can even run multiple copies of Windows 3 in a window! It is important to realise that in this case Windows 3 and any Windows 3 applications are actually only running in standard mode or in real mode (as opposed to enhanced mode - see Chapter 12.) In many cases this isn't a serious disadvantage, but there are an increasing number of Windows applications that require enhanced mode.

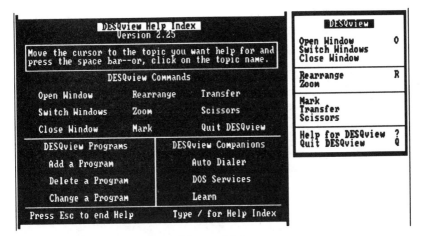

Figure 11.1
The DESQview main menu that appears whenever you press the
ALT key, and the help main menu

Installing DESQview 386 is a two stage process. First install
QEMM, the Quarterdeck Expanded Memory Manager, and
then install DESQview proper, answering a few simple
questions on the way. Starting DESQview is just a matter of
typing DV at the MS-DOS prompt. This causes the DESQview
menu to appear. This is the key to making use of DESQview
and it appears whenever you press and release the ALT key
or click both mouse buttons together - see Figure 11.1.

DESQview will only allow you to run programs that have been
installed. If you select the Open Window option from the
DESQview menu then you are given a list of installed

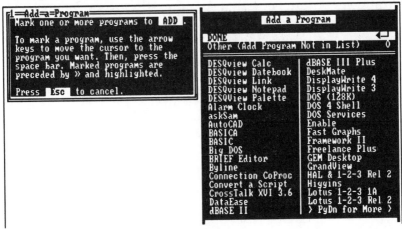

Figure 11.2
The Add a Program menu showing a some of the wide range of
standard programs supported

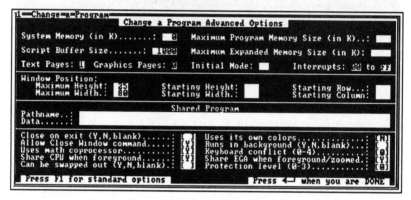

Figure 11.3
The Add a Program screens are used to customise the way a
program runs under DESQview

programs from which to select. Selecting one causes a window
to appear with the program running. DESQview supports full
screen and small windows. Full screen programs just look like
programs running under MS-DOS. Programs running in
small windows can be moved and sized.

The Add a Program option in the DESQview menu is the tool
used to configure programs for running in the multi-tasking
environment. There are a large number of preconfigured
programs listed that can be added simply by selecting their
name from a list - see Figure 11.2. If you want to add a
program that isn't listed then you have to define its
characteristics. Information about how the programs should
be run is entered into a screen form - see Figure 11.3. In the
non-386 versions of DESQview some misbehaved programs
can only be run in full screen windows but the 386 version

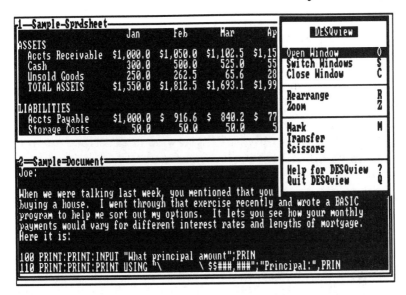

Figure 11.4
Two windows open and the DESQview menu on the screen at the same time

allows various levels of protection to be set which give the user more flexibility.

DESQview, being based on QEMM 386's memory management, is of course VCPI compatible and so it can run DOS extender-based applications such as Lotus 1-2-3 Release 3. It also defines an interface that other applications can use to go beyond MS-DOS, but the success of Windows has ensured that very little software actually makes use of this. In short, DESQview is a very good DOS multi-tasker but that's as far as it goes. It certainly isn't a challenger to Windows 3, NT, OS/2 or any other protected mode operating system.

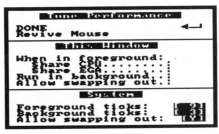

Figure 11.5
The Fine Tune menu that allows a user to alter the way a program is run by DESQview

At the time of writing Quarterdeck had announced that their successor to DESQview, DESQview X, would soon be available. This is an extension to MS-DOS that implements the Unix X Windows environment. This is so different from the current version of DESQview that it seems to be a successor in name only. DESQview X is described in more detail in Chapter 14.

Multiuser DOS

Unlike DESQview, Multiuser DOS from DR (Digital Research) isn't an MS-DOS add-on, it is a complete operating system written from scratch to replace MS-DOS. Indeed, the MS-DOS-like part of Multiuser DOS has been turned into DR-DOS and is sold as an alternative to the real MS-DOS.

There are two ways that you can use Multiuser DOS; as an open system or as a secure system. As an open system it looks just like MS-DOS. You can sit down and start using it at once, without knowing that it is Multiuser DOS at all. However, if you press Ctrl and Esc a task list appears and you are immediately aware that this isn't plain MS-DOS. By default the main machine has four DOS sessions running and you can switch between them by pressing various key combinations. Each DOS session runs full screen so this isn't a windowing multi-tasker but it does support VGA graphics and switching between tasks is instantaneous.

Of course a multi-user system is only multi-user if you add terminals. For this you need to equip the main machine with a number of serial ports. You can use standard PC serial ports or special multi-port serial cards as described in Chapter 8. With standard serial cards, or unbuffered multi-port cards, the maximum number of users is 16. Using buffered cards this number can rise to 64. In addition, each user can have up to eight DOS sessions making a total of 512 DOS tasks on a single machine. In practice it is likely that a 386/486 would run out of processing power when working towards the theoretical limit.

Terminals can be any standard dumb VDU. However, terminals are expensive when you compare them to low end PC hardware. However, you can use a standard PC as as a terminal by way of the PCTERM terminal emulation package which is included as standard. Each terminal can run up to eight DOS sessions, but in most cases one or two should be quite enough. The terminals behave exactly like standard PCs but with the restriction that graphics are limited to CGA resolution and they can't be interactive. This means you can get charts out of spreadsheets but you can't run a drawing package. This isn't at all an unreasonable restriction but it does further emphasise the point that CAD and other graphics applications are better served on a network. However, each terminal can use a mouse via additional serial ports on the main machine. All terminals can share a common printer by way of printer spooling.

Although the open system is the simplest to set up and administer, most applications will require a secure system. There are a variety of security options that you can use but the main one is the need for a log-in name and password. Access to files and directories can be controlled via Owner, Group and World access permissions. This system makes it possible to manage user and group use of the machine without too much effort. You can set disk media to be secure - i.e. not accessible from DR-DOS or MS-DOS in a dual booting system. You can make use of a console lock to leave a terminal unattended but secure without logging off. Individual terminals or DOS sessions can be restarted using Ctrl-Alt-Del without re-booting the main machine.

There are some specially written Multiuser DOS applications but Multiuser DOS implements all of the file and record locking found in MS-DOS based networks. This means that it is possible to use any network based multi-user software under Multiuser DOS without change and without a network!

Multiuser DOS is clearly an alternative to a network of separate machines. As long as you are only considering text based applications such as database or word-processing, then it is also an economical alternative.

Key points

» MS-DOS 5 has considerable advantages over earlier versions which only have limited memory management facilities.

» HIMEM.SYS is the standard MS-DOS XMS memory manager. EMM386.EXE is the standard MS-DOS expanded memory and UMB provider.

» You can increase the size of conventional memory to just over 600 KBytes using the HMA and UMBs to store drivers.

» Alternatives to MS-DOS 5's HIMEM.SYS and EMM386 such as QEMM or 386MAX offer some advantages and are easier to use if you want to avoid the technicalities of manual memory optimisation. They are also an alternative to upgrading to MS-DOS 5 for users of earlier versions of MS-DOS.

» DOS multi-taskers are an obvious step beyond simple memory management. DESQview and Multiuser DOS are the two best known. There are also a number of common task switchers including the MS-DOS 5 Shell.

» DESQview has many advantages if you want to stay with MS-DOS real mode applications. It can run a number of real mode applications at the same time either full screen or in multiple on-screen windows.

» Multiuser DOS can be used to set up small 386/486 time-sharing systems as an alternative to a network of separate machines. This is an economical alternative but it will only work with text-based applications.

Chapter 12
Windows

In the short to medium term at least, the most important operating system for the 386/486 is MS-DOS plus Windows. This combination delivers more of the power of the 386/486 and is a potential upgrade path to operating systems that release even more of its power.

Windows 3 is the source of a great deal of controversy. Some users love it, others hate it and with equal passion. On the surface the most important feature of Windows is that it is a GUI - a Graphical User Interface - but in fact this is almost the least important of its features. Windows allows you to multi-task real mode programs in much the same way that DESQview does, but it also supports a range of memory management options that allow specially written applications to run in protected mode and use more memory than the usual 640 KBytes. MS-DOS programs can also run in protected mode by making use of the DPMI DOS extender standard.

Windows applications can even make the transition to full 32-bit status, but only with difficulty and the great majority are still 16-bit applications. For the moment Windows 3 gets closest in supplying the power of the 386 along with a good range of applications to choose from. In the future Windows 32 and Windows NT will deliver yet more of the 386's power without becoming incompatible with the original.

Windows has been through a number of different versions including Windows 386, the first version specially written for the 386. However, it is important to realise that Windows 3.0 and 3.1 are very different from all earlier versions. If you are using Windows 386, or an even earlier version, then it is important to upgrade. Also, if you experienced Windows 286 or 386 and found it unsuitable then you need to re-evaluate Windows 3.1.

The latest version of Windows is 3.1 but there are still a great many copies of 3.0 in use. Windows 3.1 represents a development on 3.0 and while it doesn't support any radically new features it is still worth upgrading to it.

Modes

Windows operates in different modes depending on the type of processor and memory configuration it has at its disposal. Windows 3.0 supported three modes - real, standard and enhanced, but real mode has been dropped in Windows 3.1.

Real mode was designed to work on machines that lacked any sort of memory management or only had expanded memory. The only importance of real mode is that it allowed early Windows 2 applications to run without modification. For a 386 user real mode isn't very useful and its omission from Windows 3.1 is nothing to worry about.

The remaining two modes - *standard* and *enhanced* correspond to the 286 and 386's memory management abilities. Standard mode makes use of segmented addressing to multi-task Windows applications but it is forced to switch back to real mode to run an MS-DOS application. The time to switch back to real mode and the loss of memory management makes it slower to swap between tasks and makes it less easy to share the machine's resources. For example, in standard mode you can only run MS-DOS applications full screen i.e. not in a re-sizeable window. Standard mode is the only mode that works on a 286 or on a 386/486 with only 1MByte of RAM. In nearly all cases it is very worthwhile adding additional RAM to a 386/486 system to allow it to work in enhanced mode. Many of the criticisms of Windows 3 come from users who have only experienced it in standard mode - there is a great deal of difference.

In enhanced mode the full memory management abilities of the 386 are used to make multi-tasking efficient and safe. Each task is run on a virtual machine using the 386's virtual 8086 mode. This increases the speed of task swapping and allows the machine's resources to be shared. In practical terms this makes it possible to run MS-DOS applications in re-sizeable windows. In addition paging is used to supply expanded memory to any application that needs it and to implement a paged virtual memory system. The paged virtual memory can be used to increase the number of applications running well beyond the actual capacity of the RAM fitted by using the disk as extra storage.

On a 386/486 system you can take advantage of all the benefits available from enhanced mode. For this reason further discussion of Windows will be confined to running it in this mode. The only factor that might prevent this is lack of memory and if this is the case then you really need to invest in the additional RAM needed to run Windows 3 in enhanced mode.

Memory management

Windows 3 builds on the memory management options introduced in Chapter 10. HIMEM.SYS is used as the XMS memory manager and Windows 3 will not run in enhanced mode without it. In addition to managing the extended memory via XMS Windows 3 makes use of some UMBs of its own creating and it will simulate LIM 3.2 and 4.0 expanded memory for any application that needs it. In other words, you don't need EMM386 to run Windows. However, if you have used EMM386 to optimise conventional memory under MS-DOS then Windows will make use of this.

Windows 3 and MS-DOS 5 work together to manage memory particularly well. So much so that you should always consider upgrading to MS-DOS 5 before installing Windows 3.1. When MS-DOS 5 is installed it creates a file, WINA20, in the root directory that controls how MS-DOS and Windows share the UMA. It may seem like unfair competition but it is true that Windows 3.1 and MS-DOS 5 make a more compatible pair than any other combination of operating systems simply because Microsoft wrote both of them.

The size of the conventional memory area in each of the virtual machines used to run real mode applications is just a little smaller than was available just before Windows was started. What this means is that maximising the conventional memory under MS-DOS using EMM386 is very well worthwhile. The only problem is that if you don't leave enough free upper memory, Windows may not be able to allocate its translation buffer in upper memory and so may have to resort to using some conventional memory. The translation buffer is the area used to make the link between protected mode applications and real mode MS-DOS. That is, Windows plays the role of a DOS extender for Windows applications. If the translation buffers are placed in conventional memory then they will take up space in the memory map of every virtual machine.

As well as the translation buffers Windows will also allocate a 64KByte page frame to enable it to provide LIM 3.2/4.0 expanded memory. Notice that you don't need EMM386 to supply expanded memory to real mode applications that run under Windows. If you do run EMM386 using the NOEMS option then Windows will not be able to create expanded memory because EMM386 will have turned all of the available space into UMBs. To allow Windows to create expanded memory you should either use the RAM option or use the X option to exclude a 64KByte area suitable for use as a page frame, see details in Chapter 11.

Notice that once you have installed Windows there is never any reason to move back to MS-DOS proper. If you want to use your machine via MS-DOS then simply run the command prompt at full screen. The effect is as if you were working with just MS-DOS but with a memory manager installed. In other words, if you find that you don't like Windows applications then you can always use it as an MS-DOS memory manager!

Using Windows

Assuming that Windows has been correctly installed on your machine, then using it is exceptionally easy. Windows is a GUI, a *Graphical User Interface*, so everything is done by pointing, clicking and dragging using a mouse. The idea is that all the traditional computer entities such as file, directories, programs etc. are represented as icons that are manipulated using the mouse. This is a way of working that beginners usually find easy, but experts who have spent time learning how to use MS-DOS via the command prompt often find that it slows them down. This may be true, but the GUI way of working is not only simpler, it is also less error prone. It is harder to delete a set of files by accident if you see their names listed on the screen and actually have to select them from a list by clicking. However, as already mentioned in the previous section, not liking the Windows interface is no reason to avoid using it. It is quite possible to run programs from the familiar MS-DOS command prompt and so forget that you are using Windows until you need to make use of its special abilities.

In many ways Windows converts the PC into a machine that is as easy to use as the Apple Mac. However, there are a number of important differences in that the Mac users generally don't have to get involved with setting up their equivalent of Windows! This tends to give Windows a slightly more technical feel than the Mac's GUI. In addition Windows isn't quite as friendly as the Mac and doesn't use many of the same direct methods of representing operations. For example, on the Mac you drag a file to a waste bin icon to delete it, but in Windows you select the file and then use a menu command. In other words, Windows is not a very GUI graphical user interface. This probably has something to do with the legal need for Microsoft to avoid making Windows too much like the Mac.

In Windows, programs are represented using suitable icons and you can run any program simply by double clicking on it. Programs are organised into groups using the Program Manager. This provides a way of grouping programs together irrespective of where they are actually stored on disk. Files and directories can be manipulated using the File Manager. The File Manager in Windows 3.0 has received a lot of criticism and it is much improved in Windows 3.1 but it still isn't very good. Indeed it is this one aspect of Windows that makes it a less than successful GUI. You can get replacements for the File Manager that are easier to use.

There are a range of mini-applications included with Windows - a simple word processor, a calculator, a cardfile, a paint program etc.. None of these make the change to Windows worthwhile in themselves but they all help to increase the usefulness of the Windows system. Full Windows applications are among the most sophisticated applications found on a PC. They are not limited to the 640 KBytes of conventional memory, but they are often criticised as being slower than similar MS-DOS applications. This sluggishness is true of some badly written Windows applications but not all and the situation is improving. However, Windows applications are

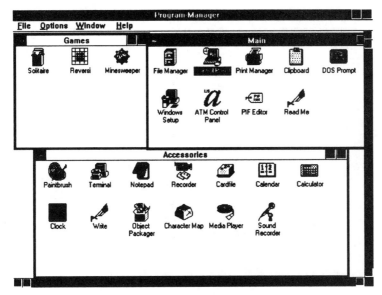

Figure 12.1
The Program Manager (3.1)

becoming increasingly greedy for memory and disk space. A typical Windows application will consume 5 to 10 MBytes of hard disk space. The demands of running Windows applications make a 100MByte hard disk a minimum requirement. However, most Windows applications work reasonably well on a 16MHz 386SX with 4 MBytes of memory - although a faster processor and more memory obviously help.

Windows applications generally automatically add an icon to the Program Manager during their installation. To run a Windows application all you have to do is double click on the icon. They can be run full screen or in re-sizeable windows and you can run more than one application at a time and switch between them almost instantaneously by clicking within the window of the one you want to be active. Data can be transferred between Windows applications using the clipboard and cut and paste operations. There is also a sophisticated way of linking applications together using a

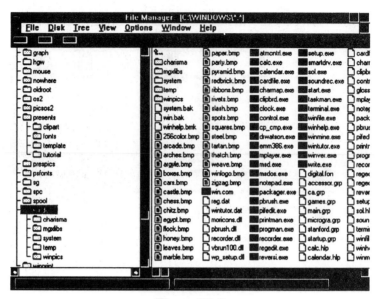

Figure 12.2
The File Manager (3.1)

facility called DDE - *Dynamic Data Exchange*. In practice DDE is often difficult to use and in Windows 3.1 it has been more or less superseded by a new way for applications to interact called OLE (pronounced Oh-lay) or *Object Linking and Embedding*. OLE allows the user to store data objects produced by one type of application within anther. For example, a picture created using Windows Paint can be embedded in Windows Write or any other OLE supporting word processor. The picture can be viewed in the word processor but it doesn't 'forget' its original association with with Windows Paint. Double clicking on it within the word processor document immediately starts Windows Paint with the picture all ready to edit. The same sort of of embedding is supported for a wide range of data types and applications. For example, if a sound card is fitted a sound file can be embedded in the same way and double clicking on it allows the user to hear the recording. OLE is clearly going to change the way that users think about data and documents.

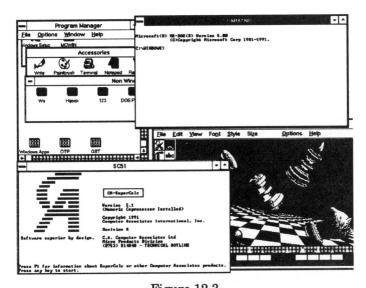

Figure 12.3
Running MS-DOS and Windows applications - SuperCalc 5
bottom left, the command prompt top right, PaintBrush bottom
right and the Program Manager top left (3.0)

Applications can also be minimised back to their icon while
still loaded and running. Obviously while minimised to an
icon the user cannot interact with the application. Double
clicking on the icon restores it to a full window.

Running MS-DOS programs

As well as Windows applications, MS-DOS programs can be
run on an almost equal footing. Of course, these are still
limited to the 640 KBytes of conventional memory but
Windows will make expanded memory available if the
application can make use of it. MS-DOS applications can be
run in two different ways. They can be installed in the
Program Manager and represented by a suitably meaningful
icon. In this case to run an MS-DOS program all you have to
do is double click on it in exactly the same manner as a
Windows application. MS-DOS applications can run in an

on-screen window so that you can see more than one application at a time but programs that use high resolution graphics modes sometimes have to be switched to full screen. For example, if you are running Lotus 1-2-3 or SuperCalc in an on-screen window then trying to plot a graph which uses high resolution mode will cause an error to be reported. However, switching the application to full screen allows the graph to be drawn. The application can then be returned to a window.

One of the problems with running MS-DOS applications in a window has been overcome in Windows 3.1. The size of the font used in an MS-DOS window cannot be changed prior to Windows 3.1 and this often resulted in unreadably small displays. In Windows 3.1 you can select a font size that will produce larger or smaller displays as required. Text can be cut and pasted between MS-DOS applications while they are running in on-screen windows.

The need to install MS-DOS applications and use them via Windows often annoys experienced MS-DOS users who are forced to give up all of the tricks of the command line prompt. In practice there is never any need to use Windows in this way. The program that manages the command prompt, i.e. COMMAND.COM, is installed in the Program Manager as standard. Double clicking on the DOS Prompt icon produces an on-screen window or a full screen display of the familiar MS-DOS prompt. At this point you can type in any MS-DOS command and run any MS-DOS program that you want to without installing it in the Program Manager. You can even run the MS-DOS 4 or 5 DOS Shell to manage programs and files if you want to! Using Windows in this way makes it entirely equivalent to using the MS-DOS prompt but with the added ability to run more than one MS-DOS prompt window at the same time.

The characteristics and requirements of each MS-DOS program to be run under Windows is determined by a Program Information File or PIF. PIFs can be set up for each program separately but there is also a default PIF that controls the way an unknown program will be run. In most cases the default PIF is satisfactory but if an application has special

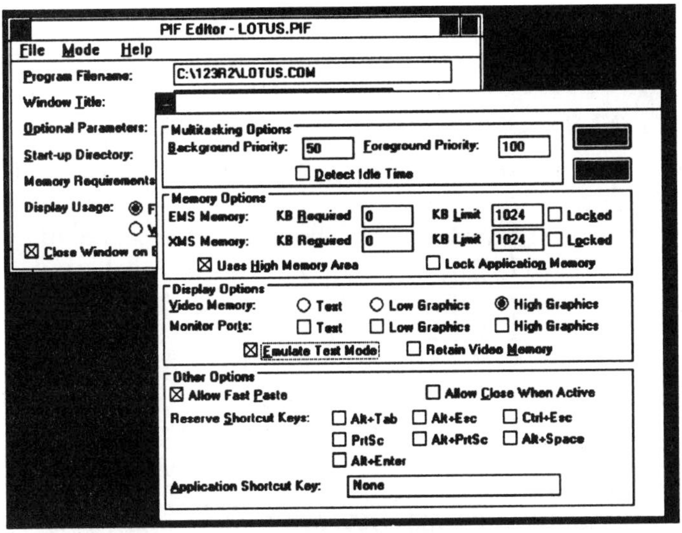

Figure 12.4
A sample PIF

requirements, or the way that Windows runs needs to be optimised, then you can make use of the PIF editor to create a customised PIF. Although the PIF form can look intimidating, most of it is concerned with setting limits on the resources to be made available such as the amount of expanded and XMS memory and whether the program should automatically be run in an on-screen window or not.

As well as the ability to multi-task applications, Windows brings a number of other advantages with it. It defines a standard interface for programs so that if you have a driver for any device - screen display or printer - then all Windows applications will work with that device without the need for an individual driver. This uniformity makes applications easier to install and reduces the risk in using non-standard hardware - if there is a good Windows 3 driver then it can be used with all existing Windows applications.

Windows 3.1 has also introduced TrueType fonts as a standard way of producing high quality text on any device including the screen. Before Windows 3.1 the same effect could be achieved by using font managers such as Adobe Type Manager but TrueType is more tightly integrated with Windows 3.1. In practice TrueType makes almost any printer

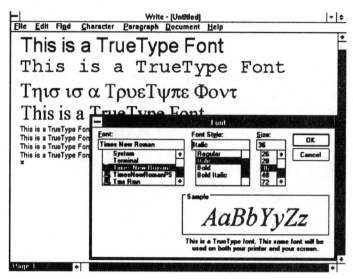

Figure 12.5
TrueType fonts on the screen

capable of using a range of different fonts at different point sizes.

The standardisation of Windows file formats has been less successful. Windows defines a range of formats for graphics files but at the moment these are not quite good enough to make proprietary graphics file formats redundant. As a result there is a great deal of confusion over which applications work with which file formats. This situation is slowly improving.

Windows 3.1 has also introduced a new set of multi-media standards. Multi-media is a difficult term to define but roughly speaking it involves the use of sound and graphics to present information. The new Windows 3.1 drivers act as a standard interface to the wide range of PC sound cards - SoundBlaster, Roland, Ad-Lib, etc.. and to CD-ROM. Multi-media is a technology that has been on the verge of developing for some time and the support that it gets from Windows 3.1 could be just the push it needs to make it commonplace.

Windows Problems - the UAE

The description of Windows 3 so far makes it sound as if there could be no better environment for a 386/486 machine. But Windows isn't without its faults. For one thing, it can be very difficult to set up to run reliably on some hardware. The trouble usually stems from the age of the design and, in the case of 386/486 machines, usually from an incompatible BIOS ROM or non-standard disk drives. The disk drive problem has more or less been cured in Windows 3.1 and it is reasonably easy to replace the BIOS ROM once you are sure that this is the cause. Even so, these difficulties have given Windows 3 the reputation for being an awkward piece of software to install.

Windows 3 may run protected mode programs, but it is built on the foundations of real mode MS-DOS and this causes many problems. Subtle errors in device drivers and in early versions of Windows 3.0 caused it to crash often when system resources were low. The problem in Windows 3.0 was put right mid-way though its life by an unpublicised upgrade release. Most early users of Windows 3.0 never knew about the change and so carried on using a not completely stable version.

Another problem that affects stability is the complexity of the Windows interface to applications programs. Many mature applications contained serious bugs that caused them to crash with the message UAE, Unexpected Application Error, if they were pushed too hard. This sort of error is quite unfamiliar to the typical MS-DOS user, although Mac users have been putting up with similar behaviour from their operating system for years, the only difference being that the Mac operating system shows a friendly icon in the shape of a bomb with a smouldering fuse for a system error! Systems and users varied in the number of UAEs that they experienced. Systems that had subtle setup errors or limited resources produced UAEs more often than standard systems with plenty of RAM and disk space. Users varied in how much they expected from the system in terms of the number of applications running and how careful they were about accessing the same file more than once! Good systems and careful users suffered roughly one

UAE every two weeks of use. Poor systems and ambitious users would see one or two UAEs a day. Windows 3.0 gained a reputation for being unstable.

Many of the UAE problems have been fixed or improved in Windows 3.1, as has the overall efficiency of the system. Windows 3.1, in enhanced mode in particular, now makes better and more careful use of MS-DOS. It checks what applications do more completely and instead of issuing uninformative UAE messages it reports specific problems or AEs, Application Errors, that the application's programmers can use to debug the software. In other words rather than causing a complete system crash errors in individual applications now tend to be localised. Instead of Windows as a whole getting the blame for the crash particular applications can now be labelled as 'buggy' and either removed, used with care, or upgraded. This isn't to say that system crashes have been abolished but they have been reduced to a level more typical of other multi-tasking systems.

However, Windows 3.1 has done little to remove the main two problems with Windows and its use of the 386/486. Windows is still a 16-bit operating system extension built on top of a 16-bit real mode operating system. It also still uses 64KByte segment addressing which makes programs slower and less reliable than they could be. These criticisms can only be met by re-writing Windows 3 from scratch to produce a fully protected mode 32-bit operating system, and this is exactly what Windows NT is designed to be.

Virtual memory

One of the best features of Windows when running in enhanced mode is its use of disk storage to provide *virtual memory*. The virtual memory is managed without applications knowing anything at all about it - even MS-DOS applications make use of it. However, there are two different ways that the area of disk storage can be allocated - as a variable swap file and as a fixed size swap file. If you opt for a variable size swap file then the amount of disk space used to create virtual memory varies each time you start Windows.

Windows creates a file WIN386.SWP when it first starts and the size of this file grows and contracts as the demand for virtual memory changes.

If you create a fixed size swap file then, as the name suggests, a fixed amount of disk storage is allocated in a hidden file called 386PART.PAR. A fixed size swap file has the advantage of being faster because the virtual memory manager always knows where it is stored on disk and the file is allocated as one contiguous block of storage.

In Windows 3.0 allocating a fixed swap file was an involved process that needed Windows to be operating in real mode and used a separate utility program to do the setup. In Windows 3.1 the procedure has been simplified and made part of the Control Panel icon. As the permanent swap file has to be allocated in a single contiguous block of storage, running a disk defragmenter before trying to create it is a good idea. This moves all of the free storage on the disk into a single area. You should in general accept the suggested size for the swap file. Windows 3.1 also added a special 32-bit disk driver that speeds virtual memory implementation even more.

If you are running Windows on a network then it is extremely inefficient to allocate a swap file on a network drive. It can be done but it is very slow!

DPMI and VCPI

Windows 3 supports the DPMI standard and any MS-DOS program, such as Lotus 1-2-3 Release 3.1, that makes use of a DPMI compatible DOS extender will run perfectly well and can make use of as much extended memory as it needs. However, Windows 3.0 doesn't support the VCPI standard and programs that make use of it will simply not work. Windows 3.1 will work with VCPI applications in standard mode. In enhanced mode you will see a warning message telling you to change to standard mode if a VCPI program is started. Memory managers that are only VCPI compatible are not suitable for use with Windows 3 but you can make use of memory managers that are both VCPI and DPMI compatible such as QEMM 386 and 386MAX. Of course, EMM386 is DPMI compatible!

SMARTDrive and DMA

SMARTDrive is the disk caching utility in MS-DOS and Windows. In the case of the MS-DOS 5 and Windows 3.0, it is indeed nothing more than a free disk cache utility, but in Windows 3.1 it also has another role to play in minimising problems that occur with non-standard disk drives.

SMARTDrive is loaded by adding the line:

DEVICE=SMARTDRV.SYS *size min*

into the CONFIG.SYS file after HIMEM.SYS has been loaded. SMARTDrive will create a disk cache using *size* KBytes of extended RAM. When Windows starts running it can ask SMARTDrive for some of this RAM back for other uses but you can also specify that *min* KBytes is reserved for disk caching. For example:

DEVICE=SMARTDRV.SYS 512 256

sets up an initial disk cache of 512 KBytes which could be reduced to as little as 256KBytes if Windows needs the memory. You can also add /A to the end of the line if you would like the cache allocated in expanded memory, but this is not likely to be an option that would interest a 386/486 user. SMARTDrive is certainly worth installing, especially if you are not making use of extended memory in any other way. However, it is worth commenting that it can be out-performed by other disk caching programs.

SMARTDrive 4.0 was introduced with Windows 3.1 and it is a considerable improvement on earlier versions. SMARTDrive 4.0 can cache all types of block device including non-standard hard disks, optical disks and CD-ROMs. The most important change, as far as performance is concerned, is that 4.0 implements a read and a write disk cache. In other words, it not only keeps tracks read from the disk in memory in case they are needed again, it also postpones writing data to the drive until the system has nothing more pressing to do. This approach speeds both disk reads and writes but it is slightly dangerous in that unless the SMARTDrive buffers are flushed, i.e. written out to disk, before switching off the machine data could be lost. If you are using SMARTDrive under Windows 3.1 then this is only a very slight danger in that closing down Windows automatically signals to SMARTDrive to flush its buffers to disk. This is one of many very good reasons for not simply switching your machine off while Windows is running! If you are working with SMARTDrive under MS-DOS then there is no special 'shut down' signal and so SMARTDrive has to be told to flush its buffers before the machine is switched off.

SMARTDrive 4.0 is loaded differently to earlier versions. It can be loaded directly from the command prompt before starting Windows or by including the line:

SMARTDRV *size min*

in the AUTOEXEC.BAT file, where *size* sets the initial size of the cache and *min* determines how small Windows can reduce this to if it needs the RAM. Notice that this is a transfer from the CONFIG.SYS file to the AUTOEXEC.BAT file.

There are also a number of other options that can be used to control the way that SMARTDrive works - in most cases you can ignore these.

Normally SMARTDrive will read cache all drives, including floppy drives and read/write cache all hard disks, optical disks, CD-ROMs etc.. You can change the cache status of any drive by including its drive letter after SMARTDRV. Following the letter by a + enables both read and write caching, a - disables all caching and using just the drive letter enables read caching but disables write caching. So for example:

SMARTDRV A C- D+

will read cache A, disable caching on C and enable read/write caching on D.

The options /e:*size* and /b:*size* set the size of the cache element and the read ahead buffer in KBytes. You should leave these at their default value in nearly all cases.

SMARTDrive can be loaded into a UMB but you can stop it doing so by adding the /L to the end of the line.

You can control the action of write caching by using the command:

    SMARTDRV /C

which writes the contents of the cache buffers to disk. You can also use:

    SMARTDRV /R

to erase the buffer contents and reset SMARTDrive - but don't be tempted to do this! Adding /? provides online help and adding /S displays the current status.

As well as providing disk caching SMARTDrive, or rather a second component of the utility, provides double buffering that makes it possible for non-standard bus mastering SCSI drives that do not support VDS to work safely. The double buffering component of SMARTDrive can be loaded by adding the line:

    DEVICE=SMARTDRV.EXE /double_buffer

to the CONFIG.SYS file. SMARTDrive automatically determines which drives need double buffering when it loads. To discover if double buffering is necessary all you have to do is read the status screen that is produced by SMARTDrive. To be completely sure you can also give the command:

    SMARTDRV

at the command prompt and read the resulting status screen.

With all of these changes to SMARTDrive it hardly seems worth using an alternative disk cache. SMARTDrive is well integrated with Windows 3.1 and is efficient.

Controlling Windows

This section describes the fine detail of configuring Windows Memory management options and can be left until needed.

As Windows 3 acts as a full memory manager for UMBs and expanded memory you would expect it to have the same range of options to control its use of the UMA as, say, EMM386. In fact it has a huge number of options that can be used to control its use of memory in all manner of ways stored in a file called SYSTEM.INI. This is a text file that can be edited using Notepad, Edit, Sysedit, Edlin or any word processor that can work with an ASCII file. In many ways the SYSTEM.INI file plays the role of CONFIG.SYS for Windows. As with CONFIG.SYS it is quite possible to make changes to SYSTEM.INI that will stop Windows from working. It is important that you always back up SYSTEM.INI before making changes to it. Most of the settings in SYSTEM.INI will be correctly inserted by the initial setup routine and you should only need to change them if you are using unusual hardware or want to alter the way that Windows is running.

The SYSTEM.INI file is divided into a number of sections by the occurrence of section titles enclosed in square brackets:

[boot]	Lists device drivers and Windows modules
[boot.description]	Lists the names of devices that can be changed using Windows setup
[drivers]	names the installable device drivers
[keyboard]	defines the keyboard
[mci]	list multi-media drivers (3.1 only)
[NonWindowsApp]	controls the way real mode applications run
[standard]	defines configuration in standard mode
[enhanced]	defines configuration in enhanced mode

There are a great many options in the [enhanced] section but only a relatively small number ever need concern the user. The option:

EMMPageFrame=*address*

can be used to set the location of the page frame that Windows uses. This is the same as the Frame= option used with EMM386. In the same way, the two options:

EMMExclude=*start-end*
EMMInclude=*start-end*

are the same as the x and i options used to exclude and include sections of memory in EMM386's handling of the UMA. Notice that in MS-DOS 5.0 and Windows 3.0 the range E000-EFFF was automatically excluded in case it contained a PS/2 extension ROM BIOS. In most cases it is safe to include this range on machines that have a 64KByte ROM BIOS. Windows 3.1 auto detects if this range is in use or not.

To limit the use of expanded memory use:

EMMSize=*size*

You should only need to use this if an application always grabs all of the memory as expanded memory when it runs. The size is specified in KBytes. To remove the expanded memory manager completely use:

NoEMMDriver=True

If the machine has any hardware-implemented expanded memory then it is possible that this will make Windows fail to work. Windows certainly cannot make use of any real expanded memory in extended mode so you might as well use:

IgnoreInstalledEMM=Yes

to correct the fault.

There are also a number of other very technical options that relate to the use of virtual memory and other aspects of memory efficiency, but these rarely have to be altered by the user.

Crashing

The really important question is what to do if Windows keeps locking up or crashing. Such events are usually related to conflicts in the UMA, although sometimes they are due to more serious faults such as an incompatible BIOS ROM. A sure sign of UMA conflict is being able to run Windows 3 in protected mode but not in enhanced mode. To test for this try starting Windows using:

WIN /P

which starts it in protected mode no matter what machine configuration is available. If Windows runs in protected mode then your only choice is to resolve the UMA conflicts by excluding areas from being converted into UMBs. Add the line:

        EMMExclude=A000-EFFF

to the [386enh] section of SYSTEM.INI. This excludes the entire UMA and stops any UMBs being created. If Windows now works in enhanced mode your only remaining task is to reduce the excluded range to give as large a usable UMA as possible but without crashing the system.

If a UMA conflict isn't the source of the problem then you should try to isolate the problem by creating a 'clean boot' disk. This is a system disk that contains the simplest possible CONFIG.SYS file and AUTOEXEC.BAT files. If Windows works when the machine is clean booted your next job is to introduce extras to the CONFIG.SYS and AUTOEXEC.BAT file until it again fails to work. This technique isolates the problem to a single driver.

You can use the same isolation technique if the problem is thought to be due to a hardware conflict - although most hardware conflicts should show up under MS-DOS before you ever get to the stage of running Windows.

As well as complete crashes there are also a range of intermediate problems that sometimes occur with floppy and hard disks. If the machine has trouble accessing a floppy then try adding:

        HIGHFLOPPYREADS=NO
        EMMEXCLUDE=E000-EFFF
        VIRTUALHFIRQ=OFF

to the [386enh] section of the SYSTEM.INI file. If this doesn't work then you most likely have an incompatible BIOS ROM which needs to be changed. The same problem with a hard disk is most often due to not using SMARTDrive. If you are using SMARTDrive then you can also try adding:

        VIRTUALHFIRQ=OFF

to the [386enh] section of the SYSTEM.INI file. Some PS/2s also need the line:

        DEVICE=DASDDRVR.SYS

in their CONFIG.SYS file. Otherwise the final treatment is the same as for the floppy - change the ROM BIOS.

General protection errors

A *general protection error* is caused by one application or system program trying to use memory that has been allocated to another program. It is exactly this type of error that protected mode was invented to detect. However, detecting a general protection error still leaves the system with the problem of what to do about it. A general protection error isn't confined to the Windows environment but can occur in any protected mode software, be it a DOS extender or memory manager.

In Windows 3.0 general protection errors usually resulted in UAEs that the user couldn't attribute to any particular cause. In Windows 3.1 general protection errors are reported as specific errors associated with the application that caused the problem. There is even an error reporting utility called Dr Watson that can be used to record the details of a general protection or any other type of application error (AE).

Using this log it should be possible to discover if the AEs are being caused by a particular application, in which case the faults should be reported, complete with the DR Watson log, to the manufacturer of the software. If the AEs are evenly spread then the fault is probably in the system configuration and most likely a BIOS ROM incompatibility.

BIOS ROM problems

The most common serious problem encountered in running Windows is an incompatible BIOS ROM. Changing a BIOS ROM is reasonably cheap and easy. You simply order a BIOS ROM from the same manufacturer as the one already fitted for the same class of machine, open the case, remove the old BIOS ROM and plug the new one in. In practice things can be slightly more complicated and you should aways seek specific advice when you purchase a new BIOS ROM.

At the time of writing the 386 BIOS ROMs known to be incompatible with Windows included:

» Phoenix - any version earlier than 1988. There are also some manufacturers versions that are at fault after this date

» AMI - all BIOSs before 1990 have serious problems. After 1991 minor serial port problems persist

» Award - all versions before 3.05 caused floppy disk errors

» DTK BIOS - problems with all versions before 36

» Peak/DM (Chips and Technologies) - there are problems before version 1.30

» Quadtel - problems before version 3.05

» Tandon BIOS - early models cause keyboard failures

» Toshiba BIOS - T3100/20, T3100e and T5200

See *Contact Addresses* at the end of this book for information on where to obtain general BIOS upgrades.

Key points

» Windows 3 is a DOS extender, memory manager and multi-tasker.

» There are significant advantages to running Windows 3 on a 386/486 based system including: multiple DOS windows, expanded memory simulation for DOS applications, and virtual memory management.

» Windows 3.1 is a significant upgrade on Windows 3.0 in that it provides a more stable and more efficient environment. It also adds multi-media support to Windows.

» Windows builds on the memory management provided in MS-DOS. HIMEM.SYS provides XMS memory and EMM386 acts as a UMB provider. Windows acts as its own expanded memory manager.

» Windows provides a disk cache program SMARTDrive. SMARTDrive Version 4.0 used with Windows 3.1 caches reads and writes and solves the problem of DMA bus mastering disk drives by supporting double buffering.

» Windows memory management is DPMI compatible but version 3.1 supports VCPI applications in standard mode.

» One of the main drawbacks of Windows is the number of UAEs, Unexpected Application Errors, that users encounter. These can be due to system incompatibilities or AEs, Application Errors. Windows 3.1 tries to convert all UAEs into AEs so that the problems can be tracked down to source.

» UMA allocation conflicts are the source of most UAEs, closely followed by BIOS ROM incompatibilities.

» Windows isn't the perfect 386/486 operating environment because it is built on real mode MS-DOS and it is still 16-bit software. Win32 and Windows NT are designed to provide a smooth upgrade path to a true 386/486 operating environment.

Chapter 13
OS/2 - an alternative?

MS-DOS isn't designed to take advantage of a powerful 386/486 based computer. Windows makes better use of it but, at present, it is still a 16-bit operating system, leaving OS/2 and Unix as the only true 32-bit protected mode operating systems for the 386/486. This chapter examines OS/2 as an alternative operating system.

Although Windows 3 is doing a good job of extending the life of MS-DOS and its associated real mode applications, there is no question that at some time in the future an alternative 32-bit protected mode operating system will replace it. The original intention of IBM and Microsoft was that this replacement should be by revolution rather than evolution. The replacement was to be OS/2, a completely new operating system that would offer the user such a huge advantage that it was worth the expense and trouble of changing the habits of a decade. However, this grand plan for the future has so far failed, and the reasons why might be a good indicator of what is to come.

The grand plan

Even when the first 286-based machines were introduced, it was obvious that a new operating system was needed and IBM and Microsoft teamed up to produce OS/2. Many of the initial problems of OS/2 can be seen as a consequence of this early start. By being designed initially for the 286, the original version of OS/2 failed to make use of any of the facilities of the 386. In particular, because it didn't use virtual 86 mode to create virtual machines to run real mode programs, its compatibility with the past was very limited. It could run MS-DOS programs, but only one at a time and in a very complex and unfriendly way. At the time the restriction to the 286 didn't seem unreasonable. The 16MByte memory limit, for example, seemed large, while the use of 64KByte segments and the lack of virtual memory seemed minor faults. Compared to what MS-DOS offered at the time, OS/2 Version 1 looked very good.

What stopped OS/2 Version 1 from being widely adopted is difficult to pin down because it was a combination of factors. At the time of its introduction memory was in short supply and this contributed to making its 2MByte minimum and 4MByte recommended memory requirements look extravagant. IBM also didn't help matters by trying to give a proprietary feel to the new operating system. It would run on PS/2s and a few other manufacturers' machines, but it was by no means certain that you could run OS/2 if you had a non-IBM PC. IBM even produced an enhanced version of OS/2, the Extended Edition, that was very definitely only for IBM machines. Many users were even under the impression that OS/2, the PS/2 and the MCA bus were all bound up together so that you needed one to make use of the others. IBM were guilty of using OS/2 as a marketing lever for their own products.

The first version of OS/2 was also primitive in the sense that it wasn't a GUI but a command line prompt, modelled on MS-DOS. The intention was to make MS-DOS users feel at home, but a command line prompt isn't a good way of making use of an advanced multi-tasking operating system. In later versions this error was put right with the introduction of Presentation Manager, or PM. However, applications software for PM has been, and still is, slightly thin on the ground.

Perhaps the final reason for the slow acceptance of OS/2 was the introduction of Windows 3.0. This gave MS-DOS users a way of releasing some of the power of the 286 and the 386 without having to buy all new software. When running in enhanced mode on a 386/486 machine, Windows 3 even surpassed OS/2 in the range of features it offered. For example, it could run multiple MS-DOS applications in re-sizeable windows. It may have been technically inferior to OS/2, but from the user's point of view it looked superior!

Windows 3 created a split between IBM, who still wanted to make OS/2 the operating system of the future, and Microsoft who thought that building on the success of Windows 3 was a better idea. Microsoft stopped work on OS/2 Version 2, which was to have been 32-bit and 386 specific, and announced its plans for Windows NT - a 32-bit 386 specific version of Windows. IBM decided to go it alone and produce OS/2 Version 2 as a direct competitor to Windows 3 and Windows NT.

Producing a competitor to Windows has forced IBM to drop all efforts at keeping OS/2 an operating system for IBM machines. Indeed, they have gone out of their way to make sure that it will work on as wide a range of machines as possible. Other changes to the basic design of the operating system have also been necessary to compete with Windows. In particular, the need to be compatible with the past now extended to running multiple MS-DOS applications and multiple Windows applications.

The history of OS/2 to date can be summarised as:

» OS/2 Version 1.0   Basic system no PM

» OS/2 Version 1.1   PM included

» OS/2 Version 1.2   High performance filing system
introduced along with improved
version of PM

» OS/2 Version 2   386/486 specific

Version 2.0

Although some users will stay with Version 1.1 of OS/2, the
majority will prefer to upgrade to Version 2.0. The minimum
system requirements are:

» 386SX or better processor

» 4 MBytes RAM

» 30 MBytes of hard disk space for the full system

However, to make good use of OS/2 2.0 you really need a
machine no slower than 25MHz, at least 8 MBytes of RAM
and a 200MByte hard disk.

OS/2 can be installed so that it becomes the only operating
system on a disk. In this case the High Performance Filing
system, HPF, can be used. If you want to keep other operating
systems active on one disk then you can either re-partition the
disk or use a dual boot option. If you repartition the disk you
will lose all of the data on it but you can then have as many
different operating systems on it as you need - i.e. MS-DOS,
OS/2 and Unix. In this case OS/2 will be able to use its new
filing system within its own partition. Many users will opt to
to install OS/2 alongside MS-DOS in a dual boot configuration.
In this case no repartitioning is necessary, but OS/2 is
restricted to working with the standard MS-DOS (FAT) filing
system. In this case you can swap between MS-DOS and OS/2
by restarting the machine.

The redesigned interface

OS/2 has a completely re-designed GUI interface and even users of OS/2 Version 1.1 will find it very different. The basic components are familiar, with icons for programs and data and menus for operations. The biggest change is that now the second mouse button is used to produce a floating menu and for some other operations, such as dragging an object to a new location.

The new GUI interface is designed to be 'object oriented'. Everything is represented on a single desktop as an icon, there is very little distinction between a program and data and any type of object can be stored in a folder. There is no division corresponding to the Windows use of a File Manager and a Program Manager. If you move a collection of program icons into a folder you have something equivalent to a Program Manager group, and storing files in a folder gives you the equivalent of a File Manager directory. However, there is no reason to stay with this strict division and a folder can contain both programs and data files. In fact, icons can be placed directly on the desktop without being grouped in a folder. This should allow users to organise their work without having to worry about the true location of files and programs etc..

OS/2's object-oriented approach sounds like a good idea but there are one or two drawbacks to keep in mind. The first is

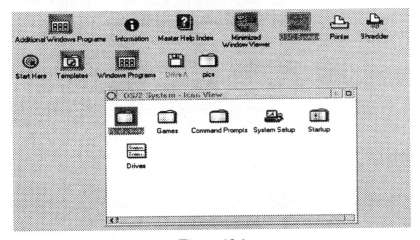

Figure 13.1
The OS/2 desktop

that while some aspects of it are easier for the beginner, there is an air of sophistication about setting up the desktop. For example, templates are used to create new objects. To create a new folder you have to drag a template folder, which is stored along with other templates in a folder, onto the desktop. You also have to configure objects by way of an on-screen form. The use of shadow objects allows the same data or program to be represented by more than one icon in different locations. All of the icons refer to, and make use of, the same underlying data.

All of this might be a good way to teach a beginner how to use a machine, but remember that one of OS/2's strengths is that it will run MS-DOS and Windows applications, and these each make use of a different way of looking at the system. Even current OS/2 applications are not object oriented in the same way and as soon as you start using one you find yourself back to thinking in terms of files, directories and programs.

On a more mundane level, many of the facilities of the OS/2 interface are already available in Windows 3 or can be added by using additional programs. For example, in both OS/2 and Windows you can run an application by double clicking on its associated data file. Windows 3.1 even adds the 'drag-and-drop' way of running or printing by dragging the data file's icon over to the application or printer icon. If a more object-oriented interface is required, Windows can be run using HP's NewWave or Xerox's Rooms. Both are alternative desktop programs for Windows that make it a more sophisticated GUI environment. In other words, the OS/2 user interface may be good, but it is neither new nor unique in the range of features that it offers. It may even be a handicap in a mixed MS-DOS, Windows, OS/2 environment.

Running DOS

OS/2 2.0 can run multiple MS-DOS sessions, each in an on-screen window or full screen. It does this by making use of the virtual 8086 mode of the 386 processor in much the same way that Windows 3 in enhanced mode does. The difference is that OS/2 simulates MS-DOS more effectively. Each virtual machine is started up, a process similar to booting a real machine, using a heavily modified version of MS-DOS. This is smaller and more efficient than the real thing. You can start each MS-DOS session using different memory configurations. You can load different drivers in UMBs just as you can with the real MS-DOS. OS/2 will also supply LIM 4.0 expanded memory to any applications that can make use of it. By restricting the graphics modes to CGA, applications can have up to 720 KBytes of conventional memory. The only problem is that some applications break the standard rules of MS-DOS and make use of their knowledge of its internal structure. To run these a real copy of MS-DOS has to be used to start a virtual machine. This isn't so efficient but it does allow an MS-DOS window to be created running a real copy of MS-DOS version 3, 4 or 5.

OS/2-DOS also supports XMS memory and the DPMI standard as well as expanded memory, but it does not support VCPI programs.

OS/2 succeeds in being more efficient at running MS-DOS applications in an on-screen window than Windows 3.0 in the sense that it is faster and places fewer restrictions on the use of screen display than Windows does. However, Windows 3.1 has improved the implementation of MS-DOS applications so that they are faster and work with all standard video modes. OS/2 is clearly an ideal environment in which to develop MS-DOS programs, but as far as the non-programming user is concerned there is little difference between Windows 3.1 and OS/2 in their ability to run MS-DOS programs.

Running Windows

It was originally planned that OS/2 2.0 would translate calls to Windows 3 into equivalent Presentation Manager (PM) operations. However, this proved not to provide sufficient compatibility. Instead OS/2 runs a slightly customised version of Windows 3.0 using yet another virtual machine under Virtual 8086 mode. The only problem with this approach is that it can be slow to start a Windows session because it is equivalent to starting up the whole of Windows. Individual Windows applications can be installed as OS/2 desktop icons, but you can also run the Windows desktop including the Program Manager and the File Manager.

There are restrictions on how Windows can be run using resolutions higher than VGA, but at the time of writing OS/2 only recognised XGA and 8514/A video modes. Until Super-VGA drivers are available it is difficult to judge the importance of the restrictions.

OS/2-Windows doesn't run in enhanced mode and so you can't make use of any of the advanced features that it offers. In most cases this doesn't matter because OS/2 provides equivalent facilities. For example, you cannot run MS-DOS applications in re-sizeable Window's windows but why would you want to when you can do the same thing in an OS/2 window! However, some Windows programs do make use of enhanced mode as part of their basic operation. For example, the LaserMaster printer driver for the WinPrinter will not run in anything but enhanced mode. Also, all 32-bit Windows applications that go beyond the DPMI standard will not run under OS/2-Windows. As time goes on, the number of programs that demand the specific services of enhanced mode Windows is likely to increase. IBM say that they are working on providing enhanced mode OS/2-Windows.

Adobe Type Manager, ATM, is standard on all OS/2 and Windows sessions so there is no need for TrueType which isn't supported. Data transfer is supported via the clipboard and DDE but not OLE, which is of course new in Windows 3.1.

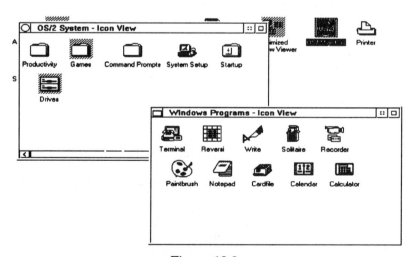

Figure 13.2
Windows 3.0 Accessories in OS/2

It is interesting to notice that all of the Windows accessories - calculator, clock, cardfile etc. are available under OS/2-Windows. There are also a very large selection of OS/2 accessories which go well beyond the functionality of the Windows accessories. For example, there is a graph drawing tool, an organiser, and a chess game.

An OS/2-Windows session is slightly slower than the real thing, but not enough to make any great difference from the user's point of view. The real disadvantage of using OS/2-Windows is that it is based on Windows 3.0 running in standard mode. IBM were prevented from including Windows 3.1 features until Microsoft launched Windows 3.1.

OS/2 applications

OS/2 2.0 is specifically designed for the 386/486 and it allows applications to be written using 32-bit instructions and without the need to use 64KByte segments. Such applications are exactly what the 386/486 needs to demonstrate its real capabilities. Unfortunately, at the time of writing the only OS/2 applications available are 16-bit. OS/2 Version 2.0 supports both 16-bit and 32-bit applications and from the user's point of view there is no way to distinguish which is which, apart from performance. A great many software companies have stated their intention to produce 32-bit version of their existing products and only time will tell if

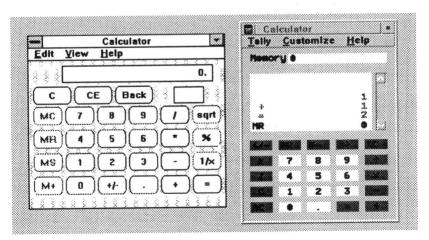

Figure 13.3
The Windows and OS/2 calculator

The BIOS and ABIOS

The BIOS (Basic Input Output System) is a set of software routines stored in ROM that forms part of the original IBM PC design. Every IBM compatible machine since the first PC has contained a ROM BIOS that implements the interface between the MS-DOS operating system and the machine's hardware. Any slight differences between the hardware of different machines can be absorbed into the BIOS routines which provide an unvarying standard that MS-DOS and even some applications programs can make use of. For example, there are many different types of disk controller card in use and they all work in different ways. This would mean that each manufacturer would have to customise MS-DOS to use the type of disk controller installed in their machine. Instead MS-DOS calls on a standard piece of software that forms part of the machine's BIOS to read and write the disk. In this case all the manufacturer has to do is to ensure that the BIOS installed in the machine conforms to the standard and can work with the disk controller.

BIOS variations are one source of problems when advanced operating systems such as Windows and OS/2 are used. Upgrading the BIOS is generally the only cure.

With the introduction of the PS/2 range IBM introduced the ABIOS, or *Advanced BIOS*, in addition to the original BIOS, now called the CBIOS, or *Conventional BIOS*, to distinguish it. The purpose of the ABIOS was to introduce a protected mode version of the BIOS that operating systems such as OS/2 could use. It is this extra ROM that takes up the 64KByte area in the UMA in PS/2s. Versions of OS/2 did indeed make use of the ABIOS but OS/2 2.0 does not, and so can run on any 386 PC, not just the PS/2 range. In most cases the memory space occupied by the ABIOS can safely be used by a memory manager to create either an expanded memory page frame or a large UMB.

these are significantly better than the existing 16-bit OS/2 applications.

OS/2 applications can be multi-threaded, that is they can contain different sections of program which run at the same time. This extends the multi-tasking offered by OS/2 right into a single application. For example, a drawing package may use one thread to implement its interaction with the user and another to re-draw the screen. This in theory at least should make it possible for the user to carry on drawing while the screen is being updated. Multi-threading makes this sort of reasonable behaviour very easy to implement but its absence doesn't make it impossible to implement. Facilities like background redrawing tend not to be included when a program makes its debut. For example, most Windows drawing packages were not interruptable while they re-drew the screen in their first versions, but subsequent versions usually found a way to implement interruptable re-draw. If a feature is desirable, i.e. likely to increase sales, then a sufficiently well developed applications program will include it, irrespective of the nature of the operating system.

A more serious problem for OS/2 is that nearly all OS/2 specific applications are available in Windows versions. For example, there is Lotus 1-2-3 for Windows and for OS/2, there is Ventura Publisher for Windows and for OS/2 and so on.. This means that there is very little incentive for the user to change to OS/2 to be able to run a particular application. OS/2 may be able to run MS-DOS, Windows and OS/2 applications but this doesn't represent a greatly increased choice unless there are OS/2 applications that are not available under Windows. It is arguable that the initial popularity of Windows was based on the fact that it was backward compatible with MS-DOS and it offered a range of additional Windows applications. What this means is that OS/2's only selling point is its stability and its performance - and both are very difficult to gauge at the moment.

The moving target

It is very clear that OS/2's major rival is Windows and IBM have done all that they can to incorporate all of Windows within OS/2. The main problem is that Windows isn't a static operating system. IBM has promised to make OS/2 a better DOS than DOS and a better Windows than Windows. They seem to have succeeded with respect to DOS and with Windows, if you are comparing OS/2-Windows with Windows 3.0. However, compared to Windows 3.1 running in enhanced mode OS/2's advantages look slight, if there are any at all!

Programmers and technicians are often swayed by the internal look of a product. There is absolutely no doubt that Windows, even Windows 3.1, is a technically poor solution to the operating system problem. OS/2 is technically sound and its new 32-bit mode gives applications programs the chance to use a simpler and faster programming environment. All of this may be true, but what matters most is how the user perceives the difference. At the moment OS/2 looks as if it delivers more or less the same facilities as Windows 3.1 with the noticeable exception of OLE. OS/2 is a more complex environment in that it can be configured to run MS-DOS, Windows and native OS/2 applications. It may provide more choice but raises questions for the user to solve concerning the co-existence of Windows and OS/2 applications. For example, how can data be transferred between a Windows and an OS/2 application. The final disadvantage is that despite IBM's best efforts there are still incompatibilities. Most are minor and nothing more than irritating but they don't exist if you use the real thing. It is difficult to see how all incompatibilities can be removed and this is true also in the case of Windows running MS-DOS programs. The difference is that OS/2 has two potential incompatibilities - with MS-DOS applications and with Windows applications!

LAN support

There is no question, however, that running OS/2 2.0 is a viable proposition and IBM will gain a substantial number of users. In particular OS/2 is the main support for the Microsoft LANManager software. Windows 3.1 will install easily on most network workstations and it can best be described as 'network aware'. It allows users access to network drives and other network facilities. What Windows 3.1 doesn't do is provide an operating system suitable for running a server. Currently most network servers run Novell Netware or

MS-DOS plus a network operating system extension. However, MS-DOS is not a good base for the multi-tasking needed to run a network server, whereas OS/2 is. OS/2's efficient multi-tasking is ideal for 'client/server' applications and this secures its role in networks for some time. Currently Microsoft have no alternative to running LANManager under OS/2 but clearly they could include such a capability in Windows NT.

Windows NT

Windows NT has already been briefly discussed Chapter 12, but it also deserves some discussion alongside OS/2. The reason is that Windows NT started under the title of OS/2 Version 3 and only later changed to Windows NT. Essentially Windows NT is a complete re-write of Windows and MS-DOS into a single operating system. The best way to think of it is as OS/2 without the ability to run Presentation Manager or OS/2 applications! Windows NT will be a 32-bit protected mode operating system that will run MS-DOS applications and both the older 16-bit Windows applications and the new generation of 32-bit Windows applications. As with OS/2, its main advantage will be stability and efficiency. The stability aspect is even being pursued to the point where Windows NT will meet the US Government's C2 security standard, the minimum requirement for an operating system to be used in government departments. To meet this standard Windows NT will certainly have to modify some of the sloppy practices encountered in Windows 3.1 and this will undoubtedly make for incompatibilities between the two. The shift from Windows 3.1 to NT may not be completely painless! Another interesting feature of NT is that it is being written in such a way that it will be possible to move it to machines outside the 386/486 family. This may not seem an important consideration to PC users, but the ability to upgrade hardware without changing operating system is one of the main advantages of Unix, and a feature that has been missing from all other PC operating systems.

Key points

» OS/2 was introduced as a replacement for MS-DOS but the early versions were designed for the 286 processor.

» Version 2.0 is a 32-bit protected mode operating system for the 386/486 family.

» The new GUI interface is unlike previous versions of the Presentation Manager manager desktop and features an object-oriented approach.

» It can run MS-DOS, Windows 3.0 and OS/2 Presentation Manager applications.

» MS-DOS applications can be run in an window or full screen and each can be fully configured as if it was a real version of MS-DOS.

» Expanded memory, XMS and DPMI are supported, but VCPI is not.

» Windows 3.0 applications can be run full screen or in a window. Currently applications that make use of enhanced mode or Windows 3.1 do not work.

» OS/2 supports both 16-bit and 32-bit native applications. Only when 32-bit applications become available will the performance advantages become clear.

» OS/2 is still essential as a network server operating system.

» Windows NT will be the first version of Windows to offer the same technical advantages as OS/2.

Chapter 14
Unix

OS/2 and Windows are both relatively recent operating systems. An alternative to creating a new PC operating system is to convert an operating system that has been implemented on other machines. The best known example of this is Unix.

Unix has been around for over twenty years and was available in a mature form when MS-DOS 1 was first introduced. It is a multi-tasking operating system, as is OS/2, but it is also a multi-user operating system. This means that you can connect terminals to your 386/486 machine via serial ports and allow more than one person to use it. This makes Unix suitable for applications where a group of people need to need to share data or programs. For example, order processing, invoicing, accounting etc.. This is not to say that OS/2 cannot be used for these applications, but generally it takes the very different route of networking a number of machines together. Unix also has networking abilities that allow it to be used in this way.

Unix runs on everything from personal computers to super computers. This is often claimed as an advantage for Unix, but it is also the source of its main problem. It is very easy to become confused by the apparent range of Unix versions and products.

History

Unix was designed originally for a DEC minicomputer and its creators made it suitable for minicomputer-powered hardware from the word go. This should be contrasted with MS-DOS, which was designed for a personal computer and has had to be replaced by OS/2 or augmented by Windows to accommodate hardware with minicomputer power - i.e. 386/486 systems. There are no memory or storage limitations with Unix. It allows you to run more than one program at a time and you can even connect terminals to your 386/486 and allow other users to share the machine and applications programs. All of this is good and well tried technology and it works. So in principle Unix is a solution to the shortcomings of MS-DOS, just as OS/2 is. It has the disadvantage of not being based on MS-DOS and hence it places MS-DOS users in a completely new environment. However, there are Unix versions of most of the best selling applications and this can cushion the transition.

The first criticism usually made of Unix is that it is unfriendly in the extreme. While I would agree with this I have to say that there is much in Unix that an MS-DOS user would recognise. Unix has hierarchical directories, uses MS-DOS-style path and file names and has pipes and filters. It is actually incorrect to say that any aspect of Unix is MS-DOS-like because Unix existed before MS-DOS and the operating system designers of MS-DOS consciously copied many of its general features.

Many MS-DOS commands do go over to Unix with only minor modifications but with different names. For example, DIR becomes LS, DEL becomes RM and so on. If you plan to switch between Unix and MS-DOS you face inevitable confusion, but once you learn the new commands Unix isn't too bad. It is generally agreed that to master Unix takes many years experience, but then again how many users ever manage to master MS-DOS fully? The main problem is that the Unix documentation is daunting - the manual is encyclopaedic. Luckily, the average user will never need to look at most of it.

Versions

In an attempt to get over the problem of a difficult user interface a number of graphical user interfaces - like Windows for MS-DOS - are in common use. The main problem is standardisation which surprisingly is also a problem for the whole of Unix. Most MS-DOS users are accustomed to the idea that there is a single standard latest version of MS-DOS. The reason for this is that MS-DOS is what Microsoft decrees it to be. Unix, on the other hand, is available from a number of sources and they have all made improvements and additions to it. The closest thing to a de facto standard for Unix is AT&T's System V Release 3.2 or more recently Release 4.0. Other versions of Unix for the 386 include BSD Unix (from the University of California at Berkeley), Xenix (now renamed as Unix) from SCO and IBM's AIX. All of these versions are recognisably Unix, they differ mainly in the extra facilities that come with them. Even so, it is still not possible to take a program out of its box and be sure that it will run properly on a version of Unix for which it was not intended.

There have been attempts to produce a unified Unix standard including graphical interfaces, but there are two major groups and so two evolving standards! Unix International is one group and the other is the Open Software Foundation. If you examine who belongs to which group you will quickly realise that this is a battle with AT&T and Sun Microsystems on one side and IBM, DEC and Hewlett Packard on the other. This situation is a serious threat to Unix being taken seriously as a challenger to the other operating systems. Even now the range of Unix versions that are available is confusing and bewildering to even the most technical of PC users.

Another important point to remember when considering Unix is that it is a multi-machine operating system. MS-DOS works on the Intel range of processors, i.e. the 8088, 8086, 80286 and the 80386, but Unix works on machines from mainframes through minis and down to desktop PCs. There are versions of Unix for the rival Motorola 68000 range of processors and it turns up on the Apple Mac and many specialist workstations. Indeed there is an argument to say that if you are considering switching to Unix then you might even consider a switch to other, perhaps more powerful, hardware. The multi-machine aspect of Unix is a strength in that it promises to eradicate the visible differences between different types of hardware. This means that one day it might be possible for software producers to write a single version of their products and expect them to run on almost any machine equipped with Unix. At the moment, though, it is something of a disadvantage because, in practice, software producers have to write down to the lowest level of support that they can expect from Unix hardware or write specifically for a particular machine configuration. If standards can be agreed this situation might change. What all this amounts to is that you have to buy a version of an application that has been produced for the particular machine and the particular version of Unix that you use.

AIX is IBM's own implementation of Unix that is available for PS/2s and other more powerful workstation products. In terms of functionality there is little to choose between AIX and other versions and you can run many standard Unix applications under it. For non-IBM 386/486 machines the customised version of Unix from SCO (Santa Cruz Operation) is the most popular. SCO Unix System V/386 combines Xenix and AT&T System V into one. It is well supported and within the grasp of the average 386 user. You can avoid many of the standards problems and arguments simply by choosing System V/386 and looking to SCO to take care of all of your needs for applications programs, advice, upgrades, etc.. The latest version conforms to many of the standards being established for Unix and there are hundreds of applications programs available, many of which will be familiar to an MS-DOS user.

To use System V/386 you need a 386 machine with a minimum of 1 MByte of RAM and 10 MBytes of free hard disk space and if you are planning to have more than one user then an extra 1 MByte of RAM and 5 MBytes of disk space is required. You can plug in extra users simply by connecting terminals to serial ports. If necessary you can add special intelligent multi-port serial cards to increase the number of users - see Chapter 8. Unix is multi-tasking and if you run out of RAM it will use disk space as virtual memory. Also recall the comments about multi-user/multi-tasking operating systems benefiting from larger cache sizes. A 64 to 128KByte cache is adequate for MS-DOS and even OS/2, but a 256KByte cache will improve the performance of a Unix machine.

Some applications will find the multi-user aspect useful as a way of sharing data. In this sense it is an alternative to networking. However, you don't have to make use of this facility. For example, if you wanted a Unix-based graphics workstation then a single user would be appropriate. There is also a well-developed Unix networking system (TCP/IP) that can be used to connect to other Unix and MS-DOS based machines. Using this an MS-DOS machine can be used as a graphics terminal to a central Unix machine via a network. In other words the MS-DOS machine displays the high resolution graphics while the Unix machine runs the applications program.

To allow you to run MS-DOS applications there is an MS-DOS simulator, VP/ix, that runs under System V/386. This allows any user to run an MS-DOS application with the benefit of simulated expanded memory if necessary.

Unix GUIs and X Windows

Unix was invented in the days when character-only VDUs were the rule and graphics was an expensive option. To bring it up to date a GUI interface is a fairly easy piece of software to add to cover up the text-based workings. Unfortunately, the Unix market has produced more than one add-on GUI desktop and there is little compatibility. The two most common Unix desktops are OSF/Motif and Open Look, but there are a great many others. Applications software has to be specifically written to take advantage of one or other of these GUI interfaces and in practice the majority of Unix applications simply go their own way. There is a standard, POSIX, which defines how applications programs should work with the Unix interface but at the moment it only covers character-based displays.

There is a Unix graphics standard, X Windows, but this is a very low level specification for how programs should interact with the display. Despite its name it doesn't specify a user interface. Indeed, all of the Unix desktops, including OSF/Motif and Open Look, make use of X Windows to do the drawing on the screen, but they look very different. X Windows is an interesting graphical standard because it also constitutes a sort of machine-independent graphics language. You can make use of an X Windows terminal on a Unix network to run a graphics program on a remote machine and see the results on the terminal. The MS-DOS world has nothing to compare with this, and all time-sharing systems are restricted to running character-based applications. (The only exception to this is Multiuser DOS when used with special hardware that allows standard PC graphics to be transmitted over high speed cables.) X Windows makes it possible to build a network of time-sharing system where the terminals have as much power as the main machine and can be used as graphics workstations. Quarterdeck has been working on DESQview X as the successor to the current DESQview. This is promised to convert a standard PC into an X Terminal capable of running Unix applications over a network or on a time-sharing system. DESQview X will have its own GUI interface but, by the very fact that it supports the X Windows standard, it will also be able to run any of the other Unix GUIs. At the time of writing it is difficult to judge what impact, if any, this will have on the MS-DOS using community, but it will clearly be important for any user with access to PCs and Unix based machines.

Unix applications

Although Unix gets over the limitations of MS-DOS, the only real benefit of this to the user is if it also offers application programs of the same or superior quality. At the moment the market for Unix applications is large but not as large as that for MS-DOS. There are over 10,000 MS-DOS applications programs and this easily makes it the best supported operating system available. There are plenty of good Unix applications, but there is a tendency for them to be rather more rough and ready than the best MS-DOS applications. Indeed, many of them resemble earlier versions of MS-DOS applications and this might seem something of a timewarp to an experienced MS-DOS user.

If you are considering changing to Unix, it is important to discover beforehand that the applications you need are available under it and that they fit your requirements. The ability to run MS-DOS applications should be viewed as an extra rather than a standard mode of working.

» Word processors

Even if word processing isn't your major Unix application, (if it was then a simple MS-DOS based system would probably suffice) you will still need some sort of word processing facility. Unix comes with an on-screen text editor, Vi, that is easy to use for general text processing tasks. One of the original reasons for the creation of Unix was to allow its originators to drive a phototypesetter and the basic publishing programs nroff/troff are still available. These are powerful but not easy to use by today's standards.

If you want a more familiar word processor then Fenix is a WordStar Professional Version 4 look-alike. You can sit down in front of Fenix and start using it as if it was WordStar almost immediately. It doesn't have the extras to be found in WordStar Professional Version 5 or 6 but it is an excellent way of making use of any investment you already have in this classic word processor. Fenix will read and work with existing WordStar files.

Microsoft Word 3.0 is available for Unix and this is the real thing not a look-alike product. If you are used to Word 3.0 with MS-DOS then the Unix product is identical. If you are a WordPerfect user then you will be pleased to know that WordPerfect 5 is also available in a Unix version and is rapidly becoming as popular under Unix as under MS-DOS.

SCO's Lyrix is a pure Unix product which is a very comprehensive word processor with all of the features you would expect - on-screen formatting, spell checker, thesaurus, hyphenation, text effects such a bold, italic, super/subscript etc. and quite a few extras such as table of contents, indexing, odd/even page headers and footers, block maths etc.. Indeed it offers features comparable to WordStar 5 or 6 or WordPerfect 5, but uses its own system of menus based on the ten function keys. There is also plenty of on-line help and prompting from menus.

» Spreadsheets

Lotus have a version of 1-2-3 for Unix and alternativelu you can run one of the MS-DOS versions under VP/ix. Microsoft's Multiplan, which is no longer supported in its MS-DOS version, is still available under Unix. The standard version of this spreadsheet has only 255 rows by 63 columns and has no database or graphics facilities and so is only suitable for modest applications. Another spreadsheet that has attracted attention in the Unix world is 20/20. This is loosely based on Lotus 1-2-3 and has the big advantage that it is available on a wide variety of machines including mainframes. The best known GUI spreadsheet available under Unix is Wingz. Versions for OSF/Motif, Open Look, Open Desktop and for the Mac and the PC are available.

» Databases

Although Ashton-Tate never produced dBASE III for Unix, dBASE IV is available. There is also a version of FoxBASE+, a dBASE III+ look-alike which uses the dBASE file and record locking methods, making it possible to take a dBASE network system and simply relocate it onto a Unix multi-user system. Although dBASE may be the most widely used database under MS-DOS, there are now signs that other database managers are becoming popular. A great many of these have migrated down to MS-DOS from mini and mainframe operating systems such as Unix. Oracle, for example is a full ANSI and IBM standard SQL database manager which available on a full range of machines. SCO's Integra is another SQL database. Database managers for Unix are inherently multi-user and therefore very suitable for medium sized multi-access systems.

» Integrated packages

There are also number of integrated packages for Unix, the best known probably being SCO Office Portfolio, a collection of modules including Lyrix and Integra. The spreadsheet component, Professional, has been withdrawn after a lawsuit from Lotus. In addition it offers MasterPlan (a project manager), ImageBuilder (a graphics package) and Statistician (a stats package). You can select any of these modules, which are also available as standalone programs, and integrate them using SCO Manager. As well as providing a calendar, diary, E-mail and scheduler, it also allows you to use a copy and paste clipboard to transfer data between applications. One alternative integrated package is the SAS Applications system which includes statistics and presentation graphics.

» DTP systems

Although Unix comes with a well known DTP system, nroff/troff, most serious DTP users will need something easier to use. There are a number of excellent DTP systems available under Unix but surprisingly no Unix versions of the best selling MS-DOS DTP programs, Ventura and PageMaker. However, Unix DTP facilities are so good that it is generally recognised that a Unix based system is what you need for large scale work. The best known Unix DTP systems are FrameMaker 2 and Interleaf Publisher. These are both WYSIWYG packages that allow interactive layout in much the same way as Ventura or PageMaker. FrameMaker is available for most of the Unix GUI interfaces.

» Languages

Although not strictly falling into the applications category it is important to know what languages are available in case you need to develop, or have developed, some custom software. The full range of Microsoft languages - including BASIC, Pascal, C and Fortran - are available for Unix and are all compatible with the equivalent MS-DOS versions. In addition there is also a range of 386 specific language compilers from LPI - Fortran 77, BASIC, Cobol, Pascal, PL/I and RPG II. There is also a range of program development tools that come with Unix, which is often described as an ideal programmer's operating system.

Why Unix?

Unix has been around for many years and was hailed as a possible MS-DOS replacement almost from the first day that MS-DOS was issued! This raises the question of why we are all not using Unix and why MS-DOS, Windows and OS/2 are not historical curiosities? Many users are indeed often worried about why they are not using Unix and feel that they must be missing something. The truth of the matter is that Unix is now an old operating system. Its initial design was good but it has needed a great deal of patching up to make it look like a modern operating system. When compared to commercial operating systems such as MS-DOS plus Windows, or OS/2, it still has advantages, but few that are apparent to the average user of applications programs. Indeed, there are situations in which Unix can look very old-fashioned and difficult to use, a reminder of the worst aspects of the days of the centralised mainframe computer. On the other hand there are situations when it can put on the face of the most advanced software available in its role as an engineering workstation.

Unix has a strong support group made up of computer academics who, due to advantageous marketing to the educational establishments, have used Unix as an example operating system for generations of students. Hardware manufacturers also like Unix because it gives them a single operating system that will work across their full range of machines. It is also true that users who need more power than a 386/486 can deliver have had no choice but to move to Unix - it being the only common operating system on other hardware. All of these pressures contribute to the 'change to Unix' message so often encountered without much explanation. If you examine the Unix market-place, however, the true situation becomes very clear - a large number of different versions and manufacturers attempting to dominate the market by the rule of the 'de-facto' standard, while on the surface claiming to support agreed standards.

If you have a specific job in mind and the software is available for a particular machine that happens to run Unix, then all well and good. You are spared the difficulties of selecting compatible products by simply buying a package of hardware and software. The same is true if you plan to have a custom software system written. Many companies run database systems designed using Unix and in this case it gives them the freedom to upgrade hardware without having to change operating system.

What all this means is that in practice Unix was and is a 'niche' operating system. It makes good sense for an engineering or scientific workstation, it makes good sense for a custom-built company-wide database but, unless there is a startling change, it makes little sense for a desktop PC with a varied and unspecified range of tasks to perform.

Other operating systems

There are a number of other operating systems just appearing but, without the volume of applications specifically written for them, they are currently of minority interest. Worthy of special mention, though, is the release of NextStep for the PC. This is the operating system, loosely based on Unix, used by the NeXT computer and now converted to the PC. This has a reputation for being advanced and easy to use but without some other support the PC version will only be of interest to users with mixed PC and NeXT hardware. Sun has also produced a 386 version of Solaris, its operating system for the Sparc processor. Again this is loosely based on Unix and in that context is yet another version of Unix to confuse the market. However, it is a technically superior operating system and will be of interest to anyone with mixed PC and Sun hardware.

Key points

» Unix has been a challenger to MS-DOS for well over 10 years. It is a 32-bit protected mode operating system when running on a 386/486 and offers many of the same facilities as Windows and OS/2.

» Unix is available on a wide range of hardware and this is its most powerful advantage.

» It is a fully multi-tasking, multi-user operating system with an excellent networking capability.

» The proliferation of Unix standards and versions is one of the main problems facing anyone thinking of changing to it.

» There is no standard for a Unix GUI although there is a very effective standard for Unix graphics - X Windows.

» Unix is very suitable for engineering workstations and custom-built systems but at the moment is not appropriate for general purpose systems.

Chapter 15
Case Studies

In this final chapter we consider the range of tasks that a 386/486 PC might be used for and examine the factors influencing the choice of a suitable machine.

One of the problems faced by anybody contemplating buying or upgrading a 386/486 PC is the degree of choice available. At the time of writing it was possible to purchase a 386SX for a modest cost and pay five times as much (or even more) for a 486DX. The key factors in deciding how much you need to spend are the requirements of the software you intend to use.

A database machine

The most important aspect of a dedicated database machine is its speed in accessing records from disk. Other desirable characteristics depend very much on the exact database package that is in use. Most database programs do not make much use of RAM memory, although many can make good use of any expanded, and sometimes extended, memory that may be available. Most don't make use of graphics beyond the standard graphics modes up to VGA. Most don't even support a numeric co-processor and even if they did this would make very little difference to the running speed of most database tasks. Of course any Windows database has the same requirements as an MS-DOS database plus the requirements of any general Windows application.

So the profile of a typical database machine in terms of the demands made on system components and specific requirements is:

	Demand or type
CPU	low
BUS	ISA
RAM	low
Expanded	low
Disk speed	high
Disk cache	preferably hardware
RAM Drive	varies
Disk capacity	medium to high
Video	standard
Co-processor	no
Mouse	varies
Printer	any
Operating system	MS-DOS

Clearly, as no co-processor is required and the demands on the CPU and memory are low, there is no need to look to a 486-based system. Indeed, a 25MHz/33MHz 386 system should be satisfactory and in many situations this will be an over-provision of computing power for the task.

If a fairly ordinary CPU will do then the situation is quite different for the disk system. The two factors to consider here are access time and transfer rate. Which is the more important factor depends very much on the nature of the database application:

» Access time - governs how fast a record can be found, most important for speedy answering of online enquiries.

» Transfer rate - governs how fast a record can be read or written after it has been located. As long as your records aren't huge this shouldn't be a noticeable effect. Transfer rate does have a strong effect on how quickly a large file can be accessed in its entirety and this is important if you are preparing complex reports based on large quantities of data.

Although you could get by with a 28ms ST-506/IDE disk, it would be better to choose a fast ESDI or SCSI drive. Although many SCSI drives are fast, there are also a number of slow ones on the market and so, if you are not prepared to shop around, specifying a 28ms or faster ESDI drive might be the simplest thing to do. Transfer rate comes down to a choice between the ISA, EISA and MCA buses. At the moment this is the most difficult part of the choice. In benchmark tests EISA and MCA buses don't consistently out-perform ISA based machines. Although an EISA machine would be a safe choice, in most cases an ISA machine would perform just as well.

The question of whether or not to make use of a caching disk controller or software disk cache is also a difficult one to answer. The effectiveness of a disk cache depends on how often the same data is reused. If your application results in very few re-reads of the same data in a single session, then a software disk cache will have little effect. In this case only a hardware caching disk controller has any hope of speeding up disk operations by scheduling writes to minimise disk head movement. However, some database packages make heavy use of the disk to run their programs once they are too large to fit into 640 KBytes of conventional memory. In this case a software or hardware disk cache would speed up the loading of database programs, but a RAM drive should do the job better.

Finally, when it comes to video most database programs are quite happy with a simple IBM compatible text display - you can use colour VGA if you have another reason to, but in most cases monochrome VGA is all that is actually required. You might even be able to acquire some of the video memory using a 386 memory manager to increase the size of the 640 KByte conventional memory to 704 KByte. In the same way a memory manager could be used to move buffers etc. into hi memory to free conventional memory.

Network server (Multi-user database)

The requirements for a network server are very similar to that for a database system. The main difference is that a network server is essentially a multi-user database and so needs a higher data transfer rate. As in the case of the single user database, the demands on the CPU are generally low unless the server is a non-dedicated server and so is being used for other applications. The exact memory requirements for a server depend on the network operating system. Most network operating systems can make use of expanded or extended memory for buffers and some can even move themselves out of the 640 KBytes of conventional RAM. Of course this is only of interest in the case of a workstation or if the server is doubling as a workstation.

As the demand on the CPU isn't high and a co-processor isn't needed, a 25 MHz or 33 MHz 386 should be sufficient for a server. The arguments for the exact type of disk needed are very similar to the single user database machine described earlier. A quick access time, 28ms or less, will ensure that the data is found rapidly but in this case a high transfer rate is important to free the disk controller ready for another operation as quickly as possible. This implies that while an ISA bus could be, and is used successfully, this is an opportunity for an EISA or MCA bus to show what it can do. A hardware caching disk controller also has the potential to speed up write operations by minimising disk head movements. Any disk cache memory has to be large to be useful because of the multi-user nature of the disk's operation. A full megabyte of disk cache per user isn't unreasonable! Most network operating systems include some built-in facility for using expanded or extended memory such as a software disk cache. Taking all of this into account the profile for a network server is:

	Demand or type
CPU	medium
BUS	EISA or MCA
RAM	medium
Expanded	low
Disk speed	high
Disk cache	preferably hardware
RAM Drive	varies
Disk capacity	medium to high
Video	standard
Co-processor	no
Mouse	no
Printer	any
Operating system	MS-DOS, Novell Netware, OS/2
Extras	Network adapter with local buffer memory

It is obvious that the critical component in any network server is its disk drive, or drives, but the performance of the network adapter is also important. This should have plenty of on-card RAM and preferably be an MCA or EISA bus product. However, the performance actually delivered also depends on the quality of the software drivers used with the card.

Finally, it is worth commenting that Novell's Netware 386 is specially tailored for the 386 and can be used to add a high power server to an existing Novell network.

Network workstation

There are no extra requirements for a network workstation over and above what is required for the application it is running. The rate of remote disk access is almost completely governed by the transmission rate of the network - e.g. 10 MBit/s for Ethernet, 4 MBit/s for Token ring, 1 MBit/s for Twisted pair networks. The amount that the network is being used and how heavily the server is loaded also affect the speed of remote disk access. So each workstation should be equipped for the application for which it is intended - CAD, DTP, program development, general office use etc. - with the exception of the hard disk component in place of which an ISA network adapter should be installed.

CAD - general graphics

Interactive graphics is the most demanding of all personal computer applications. It demands high resolution graphics, often in colour and usually over a large display area. It also needs a high rate of response and this taxes both the data transfer rate to the video RAM and the speed of the processor. Large amounts of memory are also required to store both the program and the data describing the image. At this point you might think that the disk system isn't critical but, while not as important as other aspects of the system, it does govern the time taken to save and load graphics files. If the applications program uses temporary disk storage then it can even affect the response time of the program.

The detailed specification of a CAD/graphics machine depends very much on the exact software that you are using, but the general nature of the machine is very clear. The high use of the CPU and co-processor (as long as the software supports it) suggests that a 486 is the best choice. Memory requirements suggest that 4 MBytes of extended memory is a reasonable allocation, although programs such as AutoCAD can put up to 16 MBytes of extended memory to good use. The motto seems to be the more the better and so for a CAD/graphics machine it is important to check the maximum amount of memory that can be installed on the mainboard or using expansion cards without loss of speed.

	Demand or type
CPU	high
BUS	depends on graphics adapter
RAM	high
Expanded	none or high
Disk speed	medium to high
Disk cache	hardware or software desirable
RAM Drive	often useful
Disk capacity	medium to high
Video	Super VGA/TIGA/8514/A
Co-processor	yes
Mouse	yes (or alternative - bitpad, trackball, lightpen)
Printer	Laser printer or plotter
Operating system	MS-DOS, Windows 3 or OS/2

CAD and graphics applications are characterised by loading large files. In this case the access time of the drive isn't as critical as the transfer rate. A 40ms or 28ms drive would certainly be adequate, but the drive should be an ESDI drive and if possible should be used with a caching disk controller. A disk cache, software or hardware based, will usually speed up disk operations in a CAD/graphics system more than the same amount spent on a better quality disk drive. In a budget system an ST-506 controller could be used successfully but a 1:1 interleave is desirable.

The final element is of course the graphics adapter. The type of graphics adapter needed depends on the nature of your application. If you can avoid using colour then the speed of any graphics operation will be much higher. Indeed there is an argument for using monochrome for any stage in the application for which colour isn't essential and then switching to colour for finishing. The minimum graphics standard needed for CAD/graphics is VGA or Super VGA. The main problem here is in getting the speed needed to redraw the screen in a time that makes interactive graphics interactive. A better solution is to use an intelligent graphics adapter either based on TIGA or 8514/A and even here an MCA or EISA bus would still be an advantage.

Intel have introduced a special version of the 386 and 387 co-processor - the RapidCAD chip set - optimised for graphics. Benchmarks show that replacing a 386/387 pair by RapidCAD chips halves the time it takes to render a complex image. For simple images the speed gain is much less. Another way to look at this is that RapidCAD converts a 25MHz 386 into the equivalent of a 33MHz machine and 33MHz into a 25MHz 486. RapidCAD can be fitted without any modifications to the machine.

DTP

You may think that the requirement for a DTP system is similar to that for a CAD/graphics system, but there are two big differences. The first is that even for colour publishing a monochrome system will do for most of the work involved in layout and the second is the volume and variety of high quality text to be produced is much higher. Indeed the main characteristic of a DTP system is the use of a range of fonts in different point sizes and type styles. The load on the CPU is high because of the need to manipulate fonts, but a numeric co-processor isn't generally of much use in this. However, a numeric co-processor can be used to generate libraries of screen and printer fonts for storage on disk. It can also speed up any PostScript emulator that you might want to use.

Demand or type	
CPU	high
BUS	ISA
RAM	high
Expanded	none or high
Disk speed	medium to high
Disk cache	hardware or software desirable
RAM Drive	often useful
Disk capacity	medium to high
Video	Super VGA or A3/A4 mono-display
Co-processor	desirable
Mouse	yes
Printer	PostScript or HP LaserJet printer
Operating system	MS-DOS, Windows 3 or OS/2

For a DTP system a 25MHz or 33MHz 386 is an obvious choice. If you are going to work with colour graphics then a 486 is a better choice. As in the case of a CAD/graphics system disk transfer rate is the key factor and a 28ms ESDI disk with caching disk controller is ideal. Alternatively a 40ms or better ST-506/IDE disk, preferably 1:1 interleave with a software disk cache would make a good economy system. Most DTP programs can benefit from the use of a RAM disk for temporary files and this can be as effective as a disk cache.

Although you can get by with a standard monochrome or even colour VGA the cost of an A4/A3 display will be repaid very rapidly in increased productivity. The best alternative to a special A4/A3 monitor is a Super VGA display giving 1024x768 and the Radius Pivot monitor is a good choice as it give the flexibility of having this resolution in either landscape or portrait mode. In most cases a graphics accelerator card is a good idea for Windows DTP packages.

Strangely the choice of printer influences the size of hard disk that you need for a DTP system. If you use an HP LaserJet II then many of the fonts that you use have to be stored on disk as font files - one file for each font, each point size and each effect (bold, italic, italic bold etc.). A font file is generally large and you can expect to use 10 MBytes or more of a hard disk just in keeping the font files that you need. On the other hand, if you are using a PostScript printer or an HP LaserJet III no font files are required as the font definitions are part of the printer's software. Hence a PostScript printer or similar saves 10 MBytes and more of disk space and it is simpler to use. In general most DTP software is tested using a PostScript printer and if you are going to be involved in a lot of DTP work this is the type of printer you should use.

General office use

The type of machine needed for general office use depends of course on the type of user! However, if you suppose that a general purpose office machine will spend most of its time running word processors and spreadsheets then it is possible to come up with a general specification. Word processors don't tax the CPU or need a numeric co-processor. They also don't place much demand on memory, video or disk performance. They will often make use of extra resources when made available but these resources are not essential. The speed of disk access does make a big difference to operations such as spell checking, so too much economy in this area would be a mistake. The exception to this description is any word processor that operates in graphics mode and so can show a range of fonts and graphics on the screen. Such word processors are tending toward mini-DTP packages and need machines with similar specifications.

For spreadsheets a machine needs a slightly more powerful CPU, plenty of memory and, if the spreadsheets involve a lot of computation (and not all do) a numeric co-processor. If presentation graphics are of interest then colour VGA is a good idea. Putting the word processing and spreadsheet requirements together gives the following profile:

	Demand or type
CPU	low to medium
BUS	ISA
RAM	medium
Expanded	medium
Disk speed	medium
Disk cache	no
RAM Drive	no
Disk capacity	medium
Video	VGA
Co-processor	possibly
Mouse	yes
Printer	any
Operating system	MS-DOS or Windows 3

As CPU use is low to medium a 386SX should be adequate. Memory requirements range from 1 MByte minimum to 2 MBytes.

A slightly different situation arises if Windows is adopted. This has many advantages both for the beginner and the experienced user. It shields beginners from the difficulties of MS-DOS and, as long as they can cope with a mouse, reduces training time - especially if Windows applications such as Word for Windows and Excel are used. For the expert or skilled user the most important reason for using Windows is being able to run more than one application at a time and switch between them in an instant. The only additional requirement for Windows is an increase to 4 MBytes of extended memory and a preference for a Super VGA monitor.

Scientific/engineering workstation

If the main task is producing graphs, diagrams or drawings, the specification for a scientific workstation is the same as for a CAD/graphics machine. If the need is mainly for calculation with some display of graphics then the machine profile is slightly different. The demand on the CPU and a co-processor will be high, but other requirements are less stringent. Even the demand for memory is likely to be low, unless there is a need to keep large quantities of data in memory.

	Demand or type
CPU	High
BUS	ISA
RAM	medium
Expanded	medium
Disk speed	medium
Disk cache	no
RAM Drive	no
Disk capacity	medium
Video	VGA
Co-processor	387, Weitek or Transputer
Mouse	yes
Printer	any
Operating system	MS-DOS, OS/2, Windows or Unix

The need for a powerful CPU and a numeric co-processor might suggest a 486, but if you need the ultimate in number crunching power then you would be better off selecting a 33 MHz 386 and either a Weitek Abacus co-processor or a Transputer add-on board. Of course, you then have to find the software to support such non-standard co-processors but the chances are that you would have to write, or commission, the software anyway!

If you are interested in standard statistical analysis then it is worth mentioning that most stats programs make use of a 387 so perhaps selecting a machine with a mainboard that can take both the 387 and the Weitek co-processor is the best thing to do.

In most cases a standard ST-506/IDE drive will be sufficient, unless there is a very large amount of data to process. A disk cache is generally not needed because the data files are either small enough to process in a reasonable time or too big for a cache to cope with. There is no great need for anything more advanced than an ISA bus unless interactive graphics is part of the requirement.

Multi-media or games

A machine for multi-media or games is more demanding than you might imagine.

	Demand or type
CPU	High
BUS	ISA
RAM	medium
Expanded	varies
Disk speed	medium
Disk cache	varies
RAM Drive	varies
Disk capacity	large
Video	VGA
Co-processor	varies
Mouse	optional, and joystick often used
Printer	any
Operating system	MS-DOS or Windows 3

To produce full motion graphics consumes a great deal of processor, and often co-processor power. The minimum specification for a multi-media machine is a 16MHz 386SX as most games and entertainment software runs reasonably well given that clock speed, but 25MHz is to be preferred. VGA rather than Super VGA is the accepted standard. You might also need a CD-ROM, a sound card such as Ad-Lib Gold or Sound Blaster Pro, and if you are going to use the machine to play games a joystick is essential. Windows 3 is virtually the standard for multi-media but MS-DOS is still the standard for most games packages.

Program development

The profile for a development machine is:

	Demand or type
CPU	High
BUS	ISA
RAM	medium
Expanded	varies
Disk speed	medium
Disk cache	varies
RAM Drive	varies
Disk capacity	medium
Video	standard
Co-processor	no
Mouse	optional
Printer	any
Operating system	MS-DOS or OS/2

Program development can range from writing and compiling a single module Quick BASIC or Turbo Pascal program to building a complete application from a range of modules. In the first case machine demands are low and almost any machine will do but in the second you need a little more. Compiling a large program from disk libraries makes intensive use of CPU and disk. It generally doesn't place high demands on co-processors, memory or graphics, - unless the program that results from the compilation does as part of its testing! Clearly the ideal choice for this sort of application is a 33 MHz 386. Although it is desirable to have a fast disk, program files aren't usually large and so reading them in isn't often the bottleneck in the compiling process. A standard 28ms ST-506/IDE drive with 1:1 interleave using the ISA bus should be good enough for all but the largest development projects, where a switch to an ESDI drive should solve the problem. If you are developing programs for MS-DOS, memory is rarely a problem as most MS-DOS compilers don't make use of anything more than the standard 640 KBytes of conventional memory. If the program that you are trying to develop needs expanded or extended memory then that's a different story. When it comes to program development under OS/2, having plenty of extra RAM is a good idea because it makes debugging easier if you can run the debugger concurrently with the program.

A machine for an operating system

Sometimes it is necessary to specify a machine that is suitable for running a particular operating system without being precise about the exact nature of the application. This is only possible in as much as each operating system has a typical hardware requirement which may be slightly more or less than is actually required for any given application.

» MS-DOS

It is usual to find MS-DOS on medium performance 386SX and 25MHz 386 machines, but while its applications are generally undemanding, they can benefit from the speed of a

33MHz 386 or 486 machine. A standard ISA-based architecture, with a ST-506/IDE disk drive and VGA monochrome are sufficient. The minimum RAM for a workable system is 1 MByte with the 384 KBytes above 640KByte being used for either shadow RAM or LIM expanded memory. An additional 1 MByte of extended memory converted to expanded memory via a LIMulator is also usually enough for most applications. The exception is an application that demands at least 1 MByte of expanded memory. In this case it is often thought that a 2 MByte system is sufficient. This isn't the case unless the 384 KBytes of shadow RAM can also be used as expanded memory because the LIMulator usually takes approximately 50 KBytes of extended memory which means that a full 1 MByte of expanded memory isn't available in a 2 MByte system with shadow RAM. Therefore, a 4 MByte system is to be preferred.

» **Windows**

Windows increases the demands on a system beyond that of MS-DOS so that a 25MHz 386SX or DX with cache, 4 MBytes of RAM and VGA is best considered the minimum system. Even then some Windows applications will run unacceptably slow. A fast hard disk drive helps because Windows applications can be swapped to disk if memory is in short supply. A disk cache is also a good idea and a mouse is essential.

» **OS/2**

OS/2 and Presentation Manager make more demands on a machine than any other operating system. A 33MHz 486 or better with cache produces a system with a good response time. The key difference between a Windows machine and a PM machine is simply the amount of memory needed. Although 4 MBytes is often quoted as a suitable amount of RAM for both Windows and PM, in the case of PM this is an under provision. OS/2 really needs more like 8 to 12 MBytes to sustain a reasonable performance under a wide variety of conditions. Once again a fast disk drive can help speed up virtual memory.

If you plan to run multiple tasks under OS/2 then a secondary consideration is the size of the RAM cache. While a 64 to 128 KByte cache is adequate for a single task, running multiple tasks makes it worthwhile using a 256 KByte cache. If this is the case then choosing a 486 with a large secondary cache may produce significant performance advantages.

» **Unix**

Many of the demands of OS/2 are common to Unix. A 33MHz 486 or better with cache is best regarded as a minimum system. Memory demand is more varied than OS/2, but 4 to 8 MBytes is advisable. As in the case of OS/2 a larger cache is needed to speed up multi-tasking and multi-user systems. A RAM cache of 256 KBytes is recommended for a Unix system, and a fast disk drive for efficient virtual memory.

Unix systems vary considerably in their configuration - from simple character based multi-user systems to single user high performance graphics workstations - and because of this it is less easy to characterise a typical Unix system than, say, an OS/2 machine.

The cost of changing

One of the big drawbacks of abandoning MS-DOS is simply the cost of the change. Today it is reasonable to assume that the typical 386/486 system has enough memory and hard disk storage not to need upgrading to run OS/2 2.0 or Unix. However, there is still the cost of buying the basic operating system and replacing the applications programs. To give some idea of the cost, the table below give approximate prices of operating system plus a word processor and a spreadsheet. The word processor used for comparison is WordPerfect because it is available for all three operating environments.

The spreadsheet is Lotus 1-2-3. A database isn't included because of the huge variation in cost found even within a single operating system.

	Windows 3	OS/2 2.0	Unix
Operating system	<£100	<£100	£800
Word processor	£289	£299	£500*
Spreadsheet	£295	£263	£695
Total	£684	£862	£1995

*Multi-user licence for 5 users £1000

The conclusions from this table are that Unix is still much more expensive than MS-DOS or OS/2 and this is borne out by an examination of the prices of applications software in any catalogue.

The following table compares the features of each of the operating systems suitable for a 386/486 machine.

	MS-DOS	Windows	OS/2	Unix
Multi-tasking	No	Yes	Yes	Yes
Multi-user	No	No	No	Yes
Networking	Yes	Yes	Yes	Yes
RAM (minimum)	256 KByte	1.5 MByte	4 MByte	1 MByte
RAM (recommended)	640 KByte	4 MByte	8 MByte	2 MByte
Disk space	5 MByte	1 MByte	30 MByte	10 MByte
Virtual RAM	No	Yes	Yes	Yes

Upgrade

A common question nowadays is what can be done to upgrade an existing machine. In most cases, processor upgrade involves fitting a new mainboard - and while this isn't difficult it is quite an upheaval. In the very near future Intel and other manufacturers will release upgrade chips. There is already a 486SX style replacement for the 386SX. The chip is optimised so that it runs faster than a 386SX but otherwise it is perfectly compatible with the 386SX and can simply be plugged in place of it. Intel also has plans for clock doubling versions of many of its processors. This will make it possible to replace a 33MHz 486 with a 66MHz clock doubled processor again simply by plugging in the new chip. In the future there are likely to be other new plug-in upgrade chips for the 386 and 486.

The Future - 586

Clearly the ultimate next step is the 586 which Intel should launch sometime at the end of 1992 or early in 1993. Of course there is usually a considerable delay between a processor's announcement and it becoming commonplace. It is difficult to see how the 586 can deviate radically from the basic 386 design so the most important aspects of the chip will probably be enhanced performance. The most likely improvements will be the provision of a separate data and code cache and the increased use of RISC techniques to speed up execution. The 586 and Windows NT should make good companions. However, predicting the future is never an easy task and I would draw the reader's attention to the Update Service described at the start of this book!

Contacts

Memory upgrades

Datrontech plc
Datrontech House
33 Grosvenor Road
Aldershot
Hampshire
GU11 3DP
Tel: (0252) 313155
Fax: (0252) 341939

Memory Direct
33 Grosvenor Road
Aldershot
GU11 3DP
Tel: (0252) 316060
Fax: (0252) 341939

Numeric co-processors

DMST (Distributed Micro Storage
Technologies Ltd)
PO Box 1113
Maidenhead
SL6 6RD
Tel: (0635) 247100
Fax: (0635) 247142

Intel Corporation (UK) Ltd
Pipers Way
Swindon
SN3 1RJ
Tel: (0793) 696000
Fax: (0793) 641400

MicroWay
32 High Street
Kingston-upon-Thames
KT1 1HL
Tel: (081) 541 5466
Fax: (081) 546 0614

Operating systems

IBM United Kingdom
Personal Systems Business Unit
Northern Cross
Basingstoke
RG15 1EJ
Tel: (0256) 56144
Fax: (0256) 843167

Microsoft Ltd
Microsoft Place
Winnersh
Wokingham
RG11 5TP
Tel: (0734) 270000
Fax: (0734) 270503

SCO Ltd
Croxley Centre
Hatters Lane
Watford
WD1 8YN
Tel: (0923) 816344
Fax: (0923) 817781

386 software

Megatech Software
(System Sleuth)
111-113 Wandsworth High Street
London
SW18 4HY
Tel: 081 874 6511
Fax: 081 877 1384

Quarterdeck UK
(QEMM DESQview)
Widford Hall
Widford Hall Lane
Chelmsford
CM2 8TD
Tel: (0245) 496699
Fax: (0245) 495284

International Data Security
(386MAX)
9-10 Alfred Place
London
WC1E 7EB
Tel: (071) 631 0548
Fax: (071) 580 1466

Software Paradise
Avenue House
King Edward Avenue
Caerphilly
CF8 1HE
Tel: (0222) 887521
Fax: (0222) 869209

Index

C